The Future of Banking

For other titles in the Wiley Finance Series
please see www.wiley.com/finance

The Future of Banking

In a Globalised World

Chris Skinner

John Wiley & Sons, Ltd

Copyright © 2007   John Wiley & Sons Ltd, The Atrium, Southern Gate, Chichester,
West Sussex PO19 8SQ, England

Telephone   (+44) 1243 779777

Email (for orders and customer service enquiries): cs-books@wiley.co.uk
Visit our Home Page on www.wiley.com

Other Wiley Editorial Offices

John Wiley & Sons Inc., 111 River Street, Hoboken, NJ 07030, USA

Jossey-Bass, 989 Market Street, San Francisco, CA 94103-1741, USA

Wiley-VCH Verlag GmbH, Boschstr. 12, D-69469 Weinheim, Germany

John Wiley & Sons Australia Ltd, 42 McDougall Street, Milton, Queensland 4064, Australia

John Wiley & Sons (Asia) Pte Ltd, 2 Clementi Loop #02-01, Jin Xing Distripark, Singapore 129809

John Wiley & Sons Canada Ltd, 6045 Freemont Blvd, Mississauga, ONT, L5R 4J3, Canada

Wiley also publishes its books in a variety of electronic formats. Some content that appears in print may not be
available in electronic books.

Anniversary Logo Design: Richard J. Pacifico

Library of Congress Cataloging in Publication Data

Skinner, Chris.
   The future of banking : in a globalised world / Chris Skinner.
      p.   cm. — (Wiley finance series)
   Includes bibliographical references and index.
   ISBN 978-0-470-51034-6 (cloth : alk. paper)
   1. Banks and banking, International.   I. Title.
   HG3881.S5385 2007
   332.1′5090152—dc22   2007009226

British Library Cataloguing in Publication Data

A catalogue record for this book is available from the British Library

ISBN 978-0-470-51034-6 (HB)

Typeset in 10/12pt Times by Integra Software Services Pvt. Ltd, Pondicherry, India
Printed and bound in Great Britain by Antony Rowe Ltd, Chippenham, Wiltshire
This book is printed on acid-free paper responsibly manufactured from sustainable forestry
in which at least two trees are planted for each one used for paper production.

For Dad

Contents

Preface

For the past three decades, I've lived, worked, breathed, eaten, drunk and slept around the financial industry. Sorry, scrub that last one, although a few presentations have sent me that way.

During this time, I've cut across retail and wholesale banking, brokerage, asset management and insurance, and throughout all of these transitions in my work, one thing has remained constant: the financial industry is changing faster than it has ever changed before.

For example, when I joined this industry it was in 20th Century but it could just as easily have been in the fifteenth when the first banks were being formed in Italy. Yes, banks' products and services had evolved, but automation was still to arrive.

It was only in the 1970s, only three decades ago, that we began to see the onset of new technologies. In the 1970s:

- ATMs were just arriving to automate cash dispensing;
- SWIFT had just been created to replace telex machines for settling global payments;
- the Visa card had just started to take off thanks to Dee Hock's major investment in an electronic credit card processing system;
- Fischer Black and Myron Scholes were creating the first modelling systems that became the bedrock of the futures, options and derivatives trading world; and
- most computing was being used by banks for account administration in the back office.

Today, that world has turned on its head. Today:

- retail banks are being driven by customer demands for self-service;
- SWIFT is redefining its role as its original purpose – replacing telex machines – is no longer important;
- Visa has moved from a bank-owned cooperative to a commercial, proprietary company struggling to keep up with PayPal, mobile and other payments mechanisms;
- the total value of derivatives traded by hedge funds using complex automated computing models *every day* exceeds the total value of America's *annual* GDP; and
- most computing is being used by banks to survive and compete.

By way of example, I attended a presentation in 1996 where Professor David Llewellyn, Head of the Banking Alumni at Loughborough University, said 'The industry has changed more in the last five years than in the last fifty.' This is as true in the late 2000s as it was then, if not more so, which is why I love this industry because we are in a continual state of change.

This continual state of flux is created by the very fact that financial services is based upon bytes of storage on computer discs. Banking is a digital marketplace, based upon virtual relationships electronically transacted. It was not like that when I started my worklife, but more and more we transact, relate and operate through electronic channels and electronic services.

As a result, banking is one of the few industries where technology is not only an enabler, but is its lifeblood. This is both a strength and a weakness. The strength is financial services ability to deploy, implement and support technology. The weakness is the challenge of transitioning from legacy operations and infrastructures to true electronic businesses.

I have been discussing these challenges in various outlets over the past few years through regular monthly columns in *The Banker* magazine and Finextra.com. This book represents a summary of those views and explores the challenges bankers face.

The bottom-line is that banking in the 21st Century is a technology-based business and technology is changing the rules of banking faster than ever before. That is why I love this industry, because we are in a continual state of change.

Enjoy being a Master of Change and I look forward to revisiting this space again in a few years to share some more of the trends and developments we are experiencing in this space.

In the meantime, feel free to contact me through my website www.balatroltd.com or direct via e-mail to info@balatroltd.com. I would be interested in your thoughts.

Chris Skinner
January 2007

Acknowledgements

This book would not exist if it were not for the guys at Finextra, TowerGroup and the Financial Times, and the many other clients, media and conferencing firms I work with worldwide.

At Finextra, I owe credit specifically to Paul Penrose, the editor. Paul keeps me in line. Alongside Paul are a team of great people who made this book happen by allowing me to rant and rave on their website for the last few years. By the way, if you don't subscribe to their free newsletters or tradeshow, Finexpo, then go to http://www.finextra.com/register.asp right now and enter your details. You're missing too good a thing by not doing it.

At TowerGroup are people with banker written through their soul. John Stone is one such man, and is one of the best. John used my skills to create TowerGroup Europe's service in 2002 and without that introduction I'm not sure I'd be here today.

At the *Financial Times* and *the Banker* are Mike Barker and Brian Caplen who feed me, in Mike's case literally. There's also a fine group of people including Steve Timewell, Angus Cushley, Dan Barnes, Tony Jarvis and many more seasoned professionals who produce the world's best banking journal. . .in my humble opinion.

This book is the result of my writings for Finextra, TowerGroup and *the Banker*, and also owes thanks to the many other people I connect with in this world of banking. To name a few: Tom Buschman, Emmanuel Daniel, Tom Groenfeldt, Clare Walsh, Debbie Bianucci, Conny Dorrestijn, Parveen Bansal, Katie Gwyn-Williams, Bob Fuller, Chris Pickles, Michael Baume. . .and everyone in the wonderful world of financial services we work with today who find me around the corridors of financial conferences hanging out. I should also make one other thing clear here too, which is that I often use TowerGroup research throughout this book. Although I use this research, the interpretation of what that means is entirely my own and not their opinions just in case you wondered.

One other person stands out head and shoulders in my world: Andy Coppell. Andy is a pillar of the financial community and my partner in the Financial Services Club. If you have not been to the Club, then checkout www.fsclub.co.uk. We regularly meet in London and Dublin and, should you be passing through these great cities, I would be delighted to see you there.

I'm sure I've missed a few folks, but the global knowledge base represented above has enabled me to capture the major trends in the financial industry over the last few years and, to all of you, I give my thanks.

Finally, I would like to thank my family for putting up with me, especially Jenny.

About the Author

Chris Skinner is Chief Executive of Balatro Ltd (www.balatroltd.com), his own consulting firm, and Chairman of the Financial Services Club (www.fsclub.co.uk), an organisation dedicated to understanding the future of financial services. He is also one of the four founders of Shaping Tomorrow (www.shapingtomorrow.com), the internet portal for strategists and futurists.

Chris is known for his regular columns in Finextra and the Banker, as well as other publications, and is Chairman of the Banker magazine's Technology Awards; a Judge with the Asian Banker's Excellence in Retail Financial Services; and a contributor to the World Economic Forum's scenario's programme focused upon the future of financial services.

He is a regular keynote at the world's largest financial services conferences, including SWIFT's Sibos, the Bank Administration Institute (BAI) Conferences in the USA, IIR in Europe and the Middle East, and the Financial Times in Europe. Through these keynotes, he has shared the stage with leading world figures including Richard Branson, Lou Gerstner, Gary Hamel, Meg Whitman and Bill Gates.

Prior to founding Balatro, Chris was Vice President of Marketing and Strategy for Unisys Global Financial Services and Strategy Director with NCR Financial Services. These roles sparked Chris's specialization in the future of financial services after he created the Global Future Forum in Unisys and the Knowledge Lab in NCR.

He studied at Loughborough University in the UK, and holds a Bachelor of Science in Management Sciences alongside a Diploma in Industrial Studies. He is a Fellow of the Institute of Management Services, an Associate of the Chartered Insurance Institute and a Chartered Insurance Practitioner.

He can be contacted at info@balatroltd.com.

The Current State of Banking

In this first chapter, my aim is to provide the reader with some insights into where we are with banking today, before we explore some of the future themes of banking in later chapters. So this is a whirlwind tour of banking at the highest level.

Now when my wife read this chapter she said it was pretty dry, although it did seem to do wonders for her sleep patterns, so if you know your stuff, you may want to jump to some of the other chapters as they are pretty hot by comparison. Nevertheless, I quite like this chapter, as it provides a comprehensive summary of the challenges for bankers today. So you may find it useful to read on.

This chapter also serves as an introduction to the themes we explore in this book, which is split into four major parts. The first part explores the global issues and the challenges of bank management. The other parts narrow the focus onto retail banking, payments and investment banking.

PART 1: GLOBAL ISSUES

Overall, there are four big challenges for bankers today: regulatory challenges, customer challenges, technology challenges and, most importantly, challenges to profitability.

First and foremost is regulation and compliance. I put this first because it is the biggest pain for bankers, forcing them to do stuff they do not want to do. It has come to the fore because almost everywhere you look, banks are being forced by governments and regulators to do stuff they do not want to do as a raft of regulations are being introduced, designed to protect citizens and businesses from losses, and aid governments and law enforcers to track terrorism and crime.

In particular, right now, the overarching legislative drive is Basel II. Basel II is big news because it applies to most banks around the world. Basel II is actually a framework designed to provide a complete set of risk management metrics and measures to ensure that banks have adequate capital to avoid a banking collapse. In particular, the framework aims to manage operational risk and has been adopted by banks in most developed economies.

Then we have a raft of rules drawn up by the USA and Europe to address specific problems. For example, the US has just implemented RegNMS to sort out issues in investment markets, Rule 22c-2 to stop mutual funds abusing redemption fees, NASD Rule 3011 for anti-money laundering, FFIEC's Authentication rules to ensure secure online services, and a whole load of stuff to crack down on terrorism including Michael Chertoff's Homeland Security Acts, the Patriot Act, Disaster Preparedness, the Bank Secrecy Act and more. Not forgetting the real humdinger, Sarbanes-Oxley.

You will probably be yawning already at the idea of a discussion around Basel II and Sarbanes-Oxley, SOX for short, because these two regulatory pillars have been discussed and debated in minute detail for about the past five centuries, sorry make that years, but SOX is a real sucker punch because it is estimated to have cost US firms trillions of dollars. Designed to overcome the risks and exposures highlighted by the collapse of Enron and Worldcom, SOX brought in a new regime of onerous accounting and auditing rules for any US-listed firm. This was good news for audit firms though, as SOX resulted in auditing fees for US firms increasing by 17% in 2003 and by a further 40% in 2004. Whilst audit spending in 2004 surged to $3.5 billion a new SOX Clause known as Part 404 – this Part lists the measures required by a firm to ensure that their management can prove effective internal controls – cost $35 billion alone, about 20 times more than anticipated.

You may think that bankers rocking and rolling from legislative punches from governments and regulators is isolated to the USA, but no. Europe has embarked upon a similar programme of dramatic change.

Known as the Lisbon Agenda, because it was agreed by European politicians in Lisbon in 2000, the European Commission has introduced a comprehensive range of new regulatory directives across all European countries to achieve Economic & Monetary Union (EMU), and Europe's EMU is almost as shocking as the national bird of Australia. That is because it covers every little bit of finance from the Market Abuse Directive to the Markets in Financial Instruments Directive (MiFID), from Solvency II to the Payment Services Directive . . . in totality this group of Directives are called the Financial Services Action Plan (FSAP).

The Financial Services Actions Plan is pretty much driving everyone crazy in Europe, as it tries to create a level-playing field for pan-European competition in the financial markets. In reality, this means that Dutch Banks, French insurers, German brokers and UK traders all come head-to-head in a frenzy of competition to create a market that has the scale and breadth to compete and win against the US and other global markets.[1]

A big vision and a hard reality.

Meanwhile, the Gulf Cooperation Council (GCC) is creating a similar Financial Services Action Plan for all of the Middle Eastern oil-producing nations, to compete with the Euro and the Dollar. The aim is that, by 2010, Saudi Arabia, the United Arab Emirates, Oman, Bahrain, Kuwait and Qatar have an economic union similar to Europe's, and a single currency.

Alongside these big changes are China's challenges to open up their financial markets to foreign competition and investment. For years, China has been run by State-owned banks who funded State-owned enterprises. Now, this is liberalising to comply with World Trade Organisation requirements for open markets. This means that the banks are becoming as commercial as banks in the US and Europe, and a previously non-existent capital market is being created. The result is a release of efficiency which McKinsey estimates to be worth $320 billion a year, which would raise China's GDP by as much as 17 percent and help spread China's new wealth more evenly. Similarly, India is trying to achieve the same liberalization, and has announced deregulation of their markets through 2009.

Between regulation and liberalisation, the financial markets are being radically transformed by governments and politicians. For some, this involves high cost with no return and

---

[1] Regulatory challenges are discussed in depth in Chapters 4, 5, 18, 19 and 20.

investment. It is a threat. For others, it is a great opportunity to diversify and expand business globally and so becomes a worthwhile investment. Either way, regulation is a major challenge for the world's banking community and will change the shape of banking in the future.

The second major challenge is the customer and, by customer, I mean both the retail and the wholesale client.

The retail client is a totally different beast today when compared with the humble branch visitor of yesteryear. Thirty years ago, banks had close personal relationships with their retail customers who regularly visited the branch to deposit cheques and meet staff and managers for advise. Gradually, these customers have been pushed out of the branch through technology, specifically ATMs and telephones and, more recently, the internet. This has dramatically changed the relationship between retail banks and their customers, as bankers no longer see the customer. The customer is remote and online. The result is that the bank is a commodity product provider, as service has moved to self-service. And today, the retail customer is pushing back as customers no longer accept what the bank gives them. Today, they have total choice, based upon what their home can access.

The thing you see over this 30-year period is that technology has transformed the retail banking, in fact the whole of the banking, landscape. Specifically, the retail bank customer is now the driver of technology though. This is because, 30 years ago, all of the technology the bank purchased and deployed was developed by large computing firms whose Research & Development (R&D) was driven by governmental demands for innovation, especially the Federal Government of the USA. US government drove demands for mainframes and mini-computers, security and resilience. Much of this demand was driven by defence contracts for army, airforce and navy, and the dominant players were large governmental contracted firms, such as IBM, EDS and DEC.

Bill Gates of Microsoft and Andrew Grove of Intel changed all that.

The move to PC-based technologies was fundamentally driven by Bill Gates' vision of 'a computer in every home', and this vision has come to fruition in the 2000s. The result is that most of the technologies being developed today are being driven by consumers – mobile telephones, iPods, Sony PSPs, internet and web services – rather than by governments or business. And the banks' challenge is to keep up with consumers' demands for access and service.

This is also the challenge for bank's corporate clients.

In a similar way to the challenges faced by banks, corporate clients are being challenged by consumers. Customers now order goods online, and expect regular automated email confirmations and communications throughout the whole delivery process.

The corporate client has been transformed by this process by using more and more technology-based services, and processes that allow them to manage business on a globalised, $24 \times 7 \times 365$ basis. For example, the move to outsourcing manufacturing of goods to China and services to India could not have happened without today's globalised technologies, infrastructures and networks.

This has led the corporate client to question supply chains, and the automation behind those supply chains. One such example is the invoicing process.

European businesses estimate that 27 billion invoices circulate around the European Union, with 85% of them produced in paper format costing an average of €5 to process. By comparison, an invoice processed electronically only costs around €0.21 to process. Similarly, the USA sends out around 29 billion invoices per annum, with 90% of them on paper. As a result, corporations estimate that paper inefficiencies cost their businesses around $65 billion per annum to the USA and €53 billion per annum for the EU.

No wonder they are demanding change, and banks have been heightened as both enablers and barriers to these changes.

Traditionally, banks have focused upon payments, rather than supply chains. They have dealt with treasurers rather than Chief Financial Officers. And they deliver localized service rather than globalised operations.

This is changing.

Bankers are now discussing a bank's role as being to enable supply chain automation rather than treasury automation. Banks are focusing upon the end-to-end process of purchase orders through accounts receivable, rather than just payments. Bankers are discussing einvoicing and ebilling, rather than paper processes. This is why SWIFT, the global payments network, is now delivering direct access to their network for corporate clients. Something that would have been heresy only a few years ago.[2]

Customers are creating change in banking enabled by our third major challenge: technology and, hand in hand, globalisation.

As mentioned in the opening, technology is the most critical factor in the process of banking, because banking is a digital business. Banking is bits and bytes. It is a numbers based transactional business. It originally existed to enable monetary transmissions. The most similarly aligned business to banking is telecommunications, with the main difference being that banks connect finances whilst telecommunications connects society.

As technology changes, therefore, it is a fundamental competence for banks to be able to maintain their capability to keep up. This is quite hard when retail customers are driving technology change and corporate clients are demanding direct usage of bank infrastructures.

Equally, the technology itself is shifting dramatically. It has moved from internal to Internet, from high cost and low powered to low cost and high powered, and from US technologies to Chinese.

Just as we saw the shift of technology innovation move from East Coast America to West Coast America in the 1990s, as the governmental-driven technologies of IBM and friends moved to the consumer-driven technologies of Microsoft and friends, we are seeing another fundamental shift in the 2000s. This time the shift is from West Coast America to China and India.

The purchase of IBM's PC Division by China's Lenovo at the end of 2004 powerfully emphasised this shift, whereby China's firms are generating new technologies at a tenth of the cost of US and European firms. Similarly, technology is being serviced by Indian firms such as Tata for a tenth of the cost of traditional service providers.

The biggest technological challenge therefore is to keep up with the technology innovations coming out of these new economies. China is creating new capabilities based upon next generation internet, mobile and wireless technologies far ahead of the capabilities in the USA and Europe. South Korea and Japan are also creating disruptive waves of change that will seep into the European and American banking world years downstream. Therefore, banks have a duty to maintain focus upon these economies.

However, there is another more important but less understood extreme in this changing world of technology prowess. This is the extreme of power and leadership.

---

[2] Customer challenges are discussed in depth in Chapters 8, 9, 10, 11 and 16.

Just as we accept the shift to offshore, and just as we accept that wealth and capital flow moves into these economies, we also have to accept that these economies are creating banks with world-class capabilities. Banks that traditionally languished in under-invested outfields of under-development are being transformed into shiny new leading-edge organisations. These new bank leaders have no legacy to contend with, and have scrapped tradition to learn from the best and then implement the best, and then some. You only need to look at banks like ICICI Bank in India or Alfa Bank in Russia to see the transformation. For example, Mr. K. Vaman Kamath, Managing Director and Chief Executive Officer of ICICI Bank Limited, estimates that the cost of their technology infrastructure is a tenth of the cost of a traditional bank operation in Europe or America. That means that ICICI can leverage significant cost–income advantages which, over time, surely must lead to ICICI Bank and similar BRIC (Brazil, Russia, India and China) economy leaders to takeover traditional bank brands as they move towards globalised ambitions themselves over time. It can only be a matter of time before an Indian or Chinese bank buys an American or European bank.[3]

Which leads to the final challenge for banks in the 21st century: profitability.

As regulation demands increased investment to achieve lower margins; and customers demand seamless and transparent services on a globalised $24 \times 7 \times 365$ basis; and new technologies continually erode margins of maintenance for legacy systems – established banks are concerned. Concerned about profitability, competitiveness, cost–income ratio and especially margins. Sure, bankers are always concerned about these things anyway, but the core of the issue is that the more banks focus upon their cost issues, the less they manage their income issues. It is a continual balance, but those banks that continually invest in new ideas by experimenting within a branch, product, staff or technology program are the ones that are far more likely to succeed than those that continually cut their investments in branches, products, staff and technologies.

It may sound like teaching grandma to suck eggs, but far too many bankers are not just risk-averse but investment-averse. Often the two go hand in hand. The consequence is that many areas of bank operations, especially those that are customer-facing, are under-invested whilst those that make money – capital markets – gain the attention. Many of the world's largest banks make more money out of one day's trading in the world's investment markets than they ever will out of a branch or, for some, their total retail operation.

This is the balance of focus between cost and income, frugality and service, direct dealing and investment dealing. Some banks get this balance just right, whilst others tip the balance too far in one direction or the other. And that is the challenge of banking that we explore in this book. The balance between getting it just right versus getting it just wrong. Luckily, for most banks, getting it wrong is rarely a terminal error. Few banks collapse and die, and the few that have in the past few decades tend to be those caught in illegal dealings such as BCCI.

Some would say that banks do not collapse because if they did, we would have anarchy. That is why banks are often protected by government licences to ensure they can be trusted. Others would say banks are protected by government licensing to avoid true competition.

Whichever way you look at it though, banks are faced with four big areas of challenge today: regulatory, customer, technological and profitability challenges.

---

[3] Technology challenges are explored in depth in Chapters 1, 10, 13, 14, 15, 17, 21 and 22.

PART 2: RETAIL BANKER'S CHALLENGES

Retail banking changed more in the last few years of the 20th century than in the decades that preceded, due to the explosion of communication introduced by the internet. That wave of change came to an end in 2001 when the internet went bust, or rather investing in the internet went bust as people lost fortunes on their internet investments.

What was interesting is that there never actually was an internet boom and bust – just an internet *share price* boom and bust. The innovations of the internet itself never stopped, as demonstrated by the sudden rise to fame of YouTube purchased for $1.65 billion by Google in 2006, and MySpace which was bought by News Corporation for $580 million in 2005. Of particular note is that News Corp bought MySpace in July 2005 and people thought they overpaid. If they had waited until the time YouTube sold out to Google, October 2006, they would have had to pay over four times that price.

The internet boom is back, only this is the second-generation internet termed Web 2.0. Web 2.0 is all about blogging, podcasting and connection. It is also about the reality of delivering truly integrated telephony and technology where the world has finally converged. The convergence of telecommunications and technology has taken the separation of entertainment and work and made them one and the same. We can now email through our televisions, telephone through our computers and entertain ourselves with television on our telephone. That is the new generation of the internet world.

During the period after the internet bust however, most retail bankers have taken a breather. The fast cycle change of the early 2000s had burnt many retail bankers out and there was little appetite to continue to invest in the internet frivolities. Many banks returned instead to investing in traditional bricks and mortar and went into branch renewal programmes.

What this demonstrates is the 'lemming' mentality of banking. Bankers often refer to themselves as 'fast followers' or 'lemmings'. The reason for this is that banking trades on a key tenet of being reliable, secure and trusted. This means banks have to be risk averse by nature. They therefore are often reluctant to lead, innovate or demonstrate entrepreneurialism, because these qualities require taking risks and banks exist to avoid risks by being secure, resilient and reliable.

However, the result is that banks all tend to follow each other around, looking for things that work for others and copying them fast. This is the fast-follower mentality. Fast following is often blind though. For example, in the UK, Midland Bank introduced free banking in the 1970s. Just as they realised it was a mistake because it was not profitable, all the other UK banks launched free banking because Midland Bank had taken many of their customers away from them. The result is that all UK citizens enjoy free banking and no bank dares to charge for banking as the media would rip them to pieces. Yet, they all hate free banking because it was a mistake.

The lemmings had all fallen over the cliff following each other and were stuck. The result is that UK banks make up for free banking by charging for other things such as heavy penalty fee rates for unauthorised overdrafts and late payments.

The lemming culture has demonstrated itself again recently though, in the debate between branch banking and internet banking.

What happened was that bankers all thought the branch was dead in 1996 and invested heavily in online servicing integrated with call centres. The call centre became a contact centre for email and instant messaging, whilst branches languished with zero investment and zero support. By 2000, most retail banks were closing branches to actively release funds for their technology adventures.

Then the internet explodes, so funding for the internet was frozen and investment returned to the branches. 'The Branch is dead, long live The Branch.'

Hundreds of millions of dollars have since been sunk into branches during the mid-2000s. Branch Transformation programmes have been replenishing branch operations with highly visual and exciting stimulants such as children's play centres, coffee machines, new high technology core systems and high bandwidth connections. The problem here is that the retail bankers were right in their original summation. The branch is dying. The branch is being rejected by new generations of customers, and old generations too. The branch is seen as a chore. And fundamentally, the branch, which used to be a bank's major asset, is now a liability.

Just take a look at the research, such as the 2006 survey performed by the American Bankers Association (ABA), which found that customers aged over 55 prefer to go to their branch, those aged under 35 prefer online banking, whilst one in six 18–35-year-olds see the branch as the last resort.

The branch is dead, and it is just taking longer to die than anyone ever thought. So what surprised me is that all the retail banks started investing heavily in branches shortly after the internet cycle of hype ended. This was the old nugget of 'that new fangled thing we don't understand didn't work after all so let's go back to the things we do understand'.

Yet the internet never stopped. The hype about internet firms' share prices stopped, but the actual web development continued and moved on.

The retail bankers' reversal of policy – from branch to internet and back to branch – is little like my personal experience in an electrical store in 2002. Back in 2002, I went into a mainstream UK electrical store and enquired to buy an MP3 player. The shop assistant said, 'Ah, we used to stock those but we stopped because no-one wants one; after all, who the hell would want to download music off the internet?' They did not see broadband coming and so the store did not stock MP3 players or iPods. In 2006, the same chain of electrical stores closed all their shops and is now purely operating through the internet and call centre.

The same is true of branches I am afraid. I know all the retail bankers will disagree, but just as Web 2.0 hits the streets, and YouTube sells for almost $2 billion within 18 months of its launch, most bank websites are languishing in web services dating back to the early 2000s, whilst their branches look flashy and no-one wants to use them.

Two of the chapters in this book focus upon the current and future web impact on retail banking front and back office, and these are two critical chapters. For me, they illustrate the issue of the 'fast follower' or lemming-mentality of bankers. The lemming discussion is that bankers all run after each other in packs and, if it goes wrong, they all go over the cliff together.

That is where we are right now. A lot of bankers falling over a cliff together due to the lack of web vision.

Web 2.0 is today's web, and Web 2.0 is all about podcasting, blogging, communities, participation and the long tail. It is about letting your community of participants control the flow of commerce, rather than controlling the community yourself. It is all about allowing self-expression and inclusion, not one-way marketing and minimal interaction.

So, just as retail bankers have returned to the bricks and mortar, the clicks and word of mouse is winning out. And the real issue for the retail world is that just as they get Web 2.0 and return to internet investing to catch up, the internet will have moved on again. There is already a third-generation internet on the way which I now nickname WebLife. This internet is even more disturbing than Web 2.0 because it requires a complete overhaul of a retail bank's core systems, back office, staff, organisational structure and operational structure.

Big challenges and big news.

That is not to say retail banks cannot get this right, it is just learning to live outside of their comfort zone in today's world of faster cycle change.

PART 3: PAYMENTS CHALLENGES

Meantime, in the payments market, more fast cycle change is occurring. Traditionally, banks have organised their payments groups in lots of different silo operations: cash management, cheque processing, credit cards, clearing and settlement, treasury, SWIFT, custody, and so on. This no longer works. Why? First, because retail payments are changing fast. Cash and cheques are declining, whilst prepaid, debit and credit cards are gaining. This was particularly demonstrated for me by a discussion in France where cheque usage has declined from 55% of payments to 33% between 1990 and 2005 whilst plastic card usage increased from 16% to 30% in the same period. However, the French banker who talked these numbers through with me was then lamenting the fact that customers were not moving fast enough away from traditional payments instruments – cash and cheques – to new electronic payments – direct debits, credit transfers and cards.

This is the retail payments challenge: getting the customers to move to electronic payments as that lowers costs and, potentially, increases income. Even then, even if we achieve getting customers away from their beloved paper, there are other challenges in that new technologies are driving relentless change in consumer payments. First, there was PayPal. Then there was Google Checkout. Then there was PayPal Mobile. Then there was PayPass. Then there was Pay-By-Touch. Then there were hundreds of contactless chip, micropayment, biometric payment and other services.

Very soon, we will have payments facilities integrated into chips in all sorts of devices, such as our clothing and jewellery. As a result, consumers do not need cards to pay or cash to pay, just a chip. If chips are everything, then why are banks still wedded to cards? After all, cards take up wallet space, especially if you have several card providers of both debit and credit. My own wallet is bristling with ten or more payment cards, along with a vast range of membership cards, loyalty programmes and prepaid gift cards. I actually went out and purchased a small portable A4-sized leather wallet portfolio case to carry around all of these cards, but did not feel it was secure enough.

Today, all of these cards could be condensed down into a single chip. So why are not we doing this? Because, again, we have investment in legacy card readers and infrastructures that do not make a switchover viable in the near-term. The technology is not proven, and security and authentication is not reliable enough. Ho-hum. Future retail payments will be dramatically transformed as we move further and further into chip-based payments, and I explore these themes in depth in the payments chapters.

Second, wholesale payments are changing fast. In 2004, hardly anyone talked about multinational corporations and treasury departments having direct electronic access to their bank payments processing cycles and yet today that is exactly what is happening. SWIFT, the major wholesale bank payments processing network based in Brussels, are now proud of the fact that their constituency has authorised direct corporate access to SWIFTNet, the network that provides secure and resilient global payments processing.

SWIFT is owned and operated by the banking community, and has over 7000 bank members, each of whom gets a vote on SWIFT's future. Of note then is the fact that only one bank voted for corporations to have access to SWIFT when it first hit the agenda in 2001. In 2006, 98.6% of the bank members voted for it. That is a big turn-around and reflects the fact that the corporate customer is more demanding than ever before. Corporate clients want banks that are proactive and responsive, who focus upon the value-add in their relationships with their corporate clients, and who manage and support total end-to-end supply chain automation, not just payments processing.

The payments business, in this sense, has become a commodity, and that is the payments challenge. How to differentiate a commoditized product. So, new innovations like contact-less payments, globally aggregated cash management, receivables reconciliation services, purchase order automation and einvoicing are all on the retail and wholesale agenda.

Equally, wholesale payments and treasury cannot ignore that first category of retail payments as most corporates deal with retail clients. Therefore, assisting the corporations to find it easier to transact with their customers is all part and parcel of this process, which is why banks have recognised that changing their views of, and role in, payments processing needs to reflect this.

No longer organised in silo functions, cash management, cheque processing, credit cards, clearing and settlement, treasury, SWIFT and custodial services are all coming together in most banks, under a Payments Tsar.

But that is not the only aspect of payments. There are also many discussions around the challenges in both low-value and high-value payments, and between non-urgent and urgent payments. There are the impacts of many new entrants, including the big shake-up of PayPal and the alternative processing offers of First Data and others.

Finally, there are many regulatory changes, such as the Single Payments Market in Europe and the Petrodollar zone of the Gulf Cooperation Council. In both instances, you have governments creating economically and monetarily integrated centres that can compete with the scale and size of America and China, the two dominant global economies of the 2000s. How do you challenge these economies? By creating seamless cross-border trading zones.

This involves more than just payments however. It also involves investing.

PART 4: INVESTMENT BANKER'S CHALLENGES

In the investment markets, major shake-ups are taking place to create globalised trading environments that operate on a $24 \times 7 \times 365$ basis. In order to compete in this globalised space, Europe has embarked upon a restructuring of the trading and investment markets such that the market is seamlessly integrated. The regulation is called MiFID, the Markets in Financial Instruments Directive, and will radically reshape the European landscape by allowing market-makers to compete directly alongside the national exchanges, a u-turn from the previous position in Europe where 'concentration rules' tried to concentrate all trading through the national exchanges. Equally, Clearing & Settlement is being shaken up as the European Central Bank launches their own securities clearing system, potentially in competition with EuroClear, Clearstream and other European players.

Meantime, RegNMS in the USA and a single securities regulator in Canada are causing North America to have trials and tribulations with investment markets reform. In particular, there are major concerns around over regulation, as research estimates that the USA will lose 60,000 jobs between 2007 and 2012 in Wall Street firms as Europe, and especially London, takes precedence to dominate the investment markets worldwide. Equally, the liberalisation of China opening to foreign investment is creating a brand new capital exchange, with similar dialogues across Asia around the impact of these exchanges.

All of these regulatory reforms are leading financial players to rethink processes, trading, connection and structures. In particular, low-latency technologies are the primary focus. Low latency means that any equity anywhere in the world can be tracked and traded anywhere else in the world within milliseconds, almost as though you were trading that instrument internally. In other words, the speed of trading has moved dramatically from days to minutes to seconds to milliseconds to instantaneous. That power of technology trading capability has driven two other big changes into the markets: first, connectivity overhaul through Direct Market Access (DMA); and second, trading overhaul through algorithmic trading.

Connectivity changes have been a long time coming, and has been enabled and challenged both by the nature of globalised trading but more, again, by the drive of the internet. Open systems with open access through a World Wide Web means that buy-side firms are now wondering about the value of sell-side firms when they can access trading systems direct. DMA to Electronic Cross Networks (ECNs) and Multilateral Trading Facilities (MTFs) has created a whole new business of order routing and order matching that leads to this low-latency instantaneous trading world.

It is that very technological drive that has led to automated trading increasing rapidly. Automated, program, algorithmic and electronic trading are all wrapped up in that same drive to achieve perfect markets where all players have access to all prices in all exchanges worldwide with total transparency and instant execution.

Wow!

Something never dreamed of a decade ago is now being delivered today: a level-playing field powered by Intel inside. This is not quite the case, but it is almost there, and is why algorithmic trading in particular is a critical factor.

Algorithmic trading allows investors and traders to build highly complex trading strategies across asset classes (different financial instruments) such that you can automate a trading strategy like this:

- if equity A decreases by 0.05%; and
- equity B rises by 0.1%; whilst
- $:€ exchange rates remain constant within a band of 1% change for the previous 30-minute trading period; then
- buy 10,000 units of equity A; whilst
- selling 1000 units of equity B; and
- buy a futures option on equity A being worth less in three months, equity B being worth more and $ rates increasing for a 3-month forward call contract.

or something along those lines.

Now, imagine that complexity of strategy multiplied to the nth degree, and you can see the dramatic change in the markets over the last 10 years.

First, you have very high speed trading at low costs with complex strategies. Second, you have high volumes of trading in low value. Third, the whole thing is being automated. Fourth, it is all globalised.

For these reasons, we have seen the growth and dramatic rise of two key new kids on the investment block: the hedge funds and the derivatives markets.

Hedge funds use highly complex trading strategies through globalised technology to build hugely sophisticated arbitrage. Arbitrage is similar to the above example of algorithmic trading where a change in one factor allows you to take advantage in another, whilst covering your position for any issue if the same were to happen the other way around. By way of example, if equity A rises and B decreases, buy B and sell A but take out a contract to give an option to sell B and buy A just in case. The options contract, part of the massively increased futures and options markets over the past decade, is the 'hedge' and the whole point of these funds is to find these opportunities and make a profit from hedging bets.

In addition, we have seen derivatives growing massively during the same period. Derivatives are exactly that: a derivation of another financial instrument. My aim here, though, is not to explain hedge funds, algo trading, derivatives, futures and options, but purely to give you a flavour of the investment markets, where they are and where they are going.

The bottom-line is that the combination of hedge funds and derivatives, especially credit derivatives, has introduced massive market volatility into the trading world today, as hedge funds trade trillions of leveraged dollars of investment across the global exchanges.[4]

As you can see, the investment markets are about as easy-to-understand as brain surgery except that if you strip away the complex language, they are actually quite easy-to-understand. That does not mean they are easy to work with or within, but they are understandable and I hope that some of the words in this book will strip away some of the complexity and help those of you who do not deal with these markets to understand a bit of what is going on.

THE CURRENT STATE OF BANKING

So there you have it. Seismic changes in banking are occurring as you read this book which means that even now, some of the themes explored here are out of date:

- the internet will have moved on and Web 2.0 will become passé;
- consumers and banks in China and India will change the landscape of retail banking;
- SWIFT will have begun implementation of their 2010 strategy whilst corporations will have come on board the SWIFT network to change the landscape of supply chain automation;
- investment markets will have been ripped apart by MiFID in Europe and hedge funds will have created even more market volatility through leveraging new, even more sophisticated, automated trading strategies;
- Basel II will have kicked in as will other legislative, regulatory and governmental policy changes, to ensure banking is resilient to 21st-century challenges of risk, terrorism and fraud; and
- several banks will have disappeared in a wave of mergers and acquisitions to make the big banks even bigger.

---

[4] According to Hedge Fund Research Inc., the hedge fund industry managed $1.225 trillion of assets at the end of the second quarter of 2006, an increase of 19% on the previous year and double the number of Q2 2003. Hedge funds leverage these trillions of dollars by trading based upon a 'deposit' style arrangement, as in a contract worth $100 million only needs $10 million or less of capital to cover the position. As a result, to gain arbitrage positions across the global markets, hedge funds actually control tens of trillions of dollars of global trading.

The one thing that will be constant is that banking will be changing faster in the next 5 years than in the last 50. This is as true in the late 2000s as it has been for the last 50 years. The reason is that banking is a business based upon technology today and technology has been changing faster in the last 50 years.

It was during Second World War that the first computer was invented. Known as ENIAC, the US Government sponsored the development in order to predict weather. Delivered after the War, ENIAC worked on transistors and was a huge, monolithic affair housed in a warehouse the size of an aircraft hangar. Fifty years later, the same power was in the hands of children in the form of laptop computers.

Banking is a business that has easily adapted and transformed by harnessing the power of these technologies. Visa, MasterCard and SWIFT would not exist without the technology revolution introduced by computer power. Today's global banks and global markets would not function or operate without the power of technology. And banking products, services and channels would not function today without the efficiencies in cost and service that technology provides.

Just as computer buffs discuss the idea of computing power doubling every 18 months whilst computing costs halve – known as Moore's law – there is an equal view that networking power is now doubling every 18 months whilst the cost halves. As a result, consumers, corporations, banks and governments are connecting, networking, transacting and servicing each other faster, more frequently and in more volumes, than ever seen before. That is the power of banking on technology and that is the core challenge for bankers competing in the 21st century.

Part 1
Global Issues

There are a range of global issues faced by banks today, as outlined in the opening introduction. Over-riding any discussion of global issues though, must be globalisation.

Globalisation is underpinned by the regulatory and technological changes taking place around the world over the past two decades, and has led to the rise of China and India as new powerhouse economies. In turn, China and India have pulled the economies of related regions up to new levels as they spin-off related services. For example, Russia's wealth is growing rapidly through supplying oil and gas to new and old economies, whilst Brazil is gaining capital through sourcing raw materials to China's manufacturing powerhouse.

These new economies are generally referred to as the BRICs, as in Brazil, Russia, India and China, a term which was coined by a research paper by Goldman Sachs in 2003.[1] This paper focused the world's attention upon the fact that the rise of millions of affluent consumers in Europe, America, Japan, Australia and related economies, would be repeated by the rise of the next billion affluent consumers in Brazil, Russia, India, China and other emerging economies, including Africa.

The factors driving globalisation and the discussions of the new economies are a major source of debate around the future of society and commerce, and are the focus of the first three chapters of this section.

Chapter 1 explores the impact of China and India in the world and specifically in the context of banking. Both economies will have major impacts upon core banking capabilities, from buying banks in Europe and America to creating the new generations of technology.

Chapter 2 studies a specific example of how globalisation can impact banks if they do not have tight operational controls. This particular example resulted in UBS being fined a record $100 million for supplying cash to Iraq before the Second Gulf War.

Chapter 3 reviews Islamic Banking. After the World Trade Centre attacks of 9/11, the world became aware of the needs and extremes of Islamic fundamentalism. The banking industry has responded by trying to create financial inclusion through offering Shariah compliant products.

Chapters 4 and 5 bring the focus onto the regulatory field. Regulation is a major driving factor for the banking industry, and Europe's plans for banking are the most radical. This is because they are taking an established industry, Europe's banks are the oldest in the world, and completely redefining all of the boundaries of competition.

Chapter 4 reviews the tensions this creates between politicians and regulators on the one hand, and banks and insurers on the other. Tensions that can be translated to any regulatory change agent in any part of the world.

The fifth chapter in this section looks at the European landscape and the implications of the tensions over policies related to the Euro. What would happen if the European Union ended and what would be the implications based upon the current European plan?

---

[1] Global Economics Paper No. 99, http://www2.goldmansachs.com/insight/research/reports/report6.html.

These two chapters can usefully be read in unison with Chapters 18, 19 and 20, which focus upon the key regulatory changes across Europe and the USA, including RegNMS, MiFID and the Payment Services Directive.

The final two chapters in this section, 6 and 7, then look specifically at change and technology. In this context there are issues challenging all of the world's banks, in terms of how to make processes work effectively and how to get real returns on technology investments.

1
India and China's Impact on Global Banking

We hear the stories and see the news and yet, for all we know about India and China's phenomenal growth story, how much do we really know about Indian and Chinese Banking? Shrouded in secrecy for decades, these state-owned financial behemoths are beginning to stir. In order to continue to fuel economic growth, the governments and regulators of these tiger economies are releasing the chains of their financial markets. What will this release mean to foreign banks and how should overseas banks react?

For the past few years, everyone has been talking about the powerhouse economies of India and China and, more recently, Brazil and Russia. It is not surprising that such discussions became the norm when the next billion consumers will arise out of these economies, with affluence to match those of Americans and Europeans.

The real interest in the BRIC economies – Brazil, Russia, India and China – arose from a Goldman Sachs research report published in October 2003 entitled 'Dreaming with BRICs: The Path to 2050.'[1] In this report, researchers at Goldman Sachs forecasted that by 2040 the BRIC economies would have a greater GDP than the G7; would be the main sector of growth for the next 45 years at an average 8% per annum; and that, by 2050, only the USA and Japan would remain in the G6, with the BRICs displacing Germany, the UK, France and Italy from this list of the most powerful countries in the world. The implications for the European Union appear to be grave.

The story of each economy is very different, with Brazil and Russia showing a very different form of growth to that seen in India and China, as illustrated by Figure 1.1. There is a strong relationship between the four economies however, with the ever increasing global expansion of China as a manufacturing economy and India as a services economy placing strong demand for supply of resources from Russia's oil supplies and Brazil's natural resources. As a result, increasing demand for goods from China and India is fuelling growth in the Russian and Brazilian economies.

Other factors need to be considered here too. The chart shows that India and China both have much larger populations than Brazil and Russia. India and China's workers are still heavily engaged in rural and agricultural locations, even with their respective services and manufacturing strengths, compared with Brazil and Russia's workers who are already heavily employed in service industries. And the really telling numbers are around China and India's GDP growth which have been running at 7% or greater per annum for the last decade, and are sustainable. Such growth rates for the long term are more questionable in the case of Russia, which has systemic issues of poor health due to alcoholism and drug abuse, alongside a declining population, as can be seen by the negative fertility rates. In fact, President Putin recently introduced financial incentives for women to have more than one child, although it remains to be seen whether such policies are successful.

---

[1] Global Economics Paper No. 99, http://www2.goldmansachs.com/insight/research/reports/report6.html.

Country	Brazil	Russia	India	China	USA	UK
Population	188,078,227	142,893,540	1,095,351,995	1,313,973,713	296,444,215	60,609,153
Labour force	90.41 million	74.22 million	496.4 million	791.4 million	149.3 million	30.07 million
Labour force agriculture industry services	20.0% 14.0% 66.0%	10.3% 21.4% 68.3%	60% 17% 23%	49% 22% 29%	0.7% 22.9% 76.4%	1.5% 19.1% 79.5%
Unemployment	9.9%	7.6%	9.9%	4.2% (20%)	5.1%	4.7%
Fertility (children/woman)	1.91	1.28	2.73	1.73	2.09	1.66
Population Growth	1.04%	−0.37%	1.38%	0.59%	0.91%	0.28%
Life Expectancy	71.97	67.08	64.71	72.58	77.85	78.54
GDP (purchasing power parity)	$1.556 trillion	$1.589 trillion	$3.611 trillion	$8.859 trillion	$12.36 trillion	$1.83 trillion
GDP (exchange rate)	$619.7 billion	$740.7 billion	$719.8 billion	$2.225 trillion	$12.49 trillion	$2.228 trillion
GDP real growth rate	2.4%	6.4%	7.6%	9.9%	3.5%	1.8%
GDP by sector agriculture industry, Including construction services	10.0% 39.4% 50.6%	5% 35% 60%	20.6% 28.1% 51.4%	14.4% 53.1% 32.5%	1% 20.7% 78.3%	1.1% 26% 72.9%
Inflation	5.7%	11%	4.6%	1.9%	3.2%	2.2%

Figure 1.1   The Economies Compared
Source: CIA World Handbook, http://www.cia.gov/cia/publications/factbook/geos/ch.html

For these reasons, the world's eyes remain upon the two countries with the largest populations and sustainable growth prospects: India and China. And one of the big things holding back these two economies is their banking and financial markets, or lack of them.

INDIA: SERVICES THE WORLD

India's economic success story dates back to the 1980s, when the government began investing in a critical programme of education, focused upon technology and language skills. This educational programme has enabled India's educated population to become English-speaking programmers and support providers to overseas operators and the good news is that India can keep up this phenomenal growth thanks to a population that is young, educated and growing.

The over one billion people who live in India are replenishing at a rate of 2.73 children per woman – compared to only 1.28 in Russia – with over 130 million new workers joining the Indian economy during the 2000s: a number equivalent to the workforces of Australia, Canada, Mexico, Poland, South Africa and the United Kingdom combined.[2]

Not only are seven out of 10 people under the age of 36, but they are also increasingly well educated. For the last 20 years, India's educational programme has achieved a population of 40 million graduate level citizens, 80 million achieving secondary education and nearly 150 million making it through primary education. On the other hand, two out of every five Indian citizens are still illiterate and a third live on less than a dollar a day. The challenge then is to achieve 100% literacy, which is the firm target on the government's agenda.

For example, successive Indian governments have increased investment in education consistently since the 1950s, with almost 4% of GDP placed into education since the late 1980s. This change of focus is evidenced by the fact that although two-thirds of India's over 50-year-olds are illiterate, only a quarter of under 18-year-olds are. Therefore, India's educational reforms and focus upon globalised services has been a significant success factor in their ability to achieve sustainable economic growth.

This is not to say that India relies purely upon services for its success, in that food production represents almost $70 billion of output every year and makes India one of the largest food producing nations in the world just behind China. But India is known for services due to the extraordinary success of their technology and call centre service industries, and it is these industries that can thank the educational and governmental reforms of the 1980s and 1990s.

In retrospect, these reforms were particularly visionary in terms of investment in technology and languages, as the 1990s saw the fuel of growth being delivered through globalised services via the internet. The internet boom allowed for the delivery of remote services which naturally relocated to India due to the cost savings. As a result, India has become the servicing operation to the world, with over three-quarters of global IT sourcing located in the country and most of the world's most recognised brands locating operations there, including American Express, Microsoft, General Motors, Sony, Coca-Cola, Philips, Wal-Mart, General Electric, Reebok, Boeing, IBM and so on.

The growth of India's services has been particularly noticeable in the financial community. TowerGroup estimate that total spending on offshore outsourcing amongst the world's financial institutions is rising from around $1.5 billion in 2004 to almost $4 billion in 2008, with India taking around 40% of that spend, or nearly $2 billion a year from the financial community alone. Nevertheless, financial services is not the only industry India serves, with services exports up by 71% in 2004–05 to $46 billion, of which software services represented $17.2 billion.

All of this is good news for banking, with consumer's personal disposable income surging 42% between 1999 and 2003, over 15 million credit cards issued, and four out of every five cars sold through loans. But it's not all good news.

INDIA'S BANKING: RUN BY CIVIL SERVANTS

India's banks have been fairly well protected from reform during this period. This is due to a number of reasons, with the primary reason being the Indian government's concerns over foreign ownership. Although government controls on foreign trade and investment, have

---

[2] UK (30 million), Mexico (43 million), Canada (16 million), Australia (10 million), South Africa (15 million) and Poland (17 million).

been reduced in some areas, such as civil aviation, telecom, and construction, most other areas are still subject to high tariffs. These tariffs were running at around 20% on average for non-agricultural items in 2004, and severe limits on foreign direct investment (FDI) are still in place.

In banking terms, these restrictions are potentially constraining India's competitiveness. 80% of India's banking system is government owned following nationalisation in 1969 to bring banking to the masses. The recent developments in private sector banks still only have a few names which stand out, such as HDFC Bank and ICICI Bank.

Of particular note is the fact that the central bank, the Reserve Bank of India (RBI), takes an active role in protecting India's banking system from being open to full competitive forces. For example, RBI recently attempted to restrict the operations of a new PayPal style service set up by the India Times, Wallet365.com, by enforcing Know Your Customer rules. These strict rulings severely hinder the convenience of the service, which is the whole point of providing an online wallet. Equally, RBI forced the new Chief Executive for HSBC India, Naina Lal Kidwai, to relinquish her non-executive directorship at Nestlé because it broke their strict guidelines for corporate governance, even though such guidelines would not apply to a bank executive in other regions.

For foreign banks, RBI's activities create a major barrier to effective entry. First, there are domestic restrictions such as the requirement that any bank must prioritise that 40% of all loans and advances go into agriculture and small business, the so called 'priority sectors', and that 25% of bank branches be located in rural or semi-urban areas which are typically the least profitable. RBI also limits foreign ownership in private sector banks to a maximum 5% although, under government pressure, this may be changing. For example, in March 2006, RBI allowed the first foreign institution to increase its investment in a private sector bank to more than 5%, with Warburg Pincus taking a 10% in Kotak Mahindra Bank.

Without such change India faces significant issues, as the government wants to open financial markets to more foreign ownership in order to increase capital flow. Government representatives have openly discussed financial reforms and want to achieve further liberalisation by 2009. As part of this liberalisation, they recently announced that foreign investment in domestic banks should be able to increase by up to 10% per annum to a maximum 74%. The reason the government needs this to happen is that India has a shortage of capital and capital markets.

The total value of India's financial assets including bank deposits, equities and debt securities in 2004 amounted to $900 billion. China has five times that capitalisation, with forecasters estimating that China's stock will achieve $9 trillion by 2010, whilst India will reside at $2 trillion.

The major reason for this constraint is that India's citizens do not trust banks. The culture of India's citizens is to trust assets, and so most savings goes into cattle, housing and gold, rather than into banking, deposits and savings. That is why India has the largest consumer economy for gold in the world. India's people bought $10 billion worth of gold last year, equivalent to double the amount of total foreign investment in India, whilst owning over $200 billion of gold overall, equivalent to about half of the country's total bank deposits.

It is this trust in physical assets that explains the reason why only 40% of India's citizens are borrowers or depositors and, as a nation, why India is one of the weakest nations in terms of borrowings. India's mortgage debt totalled only 2% of GDP in 2002, compared with 8% of GDP in China. Meanwhile, because of the impact of the collapse of Global

Trust Bank (GTB) in 2004, one of the larger private sector banks created during the 1990s, it is unlikely that India's people will change their minds that quickly about the stability of banks.

This causes India a major dilemma as, on the one hand, the central bank 'owns' the government debt and therefore can tell the politicians the way to go forward; on the other, the government needs to maintain economic growth of 8% or more if India's success story is to continue and this cannot be achieved if markets are artificially controlled and protected from free trade.

The arguments between the central bank and the government, along with the cultural mismatch between India's citizens and their banks, will need to be resolved if India is to succeed in maintaining momentum.

INDIA: THE FUTURE IS STILL BRIGHT

Whilst India wrangles domestically with its own banking services, one of the biggest impacts India will have on world banking will not stem from India's challenges domestically today, but from its ability to adapt and develop new services tomorrow.

As mentioned, India today controls three-quarters of the world's IT sourcing. India's National Association of Software and Service Companies (NASSCOM) states that 80 of the 117 software firms worldwide attaining the highest quality standards for software development are from India. This is substantiated by the fact that the standard by which most technology firms are measured is the Capability Maturity Model (CMM).

CMM has five levels, with the highest level – level 5 – assigned to recognise those firms who optimise software development standards, rather than just using them. Three quarters of the CMM level 5 software centres are in India. This is why India has spawned so many development centres for banking; software solutions firms for bank systems, including iFlex, Infosys and Temenos; and outsourcing and consulting firms in bank services, such as Wipro, Tata and Cognizant.

The result is that India's IT sector has been growing faster than most other sectors at a CAGR of over 30% since 2000, with India boasting over a quarter of the best IT systems sourcing talent on the planet.

This may all sound fairly pedestrian so far as yes, we all know that India has great success with IT and IT outsourcing. However, we may not all know the likely consequences of this expansion.

For example, many of India's graduates over the last 15 years have left their homes in Mumbai, Chennai and Delhi to live in Memphis, Charlotte and Detroit. As India's expatriates have grown in stature and experience, they have been charged with more and more sourcing responsibilities and experience. The result is that many of these executives are more experienced in global sourcing than any others, and are now returning to Mumbai, Chennai and Delhi as repatriates to return their knowledge to their home base. This is a natural move for many, as India's wealth and quality of living increases to match the expectations for living standards which these executives hoped to achieve when moving overseas in the first instance.

The extrapolation of this movement is that, in around 15 years, India will be teaching the world the management of operations. Some see this as an extreme but the logic is based firmly upon a similar revolution in management techniques seen during the 1950s when the Total Quality Management (TQM) and Just-In-Time Processing (JIT) revolution came out of Japan. That revolution was created by Dr William Edwards Deming.

Dr Deming was invited to Japan at the end of Second World War to advise Japanese leaders as to how to rebuild Japan's manufacturing capabilities and methods of production. Dr Deming, a statistician, introduced a range of techniques, including quality processes and JIT, which delivered high quality manufacturing over a period of years and was known as 'Deming's 14 Point Plan'. Deming's Plan has been the foundation of Japanese economic success ever since as Japan not only listened to Dr Deming's plan, but regimentally adopted it. By the 1970s, Japan was not just producing good quality products from cameras to cars, but with minimal stock and inventory control. The improvements in efficiency soon fuelled an economic boom that lasted 20 years and led to Japan becoming the world's second largest economy behind America.

This is the phenomenon that many see occurring in India today. Just as Dr Deming created a manufacturing revolution in Japan, global sourcing is creating a management revolution in India.

This revolution follows a number of phases, some of which were outlined earlier in this chapter, which lead to a natural conclusion.

The first phase is a cultural revolution inspired by government educational reform policies during the 1980s to make India become a global competitor.

The second phase is a global revolution as corporations relocate operations globally through new technological changes. The result is that India becomes the leading centre for systems developments, services and operations.

The third phase involves learning how to integrate the competencies of sourcing across financial operations. There are three distinct competencies involved:

(a) how to source – insource, cosource or outsource – a combination referred to as right-sourcing;
(b) where to source – locally, nationally, internationally, nearshore, onshore or offshore; and
(c) when to source – front office, back office, commodity, strategy, product, service, channel.

The decisions involved in deconstructing bank processes and then reconstructing them back together again in a seamlessly integrated global structure is the demanding role of today's sourcing leaders. The combination of skills required is generally referred to as 'smart-sourcing', and smart-sourcing has become critical to bank operations: how, where and when to source. And who are the world's experts in smart-sourcing? The leading proponents with these skills are Indian.

The fourth phase therefore is to use this experience and leadership to innovate the management and leadership of banking. This is India's potential – to reinvent banking based upon leadership in global sourcing techniques – and, regardless of India's domestic banking structure, is the likely major conclusion from India's IT services operations over the next decade. Should India decide to leverage that leadership domestically however, as in to use the repatriated skills returning to the country over the next 10 years, then that experience could be used to enable India's banks to become the world's most competitive banks.

The strategy for India – whether to export skills for bank structures or retain the leadership internally – will be one of the most fascinating aspects of India's developments in financial services over the next decade.

THE RISE OF CHINA

Further to reviewing India's capabilities, which lay mainly with smart sourcing technology services rather than banking, let us look at China's rise to prosperity.

China's economic prosperity is largely due to the major government reform programme of Deng Xiaoping during the 1980s. Xiaoping's vision moved China away from centralised planning and control, closed to international trade, into a thriving market-oriented economy. His government achieved this by liberalising prices, decentralising fiscal policies to local government, and increasingly allowing State-Owned Enterprises (SOEs) to act autonomously.

Xiaoping's reforms were continued through the 1990s by his successor Jiang Zemin and were paid homage to in a recent speech by the current Chinese President, Hu Jintao, who stated 'from 1978 to 2003, China's GDP increased from US$147.3 billion to over US$1.4 trillion, with an average annual increase rate of 9.4%; its total foreign trade volume grew from US$20.6 billion to US$851.2 billion, with an average annual growth rate of 16.1%; and the poverty-stricken population in the rural area dropped from 250 million to about 29 million'.[3]

Between 2003 and 2005, China's economy grew at 9% per annum, and has more than doubled in the last 10 years with industrial output increasing by a factor of nine since 1978.

Again, a key aspect of China's growth has been through targeted education, with China producing over 800,000 science and engineering graduates in 2005, more than any other nation, and expecting to rise to over a million science and engineering graduates by 2010, more than the total number of graduates in these disciplines leaving all American, Japanese, French, German and British universities.

This will continue to fuel China's manufacturing prowess and is critical to China's future growth plans as, unlike India, China has a big challenge in that its' population is getting older. As discussed earlier in this chapter, India has a rapidly growing population with 70% of the population under the age of 36. Conversely, China has a declining population. This is largely due to the Planned Birth Policy introduced by Deng Xiaoping's administration in 1979. The Policy was designed to cope with the demands of a society with scarce resources and encouraged families to only have one-child. Two decades later, the result is that 300 million Chinese who would have been born do not exist. To put this in perspective, India has 130 million new citizens joining their society in the 2000s, while China has 300 million missing.

That is why China's population growth lies at a measly 0.59% – India's is 1.3% – and why China, like much of Japan, Europe and other parts of the world, has one of the most rapidly ageing populations in the world. China will have to look hard for future workers to continue to sustain their growth phenomenon. That is not difficult though, when unofficial figures estimate that China has almost 260 million unemployed people, about the population of the USA.

China's real issues lie elsewhere, including how to manage pollution and energy supply, converting State-Owned Enterprises (SOEs) from nationalised to privatised industries, and how to rebalance the poor rural populations in the West with the growing affluent urban populations of the East. All of these relate back to China's banking structures, or lack of them.

---

[3] Hu Jintao speech to the Brazilian Parliament, 13 November 2004, Reference: http://www.fmprc.gov.cn/eng/wjdt/zyjh/t170363.htm.

CHINA'S BANKING: A RENOVATION PROJECT

Many of China's issues in restructuring to support their economic powerhouse status relate to their financial systems. For example, China currently has foreign currency reserves of almost a trillion dollars, growing at over $17 billion a month. As a result China's central bank, the People's Bank of China, regularly buys dollars from their commercial banks and substitutes them for Renminbi bonds. With so much money in government hands, is it any wonder that China is spending so grandly on major projects such as the Qinghai Tibet railway. The railroad is the world's highest, and the final section to Lhasa was opened on 2 July 2006 at a cost of $4.2 billion. China has invested over $125 billion in the Western provinces since 2000, including the controversial three gorges dam projects, and has $21 billion more planned. All of these investments are part of the rebalancing of wealth and commerce between East and West China.

Dealing with the fact that China is swimming in excess dollars is one challenge, but China's banking has more fundamental issues. For example, until 2001, the banks were wholly owned by China's government and had no function other than to take monies from China's citizens to invest in government projects and enterprises. That is why China's banks had little concept of customer services or of managing risk. If you entered a Chinese bank branch, the whole ethos is one of directing customers into queues and then leaving the customer to wonder whether they would ever get served. Interest rates on savings averaged just 0.5% for the last 10 years, even though China's citizens save almost of a quarter of their earnings.

On the other hand, China's bank lending was virtually blind, as long as it was authorised by the People's Party, with 95% of corporate loans made to State Owned Enterprises (SOEs). That lending has also been China's banks undoing however as, again according to unofficial reports, China's banks are suffering from around 40% of non-performing loans, the highest in the region. In other words, four out of ten loans are never paid off but with a trillion dollars in foreign currency reserves available from the government to bail out any bank that gets into problems, it may imply that the issue is covered, but it does lead to some major questions around China's future.

First, the government is actively trying to shift from the majority of workers being employed by SOEs to a more commercial and competitive economy. Some of these SOEs have already been transformed, such as the car industry, and many are employed in building and construction, with 40 airports, 26 underground railways, 30 nuclear power stations and over 50,000 miles of motorway being built over the next five years.

However, a third of the SOEs are non-performing and should be closed down or sold off. This would lead to a further 150 million people being laid off, and the pay-offs incurred would increase the non-performing loan rate, which is already running at almost a trillion dollars – the same amount as China's currency reserves. Of more concern is the fact that if China's banks begin to behave as banks in other parts of the world behave, then it could cause much more civil unrest and destabilise the economy.

Equally China's banks have already had to be bailed out by the government through recapitalisation of their balance sheets. Since the late 1990s, the Chinese Government has added over $215 billion to their banks reserves in order to keep them afloat. This means that Chinese banks have to generate at least $25 billion more in annual revenues to service the cost of those government borrowings, than equivalent banks would have to generate in other countries.

Second, China's financial markets have no defined capital markets or commercial banking. China's capital markets purely fund SOEs, with companies unable to borrow from the bond markets and no recognised equities markets. According to McKinsey, China only raises a third of their capital through the equities markets and, even then, half of that funding goes into government enterprises. That means that only 17% of commercial firms trade on the equities markets, compared to 60% in other emerging economies.

Even more telling is that the corporate bond market is virtually non-existent. The corporate bond market is just 13% of GDP, compared to over half in other emerging markets. Those bonds once again are funding government enterprises. This means that the funding of real business is through generic loans, with 95% of borrowing by commercial firms through bank loans.

The net result is that McKinsey estimates that China could:

- reduce their cost of capital by $14 billion a year through creating a vibrant bond market;
- that more efficient equities markets would reduce the costs of share issuing and trading by over $1.5 billion a year, even at today's small volumes; and
- that China would realise over $320 billion a year in savings through improvements from financial reform, equivalent to a 17% increase in GDP.

This is part of the reason why, unlike India, China has entered a radical reform programme of their banking operations, which began with World Trade Organisation (WTO) requirements to change in 2001.

CHINA'S BANKING: REFORMING THROUGH 2007

China joined the WTO in 2001 and made a number of concessions, not the least of which was to open their banking markets to direct foreign competition. The process allowed increasing foreign direct investment in China's domestic banks from 2001, with full competition from 2007. This is different to the Indian markets, as China is completely releasing the handles on their financial institutions once deregulation is complete, whilst India still has highly protective barriers to foreign competition.

Initially, the restrictions on foreign investment in Chinese banks was that foreign ownership could not exceed 25% of a bank and no single investor could own more than 19.9%. These restrictions will gradually be lifted and, as a result, many firms are taking the opportunity to grab a slice of Chinese banking, as illustrated in Figure 1.2.

These firms are taking a calculated risk however.

On the one hand, foreign bank investors in Chinese banking are desirous of the prospects of creating a new capital market and equities exchange as a third major business hub to match those of London for Europe and New York for the USA. They are also avaricious for the country's growing 'consumer class' which numbered almost a quarter of a billion people in 2002, or 19% of the population. These are consumers who previously could not invest overseas, did not have access to high net returns and are potentially eager for European and American banking style services.

On the other hand, China's banks are still unstable, without a strong understanding of customer service or risk management, as previously mentioned. As foreign banks enter into Chinese banking, they do run the risk that their non-performing loans are with State-Owned

Enterprises (SOEs), in other words with the government. If overseas banks begin to apply strong credit risk management techniques the result will be that they will stop providing and servicing loans to SOEs and will begin to call them in. Meanwhile, the very same banks are also likely to begin creating financial instruments that divert consumers' investments away from China's SOEs and into commercial banking or, even worse, overseas products. Either approach would cause the People's Party to rethink the reform process and potentially close down some of these 'joint ventures' with the overseas player. In so doing, the overseas investors will kiss their investments goodbye.

Nevertheless, the rewards outweigh the risks according to most bank investors and so the re-energising of Chinese banking will continue. During this renovation, a new form of banking will also appear which will teach Europe's and America's banks a few lessons.

Buyer	Seller	Deal Structure
Bank of America (US)	China Construction Bank	9% stake to rise to 19.9% in 4 years
Bank for Nova Scotia (Canada)	Xian City Commercial Bank	5% to rise to 24.9% in 4 years
Citigroup (US)	Shanghai Pudong Development Bank	5% stake
Commonwealth Bank (Australia)	Jinan City Commercial Bank	Agreement for 11% stake
Deutsche Bank (Germany)	Huaxia Bank	9.9% stake
Hang Seng Bank (Hong Kong)	Industrial and Commercial Bank of China	15.98% stake
HSBC (UK)	Bank of Communications	19.9% stake
ING (Netherlands)	Bank of Beijing	19.9% stake
Merrill Lynch (US)	Huaan Securities Co.	33% stake
Newbridge Capital, Inc. (US)	Shenzhen Development Bank	17.9% stake
Royal Bank of Scotland (UK)	Bank of China	10% stake
Standard Chartered (UK)	Bohai Bank	19.9% stake

© Balatro Ltd, www.balatroltd.com

Figure 1.2 Foreign Banks' Direct Investments in China's Banks by Buyer (2004–05)

LESSONS TO BE LEARNT FROM CHINA'S BANKS

The biggest lesson European and American banks will learn from China is in technology. Just as America has been the technology powerhouse of the world for the last half a century, China intends to be the world's technology powerhouse for the next. That is why you cannot buy any electronic goods these days without a 'made in China' label somewhere on the product, whether it be a Lenovo PC or a Konka TV. But China's real focus is to own the next generation of technologies, and the People's Party is investing very heavily in new areas from next generation internet to next generation mobile. For example, in 2006, China had 400 million mobile telephone users and 110 million internet users, over 60 million of those on broadband. This is why China is revolutionising services and products dramatically and with full government backing.

The government is also backing these changes because the last century of technology innovation by-passed China. By way of illustration, when the foundations of the internet were being laid in the 1980's, the USA created the network and dominated the system. That is why each American on average owns six IP (Internet Protocol) addresses, compared with 26 Chinese having to share one IP address, according to the International Telecommunication Union.

So China is putting dollars into technology, and big dollars. For example, IPv6 – Internet Protocol version 6 – is the chosen standard for the next generation of the internet. The Chinese government created a project that ran from the end of 2002 until August 2003 called the China Next Generation Internet, which aimed to champion China's leadership in this area. The project was supported by the National Development and Reform Commission, the Ministry of Science and Technology, the Ministry of Education and other leading government ministries, and received over $175 million investment. This gave the Chinese community a clear understanding of the implications and opportunities for IPv6. Similarly, the government lends support to leading technology providers, such as Huawei which provides internet networking facilities, and provides grants to business to experiment with new technologies.

It is not surprising that this is critical to China's future when you have a business that has jumped from 10% of the world's electronics production to 18% between 2000 and 2003 at a CAGR of 15.4% and is now worth over $200 billion a year. Similarly, China will have the world's largest broadband enabled population, with 140 million citizens on high speed lines expected by 2010.

The result is that Chinese banks are reaping the rewards of this spend. According to TowerGroup Research, bank IT spending in China increased 32% annually from 2004 to 2007, rising from $10.1 billion to $23.2 billion (USD), which is faster than anywhere else in the world. This spend is going into new core systems and into new technologies such as WiMAX, the next generation wireless standard, IPv6 and fourth generation mobile telecommunications.

One illustration of this leadership in technology was the give-away Swatch-style World Cup 2006 watch from Chinatrust Commercial Bank during the summer. The watch was given away to promote the soccer World Cup in Germany, and incorporated a contactless MasterCard PayPass chip. The idea being that you could walk around Beijing and when you saw a CD or DVD you wanted, you just flashed the watch over the reader and the product was purchased. Simple, innovative and far and away ahead of anything Western European or American banks are doing with these RFID chips so far. The watch is discussed in depth in Chapter 15, and illustrated in Figure 15.2 if you want to have a look at this sort of innovation in more depth.

The key to China is their technology future therefore. Just as America was synonymous with computing and innovation in the 20th Century, China will be the technology powerhouse in the 21st Century. Just as Wang, Data General, Prime, Digital and all the other East Coast computer firms were subsumed by the rise of Intel and Microsoft in the 1990s; Dell, Intel, HP and others will be seriously challenged by the rise of Lenovo and Huawei in the 2000s. Therefore, as a banker, if you want to see the next generation of channels, technologies and innovation: go to China.

CONCLUSION: CHINA AND INDIA ARE TWO TIGERS YOU CANNOT IGNORE

Throughout this chapter we have looked at China and India in depth, and compared and contrasted the two countries. From a banking viewpoint, both countries offer exciting opportunities as they have been closed to foreign bank entry until recently.

Neither country has sophisticated capital markets or commercial banking, and retail bank lending, savings and deposits are also relatively untapped. There are major differences, however.

India's banking systems are more cosmopolitan with some capabilities for commercial lending and equities. This could be leveraged if it were not for the concerns of India's central bank that India's banks, if opened to foreign competition, do not know how to compete. As a result, India's reform process is very slow.

China, on the other hand, has been forced to change fast as part of their accession to the WTO. Therefore, the banking markets are revolutionising with investment and foreign skills. China, in the short term therefore, will be the major market to watch.

In the long term, it is different.

China, in the long term, will be teaching American and European banks how to use technology, but their markets will gradually dwindle and wane as their citizens grow old. Conversely, India has 7 out of 10 citizens under the age of 36. Therefore, whilst China teaches the world about the next generations of technology, India will be producing the next generations of managers.

This book is called 'The Future of Banking: In a Globalised World', and you may be wondering what the vision will be for the future therefore. Well, by 2020, some are jokingly referring to the idea of a London centre being the outsourced trading operations for India's banks whilst New York provides the offshore clearing and settlement systems for Beijing.

You never know, it just might come true.

2
The Road from Baghdad to Zurich

The US Federal Reserve Board fined UBS $100 million for financial misbehaviours in 2004, the second largest penalty the Reserve ever issued. The fine was for currency trading violations when it was discovered that UBS had been exchanging US dollar bills with countries on America's blacklist economies. That may sound innocent enough, except that the investigation was triggered when US forces found $650 million newly minted American notes in a small building in Baghdad during the overthrow of Saddam Hussein. This chapter reviews some of the questions raised by the fine, the wider issues of compliance and adherence to different national, international and global regulations, as well as some of the technologies that should be considered to avoid these issues occurring in the future.

They may not have found weapons of mass destruction in Iraq, but they have found a lot of other things. In particular, US forces found a lot of cash. American cash. Apparently, the US forces broke through a wall in a small building in Iraq in April 2003 and found a number of metal boxes, each containing crisp new American dollar bills. They must have thought it was their lucky day because, by the end of that day, they had discovered 164 of these boxes around Baghdad with a value to the tune of $650 million. It may have been a lot more than that, but that is how much was declared. Most of the cash bore sequential serial numbers and had apparently been held as currency reserves by the Central Bank of Iraq. But the question that bothered the Americans is how the money got there in the first place – especially when Iraq had been subject to trade sanctions for over a decade.

The US authorities began an immediate investigation and narrowed it down fairly rapidly to a few suspects. After all, there are not that many organisations that move dollars around the world and the ones that do are called banks. Although none of the major banks dealing with the distribution of freshly printed dollars overseas had sent any currency directly to Iraq, one bank – UBS – had been trading currencies with a number of countries that were under sanctions, namely the former Yugoslavia, Cuba, Libya and Iran. These countries had then traded the currency onwards. Apparently, it is not a crime for non-US banks to trade US currency with these countries, even though they were under sanctions, and so UBS employees had been doing this since the mid-1990s. And, just to be absolutely clear, UBS was not charged with any criminal matters as a result of the enquiries, but was given the hefty fine primarily to demonstrate the Federal Reserve's displeasure at its activities.

UBS itself conducted an extensive internal audit of what had happened and attributed many of the issues to a small group of employees who either no longer worked for the bank or were asked to find alternative positions.

So, that is the end of that you might think, but let's not be so hasty.

First, this appears to be yet another instance of poor regulation and audit. In fact, many US political advisors are saying the fine was not strong enough and that the Fed has not been doing its job up-to-scratch. There is now an ongoing debate about sudden audits and on-the-spot checks of banking back offices by Federal inspectors, as well as a big sharpening of the Fed's teeth in order to better manage the banking fraternity.

Second, this also appears to be yet another instance of operational risk caused by human interaction in the process.

By way of example, when Barings Bank went belly-up, the issues were caused by operational risk. In that context, it was Nick Leeson corrupting the system by being the same person running the back and the front office, in effect becoming both the salesman and the order processor. As a result, he could take sales orders, hand over his sales order to himself and process the order, pay himself the commission and tally the accounts in his favour, and do all of this without being traced. . .until it all backfired.

In this instance, UBS employees had just got into a way of doing business that no-one had bothered to consider might be out of kilter with the US authorities. No big deal – well actually a $100 million deal, as that was the size of the fine – and yet another issue of operational risk caused by the human hand.

The result is that regulators are getting harder and harder on financial misdemeanours, whilst legislators are getting tougher and tougher on tightening the noose on the banking fraternity.

On the financial misdemeanours circuit, you only have to look at the amount of fines for the year meted out by the major regulatory authorities, such as the Securities and Exchange Commission (SEC) in the USA and the Financial Services Authority (FSA) in the UK, to get an idea of the scale of what we are talking about. The SEC fined US financial firms over $4.5 billion in the first six months of 2004 – that's more than the whole of 2003 combined, and compares with a paltry $332 million in fines in 2001. The FSA's total fines also doubled in 2004.

Meantime, we see core legislation tightening between the risk reporting requirements of Basel II, the audit and accounting requirements of Sarbanes Oxley and the anti-money laundering and fraud requirements of the Patriot Act. The latter two may be US domestic policies but do not discount them too fast as these regulations are being followed fast by European and global equivalents. For example, Sarbanes Oxley is being shadowed by the Higgs Report and Companies Bill in the UK, the Nørby Committee in Denmark, the Aldama Report in Spain, the Cromme Code in Germany and so on.

Between this cocktail of operational risk and hammer-to-crack-a-nut legislative and regulatory punches, some banks are in danger of suffering a total knockout punch unless they do something drastic. But what is it they should do?

Well, I guess the answer is back-up, back-up, back-up and index. Banks must be able to show compliance and audit within every part of the process. Banks have to plaster over any cracks in the process to ensure there are no breaks, splits or spillages. Human trade-offs and subjective decision-making has to be recorded, audited and managed in a manner whereby any bank representative can stand-up, hand-on-heart, and be willing to declare that they are confident the bank's operational procedures and processes were being adhered with. Any failure to do any of these things will no longer be tolerated, especially if you are caught in non-compliance.

Now, the danger of this is that many firms just do not have the technology infrastructure in place to be able to achieve straight-through compliance. For example, how do you capture all currency exchange movements between countries if employees do not record these movements electronically? Answer: no currency movements should take place unless they are recorded electronically and authorised. Sounds simple but it is not.

Let's take another example. Of all the e-mails, instant messages, text messages, telephone calls and mobile calls made be the hundreds and thousands of employees of your bank each and every day, how many are backed-up and indexed on your systems? How many should be? If you were asked tomorrow to retrieve the call made by John Doe at 1:15 p.m. with the subsequent instant message discussion that took place at 1:28, could you retrieve it? How fast and how accurately?

That is really what all of this boils down to, namely the instant retrieval of any communication between your bank's representatives and any other third party on demand. And that is the task challenging banks today in this world of heightened fear, over-regulation and proliferating communication channels. After all, if you are not managing your processes, auditing your communications, complying with local, national and international regulations throughout every step of your operations, do you really feel confident in your trading abilities? The answer is that you will do, only if you back-up, back-up, back-up and index. That is why JPMorgan Chase back-up and index over one terabyte of communications every day.

The corollary of this challenge is that if you are not managing all of these things at the micro-level, with back-up and indexing throughout every step of your operations, then you will get caught out. For example, SEC Rule 17a-4 and NASD 3110 states that broker/dealers and exchange members 'must preserve all electronic communications relating to the business of their firm in a non-rewritable, non-erasable format for three years, two (years) of which must be in an easily attainable place'. An 'easily attainable place' translates to you must be able to deliver any piece of electronic communications within 24 hours. That's another reason why you just might want to start auditing everything, backing up everything, indexing everything and storing everything.

Between the tracking of currency movements, the potential for human error, the opportunity for operational risk, the fear of terrorism, the threat of regulation and the hand of legislation, the excuse that you just forgot to manage the process no longer cuts ice.

3

The Rise in Islamic Banking

Following the 9/11 attacks in America, many changes occurred in how we view and treat the needs of Muslim communities in the banking industry. On the one hand, the USA introduced legislation to regulate the Hawala method of transferring money between American immigrants and their families in Asia and the Middle East. On the other, the UK government decided to endorse the opening of Europe's first fully-compliant Islamic bank with a local mandate. So what are the implications of the Islamic faith in banking, and what are banks doing to exploit the opportunities these create?

Before discussing the implications, it is worth explaining how the markets we are going to discuss operate.

First, there is Hawala – an ancient method of transferring money between people in Asia. Today, it is a method of transferring money overseas that does not involve complex payment infrastructures and processes, but more of a trust with traditional ways of doing business.

In the context of the USA, Hawala is primarily used for transferring money between American immigrants and families in India, Pakistan, the Middle East and Asia.

The way it works is that you go to your local money broker – a 'Hawaladar' in New York, Miami or wherever you live – and ask for the transfer of money to your family overseas. The Hawaladar is often a friend or contact who has a mainstream occupation in the USA, whilst offering Hawala dealings as a second business. The Hawaladar will quote you an exchange rate and a fee which will be far more competitive than a usual bank rate. Rather than taking the first rate offered, it is more likely that you would then ask a few more Hawaladars for their rates, until you find the price and fee that is the most competitive. At that point, you pay the Hawaladar your money and they ring their contact in the town you want the payment made. Their contact makes the payment in local currency to your relatives and keeps the amount paid 'on account'. The account is settled at some point in the future, when the Hawaladar meets his contact face-to-face. All of this is held together by trust and book-keeping of accounts, which has worked for centuries.

Second, there is the growth of Islamic banking in the 'Western' world. In its current form, Islamic banking traces its roots to the Mit Ghamr Saving Bank in Egypt, which created the principles of Islamic banking in the early 1960s. However, the concepts only really began to gain traction in the early 1970s when banks in Jeddah, the United Arab Emirates and Bahrain began to trade seriously in Islamic financial instruments. Today, more than 75 countries operate Islamic banks in an industry worth over $230 billion and growing by more than 15% per annum. As a result, many Western banks have started to look at this area as a future growth opportunity.

The way Islamic banking works is that the mainstream Western financial instruments that are interest-bearing, such as a mortgage, credit card, loan or savings account, are forbidden. Interest, as with usury in traditional Christian and Catholic traditions, is considered to be evil and under the Koran, interest – or riba – is specifically prohibited. Therefore, other ways to buy a car or own a house are used in Islamic banking, with the majority of financing being placed through a Murabaha contract. In this contract, the bank buys the asset, for example a car, on behalf of the customer and then sells the asset to the customer with a mark-up, payable on a deferred payment basis. The result is similar to a car purchase scheme from your local garage, except that the Murabaha contract fundamentally excludes any interest payments.

The reason for this brief discussion is that it helps us to understand why there is a growing interest in these areas of financial services. On the one hand, following 9/11, the US authorities determined to stop Hawala dealings as they were a major source of concern over Al Qaeda funding and money laundering. On the other, the UK government was persuaded to change their banking laws to enable the opening of Europe's first official Islamic Bank, the Islamic Bank of Britain.

Hawala was targeted by the US authorities because it is an anonymous network. No monies actually physically move around borders, but everything is done through contacts and connections. As a result Hawala could be capable of funding both legitimate and illegitimate activities. It is this latter concern, and Hawala's anonymity, that sparked the US government's interest. For example, worldwide remittances from rich countries to poorer ones were worth more than $100 billion in 2003. Hawala is one of the primary means of moving that money and the concern was that, even if it was just a small amount going towards terrorist activities, it was an amount too much. To illustrate the size of the money transfer market in the USA using Hawala, US customs agents estimated that over $50 million moved between Michigan and Yemen alone in 2002.

The result was that the US Patriot Act, passed in October 2001, gave the FBI and other agencies increased powers. The Act specifically made failure to register with the US Treasury's Financial Crimes Enforcement Network (FinCEN) a crime for businesses engaged in remittance services, such as Hawala businesses. The result is that Hawala activities have been subject to supervision that, until 9/11, went fairly unnoticed.

Meanwhile, the UK government was persuaded to change its approach to banking in the UK because there was no way for Britain's two million Muslim citizens to maintain their religion in their banking operations. British Muslims either had to use normal UK bank financial products and services which were interest-bearing; or Islamic banking services that were not 100% compliant with the religious laws of Shari'a. On top of this, the lack of Islamic banking principles meant that the Muslim communities were being subjected to much higher tax rates. For example, if you purchased a car, you paid tax twice: once on the sale of the asset to the agent who purchased it for you under the Murabaha contract, and once again when the agent transferred the asset to your ownership under that contract. The government's view was that the assets had been sold twice – once to the agent and the second time to you, the customer – and hence were taxed twice. That may not be a big issue on a small loan, but when it came to buying a car or a house, that's a large chunk of taxation for reasons that did not make sense.

As a result of a greater understanding of the needs of Britain's Muslims, legislators were persuaded to change the law in the UK to allow fully-compliant Islamic Banking products and services in the mainstream banking system. This meant changing legislation, taxation and banking regulations, and resulted in the launch of the Islamic Bank of Britain in August 2004.

So, two systems – one official, Islamic Banking, and one unofficial, Hawala – that work closely in line to allow the free flow of funds between global Muslim communities. So what?

Well, what is interesting is that we now see Western financial providers muscling in on the Islamic financial markets. Thanks to the greater understanding of the needs of these communities and the flow of funds between Western and Islamic financial centers, there are a range of banks and firms now offering Islamic Banking and Hawala-focused trading. For example, type 'Hawala' into google and you will see a sponsored link to Western Union's remittance services. Equally, since the launch of the Islamic Bank of Britain, we now see Lloyds TSB – a traditional UK bank – offering Shari'a-compliant mortgage services in their branches. . .because they can. The laws have been changed to make it easier for banks to follow the leadership set by those who were first to market. As a result, the Islamic Banking products offer new lines of business to grow market share through appealing to a community that represents 5% of Britain's citizens.

And these offerings are likely to grow. After all, few banks can afford to ignore a market that is under-served and offers great opportunity. The opportunity is an industry with over $230 billion of assets that is growing by more than 15% per annum. The numbers being under-served represent the second largest religious group in much of Europe and the USA, with estimates of up to 10 million Muslims living in North America. This therefore has to be a space to watch for both banks and solutions providers.

In conclusion, a much greater understanding of Islamic needs, laws and religion has been introduced as a consequence of 9/11 and subsequent activities. This is leading to opportunity for many Western financial institutions, as they learn to change and adapt to support the financial needs of the Muslim communities in their countries. In particular, the Western interest in Islamic Banking as a growth market is a new phenomena, but is one that will become significant in those markets over the next decade.

Bankers versus Regulators:
When Two Tribes Go to War

In the UK, there's a massive feeding frenzy over faster payments, best execution benchmarking, soft commissions and bundled brokerage. This reflects the changing regulations across Europe where the Markets in Financial Instruments Directive (MiFID), Solvency II, the Payments Directive and the Financial Services Action Plan are driving everyone crazy.

The USA is no better with RegNMS, FFIEC's Authentication rules, Rule 22c-2, NASD Rule 3011, Michael Chertoff, Homeland Security, Disaster Preparedness, the Bank Secrecy Act and more.

Meanwhile, the Gulf Cooperation Council (GCC) is rumoured to be creating a Financial Services Action Plan for all of the Middle Eastern oil-producing nations, which would compete with the euro and the dollar. China is deregulating through 2007 to comply with the World Trade Organisation's requirements. India has announced deregulation of their markets through 2009.

Overriding all of this is the fact that banks globally are dealing with Basel II, and all of these changes have to be completed by around 2010.

ARE WE MAD?

I could go on and on about all of these individual regulations, but I'm not that sad. What prompted me to think about this in the first place was a debate between the European Commission and the Banking and Insurance Community.

The debate asked the question: 'Do we need a pan-European regulator', and comprised a panel of stature.

In the financial services corner were Rolf Breuer, former chairman of Deutsche Bank, and Henri de Castries, chief executive and chairman of AXA Group.

In the politician's corner was Alexander Schaub who recently retired as one of Charlie McCreevy's troops in the European Commission's grand plan for European Financial regulations, and Ieke van den Burg, a Member of the European Parliament (MEP). On the regulator's side was Fabrice DeMarigny, Secretary General of the Committee for European Securities Regulators (CESR), which drew up MiFID.

The referee was Antonio Borges, vice chairman of Goldman Sachs International.

What followed was one major punch-up between financiers and politicians. In fact, it was a little bit like the boxing match in Frankie Goes to Hollywood's 1980s hit, 'Two Tribes', where the chorus goes: '*When Two Tribes go to war, a point is all you can score*', and boy did these two tribes try to score some points.

ROUND ONE

The match opened with Rolf Breuer of Deutsche Bank addressing the question, 'Do we need a pan-European regulator?' by saying something to the effect of:

> There are three issues in financial markets supervision – effectiveness, efficiency and accountability. The effectiveness of financial markets supervision is concerned with key decisions being taken at the group level, not the subsidiary level, because we need to look at group-wide rather than national supervision. The efficiency of supervision is that highly educated resources are needed, which are scarce and costly. The duplication of resources is a waste and creates a non-level playing field where competition can get distorted and unnecessary supervisory burdens create unnecessary costs. The accountability structure is also unclear.

This makes sense and scores a point – bankers 1, politicians 0.

Breuer followed up with another scrunching blow to the stomach:

> For the near term, there should be a lead supervisor for firms such as ABN Amro, BNP and Deutsche. These firms should only have one point of contact in their home country for all operations across Europe. For banks that are only national players, the national supervisor should be their contact point and regulator. In the long-term, there should be transparent, stable and consistent EU supervision. The result would be a pan-European range of supervisors comparable to the Eurosystem for Central Banks. A Euro-FSA in other words. The Euro-FSA would then resolve national regulatory conflicts and release rule-sets such that member states work to a common set of rules, with national regulators purely supervising national banks and applying those rule-sets.

Another good point – bankers 2, politicians 0.

END OF ROUND ONE

A good opening salvo for the bankers which made me think about Fabrice DeMarigny's CESR Committee, who I suspect had sparked up the whole debate, about whether there should be a pan-European regulator.

The debate has been fuelled by CESR's A-bomb piece of regulation called MiFID (see Chapter 20, 'Make or Break for Europe's Equity Markets'). MiFID is intended to make Europe's pre-trade operations as competitive as the US's through best execution and price transparency. The only problem is that the Directive is being implemented across Europe by member states that have their own discretion as to how they implement it.

As one banker recently said to me:

> I went to the Committee of European Securities Regulators (CESR) and asked them to define the phrase 'facilitates consolidation', a term used in the wordings of MiFID. The response was, 'it will be up to your competent authority'. I asked whether 'competent authority' was my home regulator, my host regulator or the regulator of the most liquid market of the stock that I'm consolidating?' I had a standard politician's answer, which was to ignore that question.

Considering the question he asked, I would have probably said: 'I don't know what the question means' because it gets far too complicated. In fact, how politicians, regulators, bankers and corporates get to talk through this stuff at all, in a common language, amazes me. Maybe that is the problem, there is no common language; and no common language means no common rules.

Hence, the argument over national versus regional versus global regulation. By way of example, another banker recently said to me:

> Charlie McCreevy has said that the Financial Services Action Plan is the last regulatory development in Europe but then we also hear people saying 'we may have got this wrong'. We, as bankers, should be asking Europe for a single regulator operating under a single series of controlling rules, regulations and procedures.

This banker's concern was that the countries around Europe can define their own rule-sets. This is also the concern of Rolf Breuer and most other bankers.

ROUND TWO

Round Two began with Fabrice DeMarigny, Secretary General of CESR. Fabrice, surely we need a pan-European regulator?

> CESR will force supervisory convergence. A precondition for this to work is that all supervisors should be networked with equal powers...where two national regulators disagree, they can talk to a group of peers to gain a decision.

Urmmmm...

In other words, if two regulators disagree, go and get a decision from your friends and, if you don't like their views, then what do you do?

Sorry, can't give you a point for that one.

But it turns out M. DeMarigny had other priorities:

> CESR will go through a metamorphosis by focusing on operational areas and creating common working methods and prioritising where these can be integrated. Our priorities for supervisory convergence are based upon risk, EU-wide impacts and the ability for CESR to manage these. Therefore, the areas we shall focus upon will include a moratorium on home-host issues; developments of IT data sharing of cases and data management overall; the implementation of MiFID; the consistency of IFRS implementation and asset management; the corporate governance Directive; and cross-border bank activities with a view toward opportunities for self-regulation.

OK, he has enough on his plate but still nil-point. What do you think European Commissioner for the Internal Markets, Mr Alexander Schaub?

> A single EU supervisor has gone away as a term because it takes us back to the idea of single structures and single EU markets. That is too simplistic. In some circumstances, harmonisation is the right answer. In others, it is only part of the answer. In others, it is completely the wrong answer.

I think you are hedging your bets. Come on Alex, what do you really think?

What we need to develop is a European system of supervision, which does not mean a single supervisor. It means a European system of common rules that can be implemented nationally.

Got it.

So what you think we need is a way to avoid political confrontation. After all, if you start taking Brussels Directives and saying, 'Dear British Prime Minister, we are taking over the FSA whether you like it or not and dear German Chancellor, the same goes for BaFIN and oh, by the way cher Premier de France, AMF is ours too' and so on, you end up in a political war.

Let's throw it back to the bankers and see if they can make it work.

Nope, no points there. Bankers 2, politicians 0.

END OF ROUND TWO

In fact, what really struck me at this point was how the politicians were sitting next to the bankers and the juxtaposition of their earnings.

How much does Mr Schaub earn per annum: €100,000 a year? €200,000?

And the gentleman sitting next to him, Antonio Borges, Vice Chairman of Goldman Sachs International? €10 million a year? €20 million?

No wonder bankers and politicians and regulators do not get on. I mean, the financial guys are making all the money out of the impoverished politicians and citizens, aren't they?

Maybe this is the point.

The politicians see bankers and insurers making loads of dosh (if you prefer moolah, spondulicks, you name it) out of the citizens, so they whip the regulators into action. The regulators try their best to interpret what the politicians want but are purely acting as go-betweens between politicians' dreams and market realities. In other words, the regulators will never win.

Alongside all of this, the industry may complain about the cost of regulation but continue to rake in the profits. The Top 1,000 world banks showed record pre-tax profits of $544.1bn and a record return on capital of 19.9% in 2005, after-tax profits grew by 30.3% compared to 65.4% in 2004. Not great, but still a healthy delivery of cash.

The industry claims this is a temporary bull market high and various folks were predicting a banking bust in 2006 but no. Almost all of the Tier 1 major banks were reporting double digit growth instead, including HSBC, Goldman Sachs, Lehman Brothers, Bear Stearns and Morgan Stanley, and the City of London enjoyed the biggest bonus pools ever. Nevertheless, the doomsayers in the banks keep saying 'this cannot last'. This would be due to a variety of factors such as consumer demand for lending reaching breakpoint, the housing sector going belly-up, interest rates and inflation rising, stock markets blowing apart through hedge fund systemic risk and so on.

But it has not happened. . .yet.

However, the fragility of the markets is one of the reasons why all these regulators are hitting us with regulation – to try to avoid a banking meltdown. Not forgetting the other objectives, such as to liberalise their markets, promote free trade and increase globalisation and competitiveness.

The result is that to be in banking, banks need licences from governments and regulators and, to get those licences, they have to comply and spend.

- The average bank has to keep up with over 100 regulations from dozens of regulators.
- One in five Tier 1 European banks are spending over 15% of overall costs on compliance.
- 45% of Europe's biggest banks will spend over $60 million in 2006–07 on Basel II.
- 36% of that spend will be on IT systems and interfaces.

They have to spend to be in banking to get the great returns when risk is minimised and markets are liquid.

Another reason they have to comply and spend is that, during these buoyant periods of high returns, banks can get greedy. Shockingly, some might even abuse their clients. Names like Frank Quattrone, Henry Blodget and Jack Grubman come to mind. No time to explain here but these guys weren't very popular with State Attorney General Eliot Spitzer of the USA during the early 2000s.

The politicians want fairness, while citizens want safety, open community and respect. They just do not trust the financial institutions to provide this without being forced into it.

Bang goes any idea of self-regulation.

Therefore, as regulations create a sea change in the financial markets worldwide, all I can think about is where will we find stability and growth? The more the regulators meddle with the markets, the less stable the markets become. After all, as you change things you create instability, and markets and people want stability. We do not like change.

Oh well, we droned into Round Three of our Euro boxing match.

ROUND THREE

Round Three was running around the final comments until Henri de Castries, chief executive of the largest global insurance firm AXA Group, piped up. Mr de Castries made many highly lucid points such as:

> Supervision should mean safety, not stability, at the right cost and with the right levels of capital. The right level of capital means the right level. Too little creates risk and too much creates wastage. There should then be incentives to make investments of that capital in the right categories of assets. All of this should be supporting innovation, rather than creating stagnant markets. . .We are starting to create a world where we are spending too much capital on a system that is not supporting the safety of the customer.

As the point sank in, I think I saw a little wobble amongst the politicians.

He then illustrated the consequences of the meddling with the markets with a potentially lethal point for Europe. . .and the rest of the world's markets.

> Every national regulator, every quarter, adds bells and whistles to the European framework. This means we are less and less convergent at higher and higher cost. For example, European Solvency II regulations mean that AXA has to reserve €23 billion to cover capital requirements for solvency. An equivalent USA insurer with a Triple-B S&P rating only has to reserve €19 billion (AXA is A3a rated) according to our risk models. That means AXA is reserving €4 billion more than it needs to because the EU does not recognise the strength of our diversifications. If that €4 billion were invested, we would realise €900 million a year in additional growth of investment funds. The result is that we lose €900 million a year in lost opportunities on that €4 billion.

In other words, the European Union is forcing our institutions to invest in weak assets and poor returns in order to comply with regulations. As this occurs, global firms with global ambitions could relocate.

The politicians fell to the floor but managed to stagger up again slightly shakily.

At this point Henri de Castries, in a kind of Rocky Balboa moment, launched in with a right hook to the chin:

> The benefits of the EU construction of the FSAP must be for the EU constructors. If the EU penalises EU firms, compared to other regions, then capital moves and companies move to where the markets are the most efficient. This means that prices rise in those markets that are inefficient.

The politicians were down and out for the count.

A CLEAR KNOCKOUT, BUT WHO CLEANS UP?

In the small skirmish I saw in Brussels, the financial industry clearly won on points, but they do not own the governmental controls, the legal authorities, the issuing of licences and the regulatory mandates.

The politicians and regulators are shaping the markets the best they can and know that somehow they have to make this work. The question is how?

The answer is that they do not know how. They are trying to compromise, to gain agreement amongst warring cultures, countries, companies and markets. It is not a pretty sight to watch because in any boxing match, there will be blood on the floor.

Some will be from the banks, some from the banks' customers, some from the banks' home countries and some from the banks' host countries.

As we look worldwide at regulatory change, we see the bouts of upper cuts and stomach blows happening in all geographies. American banks are beaten up with post-9/11 sticks. China is opening up through world trade ambitions and their banks are being knocked out by foreign bank investments. Kuwait, Saudi, UAE and the rest of the GCC seek to leverage their petrodollar billions and will find dollar and euro goliaths waiting in the wings to take over.

Just as Rocky Balboa got knocked out by a Russian, banks around the world will be knocked out and consolidated, merged and acquired. During this dramatic reshaping of our markets, only a few will win and, just as in war, the only folks who make money are the arms dealers.

Who supplies the arms to each side here?

5
The European Union Unravels

A critical component of Europe's plans to be an economic powerhouse is to achieve a single, integrated financial market. This plan is being driven by a variety of Directives which, combined, are known as the Financial Services Action Plan (FSAP). However, there has actually been little progress towards this unification of the financial markets. This may be viewed as bank resistance or, more likely, a fundamental question around the overall objectives of where Europe is heading. In light of the rejection of the European Constitution by the French and Dutch referenda of 2005, and the consequent political fall-out at the EU Budgetary meeting, is any of this worth discussing anyway?

When the European Commission introduced the concept of the euro currency, it implied a lot more than just dropping the French franc, the German mark and the Spanish peseta. There were cultural and infrastructural changes, as well as a need to change practices to enable transparent movement of currencies across borders. This need became a focused desire amongst European leadership to create a single financial market across the Eurozone. This market would be the cornerstone foundation for making Europe a leading global economy by 2010.

After consultation with the industry, it was soon realised that creating such an integrated marketplace would not be simple. For example, it would require a complete restructuring of virtually all financial market activities within the region, from mergers and acquisitions to securities and settlements, from electronic transfers between deposit accounts to insurance sales.

Such change would not be simple, as domestic financial institutions had been making significant margins through cross-border activities for many years. These margins were not just represented by currency transaction handling, but any movement of financial instruments across borders from making a payment electronically to dealing in equities across different exchanges. If the European Commission were to make the European Financial Markets behave as one, then they would face considerable resistance. First, because it would imply significant infrastructural change and, therefore, cost. Second, because the nature of such change would be to reduce margins and profitability.

The only way to achieve change that requires increasing cost for reduced returns is to force it through via legislation, which is exactly what the European Commission realised when they created a set of legislative changes in the form of the Financial Services Action Plan, or FSAP.

The European Commission produced the first FSAP Consultation on 11 May 1999, as the euro was born. The Plan has three major objectives:

- to create a single market for wholesale financial services;
- to provide an open and secure retail market;
- to establish leadership through a Eurozone-wide set of rules and regulation.

The FSAP was subsequently adopted by the European Council in Lisbon in March 2000 and has been an ongoing source of discussion and dialogue, meeting and mediation, conference and consideration ever since.

For example, the plan now incorporates a whole range of regulatory Directives, most of which have been accepted by governments but some are still to be implemented by the financial industry. For those who were not aware, here is a brief list of some of those key Directives:

- Directive on Transparency Obligations for Securities Issuers;
- Directive on Investment Services and Regulated Markets (Upgrade Investment Services Directive);
- Directive on Takeover Bids;
- Legal Framework for Payments Directive;
- 10th and 14th Company Law Directives;
- Risk-Based Capital Directive;
- Third Money-Laundering Directive;
- Directive on Insider Dealing and Market Manipulation (Market Abuse);
- Regulation on the Application of International Accounting Standards;
- Directive on Financial Collateral Arrangements;
- Two Directives on UCITS;
- Directive on the Prudential Supervision of Pension Funds;
- Directive on the Distance Marketing of Financial Services;
- Directive on Insurance Mediation;
- Directive on the Reorganisation and Winding-Up of Insurance Undertakings;
- Directive on the Winding-Up and Liquidation of Banks;
- Electronic Money Directive;
- Directive on the Supplementary Supervision of Credit Institutions, Insurance Undertakings and Investment Firms in a Financial Conglomerate;
- Directive on Prospectuses;
- the Money Laundering Directive;
- the Investment Services Directive (ISD).

No wonder Europe's financial institutions feel battered and beaten by regulation.

Add onto these Basel II, Sarbanes-Oxley and the domestic regulatory changes – such as the UK FSA's recent changes to insurance company reporting and brokerage commissions – and you have a real mix of confusion, consternation and irritation caused by these regulatory overheads.

What may be surprising therefore is that nearly all of the Directives have been adopted by the governments of the European countries and, of the Directives currently being implemented, the two that are of most interest are the Payment Services Directive (PSD) and Markets in Financial Instruments Directive (MiFID), as they imply the most significant changes.

The PSD, also known as the New Legal Framework for the Internal Markets, is not actually the change programme for banks, but is just a legal backdrop to SEPA – the Single Euro Payments Area. SEPA is the change programme being implemented by Europe's banks to support the European Commission's desire to have all euro payments treated as though they were being made within one country area.[1] As a result, all euro payments will be charged and processed as though they were domestic payments in the Eurozone countries.

Initially, that resulted in a lowering of margins. For example, banks could no longer charge non-domestic customers €4 for withdrawing €100 from a euro cash machine (see Chapter 18, 'The Future of European Payments'). Now, it looks like involving a lot more than just reduced margins.

As existing national clearing systems are dismantled, and new infrastructures come into play, the banking industry is faced with a significant bill to conform to the new Eurozone clearing and settlement systems and structures. For example, the new European Central Bank's Real-Time Gross Settlement (RTGS) system TARGET2, along with new Automated Clearing House (ACH) and Direct Debit (DD) systems are being launched across Europe. The latter are known as PEACH and PEDD, as in a Pan-European ACH and DD system. As a result, most banking payments organisations will require some refreshment to move away from existing domestic ACH's to the new structures. TowerGroup estimate that European banks need to increase spending on Payments Infrastructures from $6 billion per annum in 2005 to $10.5 billion in 2007–08 to achieve these infrastructural change requirements for SEPA, and at least half of this spend will be on new functionality to cope with the SEPA vision.

All that for increasing competition and reducing margin? Makes sense oui?

Similarly, MiFID is the Markets in Financial Instruments Directive (see Chapter 19, 'Best execution with best intentions').

MiFID appears to have the most impact upon exchanges and broker-dealers. Exchanges are impacted as they are no longer protected from competition but need to compete across Europe and, in many instances, head-to-head with the broking community. This is because all pricing for equities need to be published, whether those prices are on-exchange or off-exchange. MiFID also implies massive changes to the sell-side operators' business because it states that all investment banks, broker-dealers and securities firms must now prove best execution for all trades enacted on their clients' behalf. In order to prove best execution, under MiFID's terms, all organisations trading in Europe will need to keep all of the prices for all of the exchanges and sellers for all of the instruments that they deal in, throughout the day in real time and online, for the next five years.

This will create a need for huge amounts of storage and bandwidth. By way of example, JPMorgan Chase stated in 2004 that it backs up over a terabyte (one million gigabytes) of communications per day for SEC purposes. Under MiFID, the bank will probably need to be storing petabytes (one billion gigabytes) per day rather than terabytes. However, this is not an issue as storage is cheap, and getting cheaper by the day. As is bandwidth via Internet Protocol communication systems.

A corollary implication of MiFID is not so easy to deal with as MiFID implies deeper shifts in market structures and pricing. For example, many investment bankers believe that MiFID will create a transparent playing field where buyers will be able to see all the pricing for equities and other investment instruments simply and easily. That is the intention of the Directive. As a result, sell-side banks will no longer be able to trade profitably off their own book, and margins will be squeezed until only a few key players exist. Those players will be

---

[1] Countries using the Euro began with twelve countries in 1999: Austria, Belgium, Finland, France, Germany, Greece, Ireland, Italy, Luxembourg, Netherlands, Portugal and Spain; this increased to thirteen in 2007 with the inclusion of Slovenia; Cyprus, Malta and Slovakia join in 2008; Bulgaria, Estonia, Hungary, Latvia, Lithuania, Poland and Romania are expected to join between 2010 and 2014.

the ones with European size and scale, who already operate a transparent book of business and know how to leverage technology to manage change. There are at most eight banks that fit that profile.

In fact, TowerGroup estimate that, under current terms and conditions of MiFID, it will cost European providers upwards of €5 billion to comply with this Directive to cover all of the infrastructural changes and the warehousing of data therein.

All that for increasing competition and reducing margin? It does not make sense, non.

So, should we be 'oui' or 'non' for the Financial Services Action Plan?

Well, if Europe were to continue in its formation as of 2004, then the FSAP made political sense. However, with the 'non' and 'nee' votes in France and Netherlands to the European Constitution, combined with the political in-fighting and back-biting of the EU leadership as seen at the Brussels EU budgetary meeting, then no, it does not make sense.

In particular, there are questions that are being raised more fundamentally around the euro's future as a result of these recent developments. First, there was Germany's Stern magazine reporting that the Bundesbank and German Finance Ministry were discussing scenario's for moving forward if the euro should collapse and the Deutschmark needed resurrecting. Meanwhile, you have a political party now formed in Italy – the Northern Leagues – whose explicit focus is to destroy the euro. Add on to this Europe's economic challenges in terms of unemployment, zero growth and fractious politics, and we see the results with an 11% drop in the value of the euro against the dollar in the first half of 2005. Sure, it has bounced back since then, but it does show how fragile the euro alliance might be, especially with significant EU countries such as the UK, Sweden and Denmark determinedly remaining outside the Eurozone.

The result is that the euro is facing its most serious challenge since its inception in 1999 and, as a result, so is SEPA and the FSAP.

Between the euro regulators forcing through an overwhelming number of Directives into the financial markets and the euro politicians losing referendums and tempers, it is going to be interesting to see what happens. In particular, what will happen to the FSAP?

The answer is that there are some real obstacles to overcome if the FSAP is to achieve the change to the industry it is attempting to mandate.

The first obstacle is the legitimacy of the nature of these Directives when Europe and the euro's future are uncertain. Is it really worth shaking the industry up so hard when it may all be thrown to one side?

The second is the aggressive timelines for these Directives. Are banks really expected to be compliant with legal requirements that effectively restructure industries, markets, products and services, when all too often the rules the regulators are drafting are only being issued a year or less from the timescales for implementation?

The third will be the alignment of the pieces required to make the FSAP happen. How can a bank implement the infrastructures, technologies, products and services required for these Directives, if the legal frameworks needed to support them are yet to be put into place?

All of these obstacles can be overcome. However, with the European political landscape looking far more extreme than seen since Maastricht, it may be worth waiting a while before we tackle them.

6
Enterprise Change: The Age-Old Challenge

Almost twenty years ago, the hot topic on everyone's agenda was Business Process Re-engineering. Suddenly, it's back on the agenda big time. Is this because no-one got it right the first time?

In the early 1990s, Margaret Thatcher was Prime Minister of Britain, the Intel 80286 chip was about to be superseded by the 80386, 16Mb memory was considered turbo-speed, smart people had upgraded from vinyl to compact discs and, in business circles, a buzz had started. The buzz was created by a seminal paper published in the Harvard Business Review by a chap called Michael Hammer. The article had exhorted the benefits of analysing and re-thinking processes from end-to-end. The methodology was named 'Business Process Re-engineering', BPR for short, and it became the next big consulting bandwagon following on from Total Quality Management (TQM), the management fad introduced by Tom Peters.

Almost twenty years later, BPR is firmly back on the corporate agenda. This is, in part, because the job was never finished first time around but it is also because BPR, this time around, is different.

In the 1990s, when BPR was first being discussed, the concept was to achieve radical results, to turn the business on its head and to redesign the business from the customer's viewpoint. The aspiration was to identify all customer interaction points and design the business from scratch around those customer interactions. The achievement would be a customer-centric business and the journey to get there would involve tearing up the current business roadmap and starting again from scratch.

However, few BPR projects came anywhere close to achieving radical results because few projects re-invented the business. The majority changed business processes for incremental efficiencies and cost reduction purposes, but did not fundamentally change the business to make it truly customer-centric for revenue growth. It was the latter that many hoped would happen, but it was the former that became the reality. The reason is that no-one wanted to shake up their institution and transform it. It was just easier to implement incremental improvements to processes within functions, than to re-engineer the whole business.

By way of example, I was working with a bank in 1992 where we had the opportunity to either re-engineer the money transmissions process or the mortgage process. The former was simple because it was owned by the payments group whilst the latter was difficult because it cut across all functions, products and services within the bank. So guess which one we took? Yep, the money transmissions process. The reason we chose money transmissions was because it meant dealing with only one department within the bank and therefore avoided the political conflicts between the different business owners which would have been demanded by the mortgage process. In addition, the complexity of the mortgage process and the systems issues it would have confronted also meant it was to be avoided.

In other words, we opted for the process that allowed for improvement rather than transformation. Transformation requires revolution to achieve radical results and businesses, or more importantly people and management within those businesses, seek evolutionary change rather than revolutionary. That is why we went for the process that was easier to manage and change and, as a by-note, the mortgage process in that bank is still pretty much untouched today.

However, that could be about to change because BPR today is looking at a more fundamental revolution of processes. The reason BPR is different today, and therefore can tackle more fundamental change, is because the systems issues are different today and are more easily addressed through 21st Century architectures.

In the early 1990s, systems constrained true business transformation because we were dealing with hard-wired technologies and programming environments from the 1960s. Sure, client-server systems were around, but networked architectures, modular design, component-based methodologies and truly open systems were just a glint in the eye of a few technologists on the west coast of America.

That has been the most dramatic change in the last two decades. Today, Service Oriented Architectures, Web Services and related developments have made it much simpler to develop pieces of the re-engineered business and slot those in where needed on an evolutionary basis, rather than on a revolutionary basis. That does not mean to say that transformation is easy, but it does mean that the systems issues are much more manageable today.

But it is not just for the reasons of more manageable technologies that BPR is back. BPR is back because many of us feel that the time is right to re-engineer. After all, it has been over a decade since many processes have been touched. As a result, some bad practices have developed.

For example, how many internet banking sites reflect the bank's internal processes and systems rather than the dynamics of the blogging and entertainment oriented internet that we use today? How many banks offer online services designed for dial-up rather than broadband? These two points alone reflect the drive for continual re-engineering for 21st Century business. After all, if we do not do it, our competition will.

In addition, many of the re-engineering programmes of a decade ago got dumped before they were completed due to other things coming along. During the mid-1990s many banks were heavily engaged in re-engineering and just as those programmes were getting interesting – as in tackling the big issues like the internal politics and the legacy systems – a couple of more urgent priorities came along like the euro and Y2K. Then we had the internet bubble and burst and CRM. All these 'fads' came and went until we finally got some breathing space.

Today, we still have big challenges, but these challenges should be such that we are mandated to take the time to review where we have been and where we are going because there is no big blip, consulting fad or technological roller-coaster hitting our radars. Therefore, many of us are going back to basics and realising that our processes are still in a mess.

We still have silo-based systems and departments, baronial powerlords running functions and spaghetti systems that have cemented old structures in place. But the biggest difference with today's world of re-engineering is that we can tackle processes end-to-end on an enterprise basis without breaking apart all of the old ways of doing business. That means that we can potentially transform the business without creating revolution or being revolutionary. For the beauty of this change is that it can be achieved on an enterprise basis in an evolutionary way.

Using SOA, we can evolve the enterprise. Using component-based developments, we can build the pieces and slot them into place gradually. Using business blue-printing or whatever terms you would like to use, we can build the enterprise piece-by-piece. That is the major change in today's re-engineering programmes and yes, as a result, it will lead to business transformation.

However, there is one caveat to achieving an evolution towards enterprise renewal. It still will not happen unless the management team within the bank – the leadership team and the CEO in particular – make it happen.

Think about it. Most major enterprise change projects fail. BPR, TQM, CRM – you name it – four out of five fail. Most projects crash and burn because the change programme is delegated or designated to a department.

For example, let's think about a 'Customer' project. The Customer Project could be under any of the change banners – BPR, TQM, CRM, or any other modish acronym. The Customer Project may have been created by the head of customer services. As a result, it becomes a customer service change programme so the customer service folks deal with it. Because service people design and implement the programme, it does not get the buy-in of the sales people. However, as it turns out, it's the sales people who have to do 10 times the administration to support the service programme. If the sales people don't enter all the customer information upfront – which adds a major administrative overhead to the sales process – then the service people do not have the right information to do their job. Net result: failure.

With any such project, the minimum support required is to have all of the functional heads owning the project. By ownership, that means that there has to be real commitment, and the only way to get real commitment is to make sure it hits the wallets of those involved. Therefore, to ensure the success of the change programme, there must be a tangible impact on management bonuses, commissions and earnings. That way all of the team players have skin in the game for the project's success or failure. However, to change an executive management team's earnings structure can only be achieved if the CEO owns the change programme.

The CEO is the individual at the top of the tree and is the only person who can make change happen across the enterprise. A functional leader can make change happen across their function, but not across the enterprise. The buy-in and the ownership has to be across all functions for enterprise change to happen, and the only person who owns all functions is the person at the top of the tree. The CEO.

And that is where nothing has really changed. In the early 1990s, four out of five change programmes failed because they did not have the ownership of the CEO to make them succeed and the same message holds true today.

Even with the revolution of the internet, broadband speeds that are light years ahead of those from two decades ago, processing speeds on chips the size of fingernails that would outperform a mainframe from 1990, the message stays the same. To achieve enterprise change, you have to have the enterprise owner firmly engaged in the change programme. And by 'firmly engaged' we mean committed. The CEO must be passionate and must want to be a part of making change happen by being hands-on. The CEO must live and breathe the change programme – they cannot just buy it or delegate it. The CEO becomes the ultimate leader in the enterprise change programme.

Therefore, if you are engaged in a programme that has either the word 'enterprise' or 'transformation' involved, just make sure it has the ownership of the person who sits at the top of the tree. Make sure that that person wants to hear how it is going every day. Make sure that they are willing to drop all other matters to ensure the project's success. Otherwise, go back to doing something more evolutionary at a level that can be managed within a function.

7

Demonstrating the Value of Technology

Citigroup's Global Head of Strategic Solutions told me that the financial models we use to justify IT investments are fundamentally flawed. He summed it up by saying: 'We have these elaborate and sophisticated financial models using ROI (Return On Investment), IRR (Internal Rate of Return) and NPV (Net Present Value), but the margin of error that leads to decisions is substantial. At the end of the day, you are taking a bet.' In the 21st Century, surely we cannot still be making multi-million dollar bets?

I entered the IT industry in the 1980s believing that technology was the future. Well, it was the future then and still is now. During my first years in the industry, the main issue we came up against was the lack of understanding of technology with the users. The business community was typically very hands-off and had little or no understanding or interest in dealing with technology. That was back then when words such as CICS, IMS, ASSEMBLER, FORTRAN and PASCAL would send shivers up the spine of even the most stalwart techno-enthusiast.

We ended up in this long debate about why business people did not understand the value of technology and why technologists did not understand the needs of business. A debate we still have today. The focus of that debate was really around who really understands the value technology could deliver. Back then, the answer was no-one. Not the vendors, the technologists, the IT department, and certainly not the Managing Director, CEO or business community they served. The reason was simple. Technology was originally introduced because it delivered obvious benefits in the automation of manual processes. The efficiencies of taking humans out of the process became a major focal point in most firms.

Therefore, the cost benefit analysis back then was pretty easy. Ten clerks performing administration of accounts costing $25,000 a head can be replaced by a small data processor costing $300,000 with a payback in less than 18 months.

However, even then, it was not that simple. I remember talking to a group of bankers in the mid-1990s about data warehousing. The simple fact was that data warehouses were viewed as expensive. So I asked the question of the vendor, 'How much does your system typically save a bank?' Suffice to say the answer was amusing. After a dumb silence of about 10 minutes, and a major consultation between the CEO and his marketing head, the answer came back 'We don't know.' They did not know because no-one really measured the savings. They justified the investments but did not measure the returns once the investment was signed-off.

The result was that that particular vendor invested in a major exercise to quantify the value of the solutions they delivered. That also sounds easy but it was not. Quantifying the value that solutions deliver is never as easy as it sounds.

For example, there is the original pre-implementation dream. This is the work of fiction known as a Cost-Benefit Analysis (CBA) that ensures for every $1 invested at least $2 is saved or generated. Savings are in terms of headcount – or these days, systems consolidated and maintenance and legacy $'s reduced – and income is found through a sudden flock of customers through the door because they love the way the new technology gives them better service.

So far, so good.

Having done all that work and generated the dream, the management team sign on the contract and everything is then forgotten. That is the reason why most technology firms 'don't know' the value of the systems they sell, because no-one measures the value once it is delivered. The reason no-one measures the value is that it can often be quite scary. The vendor does not want to measure the value in case the solution does not deliver. The client often does not measure the value because the ones who cost-justify the systems are also the ones with their heads on the block if it all goes wrong.

That has to change, because we can no longer afford to continue making bets. We need more certainty, if nothing else to generate credibility and confidence in the technology function and remove uncertainty and risk. Therefore, the biggest way to lock-down future ROI in technology investments is to create a track record of measuring the margin of error made in calculating the ROI for historical technology investments. For many, that can only start today because they have no track record of measurements.

The question then is what should you measure?

I believe there are four things you should measure when identifying the value of technology, or for that matter any other investments. Money, staff, customers and risk.

Monetary measurements are the obvious ones – how much did we spend; did it save us more than we spent; did it generate any revenue; how much in total?

Although monetary measurements are obvious, it still amazes me how few organisations actually measure that one. Go back to almost any major technology programme two years down the line and ask 'what's the ROI on this then?' and typically the answer comes back, 'we think it's a lot, but cannot work out whether the revenue generated is down to the new technology or changes in the market or the fact that diddlysquat bank slipped up on that banana skin'. That just goes to show that no-one really understood the financial models in the first place and certainly did not track them through.

If you cannot measure money effectively, just think how difficult it is to measure the other things – staff, customers and risk.

Staff measurements should identify how the technology implementation improved staff morale or otherwise, through tracking employee retention, productivity and satisfaction. Customer measurements should track the costs of acquisition, retention, maintenance, cross-sell and advocacy. Risk should measure the ability of the bank to adapt to change, implement compliance on time, respond to new competitive pressures and avoid industry exposures or reputation impacts.

All of these areas – money, staff, customers and risk – are assisted or hindered by technology. All of these areas provide ROI and payback if you implement the right technologies. All of these areas are what you should be measuring before, during and after making major technology decisions – both as a bank and as a provider to a bank.

Why? Because, as a bank, it will help you to get more decisions right in the future and take less bets. As a service provider, it will make it easier for you to sell more solutions to your clients because you will have a proven track record of delivering value.

The question then is whether to measure all of these areas or whether to pick out the key areas that represent the most value and return on investment for what you are trying to achieve. This brings in the final dimension of value, which is to measure the value based upon the specifics of each and every implementation.

Every implementation's benefits analysis will be different – both before, during and throughout the project. That is why I get so frustrated when I keep hearing the same old comment about the value of technology, namely that you cannot measure the value because too many other conditions are involved: the markets change, the customers change, the competition changes and so on. I get frustrated because it is exactly for this reason that you need to make the value measurement clear from the start and adaptive during the process to incorporate other impacts and influences. The system needs to cater for these changes as they occur, but still have a clear focus upon the measurement of the technology delivery involved. That is also why you cannot build value measurement systems as a one size fits all.

Equally, it cannot be a one size fits all because each financial institution is different. Some financial institutions have already improved their operations through automation and reengineering, whilst some have not. Some financial institutions already have sophisticated value measurement systems in place which link key performance indicators to overall objectives, whilst some have not. Some financial institutions have manual processes which are less automated. Every institution is different, both in their measurement capabilities, financial sophistication and automation. Therefore, there is a great importance in measuring the right parameters that are specific to the situation. These 'situational' measures may even vary within organisations, by function, line of business and geography. If what you measure is 'situational', the key is to link the technology benefits with the specific business metrics impacted in that functional, line of business, geographic application.

The result is that different models apply to different business types, sizes, organisation structures and efficiency levels. The most important factor is that, overall, you understand how to measure – and what to measure – to determine the value and return on technology investments before, during and after the project delivery.

Today, most firms tend to only measure and analyse the value and return enough to get the senior executive vice president to sign-off on the deal. The result is, as my colleague from Citigroup said, 'we have these sophisticated financial models but you are taking a bet'. Tomorrow, taking bets will not cut to the chase so stop taking bets and start working out how to measure the right things.

Part 2
Retail Banker's Challenges

Retail banking is the area where many of us can make a comment, as we all experience its virtues and annoyances daily in our own lives. The fact you purchased this book means that you probably have and use a bank account, and many of us will love or loathe our bank; some of us will think they are all the same; and a few of us will feel that our bank is the one thing we can count upon. These themes are explored in the opening two chapters of this section, Chapters 8 and 9.

Chapter 8 points to some interesting research which is updated annually by the Bank Administration Institute (BAI) of the USA. BAI run one of the largest retail bank conferences in the world, Retail Delivery, and regularly has attendance in excess of 5,000 people. It is a show that I enjoy because it tells me the latest and greatest about retail bank technologies and best practices and I would recommend it to all of you. Especially as it gets you to places like Las Vegas, Orlando and other US 'party' capitals in mid-November every year.

I have attended and presented at the Retail Delivery Show for over 10 years and can tell you that the bottom-line appears to be that retail bankers love technology, and try to use technology more and more to make their customers love them in return. CRM, aggregation, internet and Web 2.0, the mobile phone – or cellphone as it's called in the USA – and all that stuff is the core dialogue at Retail Delivery.

These technologies are discussed in depth in later chapters in this section, but these first two chapters show that retail banks' love of technology has resulted in two potentially critical failings. First, that retail bankers do not know their customers or what their customers want; and second, that when retail bankers deliver technology, they often do so at the expense of the customer relationship. Obviously, this is not true for every single retail bank . . . just for many of those I deal with or whose customers have emailed me.

The first point is illustrated in several chapters in this section, but particularly Chapter 12. If bankers knew their customers, then how come we have so many problems with fraud and identity theft? Chapter 12 demonstrates that the more retail banks use technology to relate to their customers, the less they know about their customers. It goes with the old saying that 'no-one knows you are a dog on the internet' and no matter how much retail bankers try, they are continually challenged with how to minimise fraud and manage identity authentication.

Chapter 8 shows that because bankers don't know their customers, they therefore think their customers want relationships. As more and more technology pushes the customers out of the branch and away from the human-to-human bank interactions, this makes sense. However, the net view of the customer is that they do not want relationships! Do banks know what their customers want?

Meantime, Chapter 9 makes a different point, which is that the more banks implement technology for their bank-to-customer dealings, the more likely they are, as with all other businesses, to mess up the customer relationship when the technology cannot deal with the issue at hand.

That is not to say that technology is inappropriate or wasted. There are many technologies that retail banks should consider and these are reviewed in the remaining chapters.

One of the most critical technologies for retail banks over the next decade will be video communications. Chapters 10 and 11 explore the implications of video call centres, as 3G and broadband enabled telephones, PCs and TVs enable high definition video calling between consumers and banks.

The channel of communication for the future will definitely be visually based, and that visual connectivity has huge ramifications for bank processes, structures and operations. Some banks will get this videochannel wrong, as illustrated jokingly by Chapter 11, but the few with foresight to get it right will be the most competitive of all retail banks through the mid-2010s.

Meantime, the biggest issue of the 2000s for retail bankers has been fraud and identity theft, if nothing else because the media has made such a deal out of it. Fraud will continue through the 2000s, but there are ways to minimise it. Chapter 12 looks at this area in depth, and comes to some radical conclusions about giving your bank the finger!

The final two chapters, 13 and 14, are probably the best two articles I have written in the areas of current and future technologies in the retail bank front and back office. These articles were commissioned by Hewlett Packard TowerGroup during 2006, and an abbreviated version is presented here.

The reason why these chapters are so critical is that they really lay the foundations for understanding the technology challenges and opportunities that exist for retail banks today. They cut across many of the other themes explored here, from identity authentication technologies to payments technologies, from branch technologies to video call centre operations and so on. In many ways, if you really want to know what is happening in the world of retail bank technologies over the next few years, Chapters 13 and 14 will show you.

8
Strained Relationships

Based upon extensive research by the Bank Administration Institute (BAI) in the USA of bankers and consumers, there is a major disconnect between bankers, who say their number one driver is to create relationships with their customers, and customers who apparently do not want relationships with their banks. What are the implications of this schism for retail banks and retail bank operations?

At the BAI Retail Delivery Tradeshow a range of topics are discussed, with the critical focus being upon how retail banks can more effectively compete in a world of cut-throat competition. As part of this programme, the BAI conducted research in 2005 with 3,700 US retail bank customers and discovered an interesting nuance that 69% of bank customers do not want a 'relationship' with their bank. Apparently, only 31% of customers are receptive to a relationship, 29% are indifferent and 40% are actively sceptical.

This contradicts previous figures from BAI's research in 2004 520 senior retail banking executives were surveyed and 90% said that relationship banking and service quality were their primary value proposition. How can a bank emphasise relationships as their value proposition if that is not what a customer wants?

In fact, the research really raised a different question for me. If 69% of consumers are indifferent or sceptical about a relationship with their bank, is that because they are happy to be stuck with a nameless, faceless institution that treats them as a number? And are the 31% who are receptive to relationships with their financial providers, or even actively seek such relationships, the same customers who visit branches and talk to the branch staff regularly?

This is not researched in depth yet, but it does strike a chord. For example, the sceptic probably feels that they put up with their bank, for all of their vagaries and irritating habits, because they cannot be bothered to switch to someone else. After all, if all banks are the same, what's the point? The indifferent is likely to stay with their bank because, although they might get a better deal elsewhere, is it worth the effort? Whilst the receptive is actively seeking to find a bank that makes them feel valued and special.

That means that the sceptics and indifferents are swathed in inertia and explains why most retail bank customers are more likely to leave their spouse than their bank. That inertia has so far been the backbone of the industry. So long as banks can be trusted to safely transact payments, customer care goes out of the window.

But this will not work with the customer segment who want a relationship. The 31% who are receptive to relationships with their bank. These customers are different. They are actively seeking a relationship connection with their bank staff, more than just transacting securely. They want advice. They want to talk. They think their bank has credibility and they want staff at the bank to show them what they could do better. They want to walk into the branch and be called by name, and they want to telephone the contact centre and know that the person at the other end will not only know their name, but their last transactions and contacts with the bank. The more their bank delivers on those expectations, the more they trust them, the more they seek advice from them, the more business they give them and so on. A virtuous circle.

The issue for the banks is that doing that relationship stuff is hard and expensive. Especially if you are a big bank, a national bank, an international bank or a global bank. That is why most of the community banks and credit unions were sitting smiling smugly during all of these discussions, because these financial providers – like the small UK building societies – pride themselves on being local, community oriented and friendly. They pride themselves on branches with managers who know each of their customers by name. They pride themselves on the fact that they can pretty much talk about the town or city in a way that demonstrates they are part of that town or city, rather than part of a brand or operation. That is the unique value proposition of the local operator.

Meantime, the large banks, the universal banks, the megabanks are institutions who thrive on dealing with the indifferents and sceptics who are happy to have a nameless, faceless relationship because they do not want a relationship. They just want a transaction done safely and securely. This does not mean that all large, universal banks behave as nameless and faceless institutions – although I know many that do and who are – but that many customers think of these institutions this way.

Now maybe this distinction is a little harsh on our major, proprietary bank operators who focus upon shareholder value and cost-income ratios, but it is meant to be harsh. After all, that focus upon the bottom-line is often at the expense of the top-line. That is why the mutual organisations, who focus upon their members rather than the shareholders, prosper in a world of receptive relationship banking.

The real message is that a bank has to make strategic choices. As the major keynote presentation at the BAI's conference stated, 'You've got to see strategy as something where you make choices.' The keynote presenter who made this statement was Michael Porter and, if you do not know his work, Porter is a Harvard Business School professor. He is also the most recognised authority on business strategy and competitive differentiation.

The focus of Porter's keynote was that most banks compete in the same territory and on the same turf and he believes that is wrong. Most banks have 'me-too' strategies that do not differentiate, except on rates and channels, and that is wrong. That is not strategy, it is just tactics. It is not differentiation, it is just competition.

Michael Porter reckons that retail bankers will continue to do this at their peril as the years of bank's being able to grow through acquisition are over, and the industry will soon be entering a re-defining period of 'strategic positioning', where banks will need to differentiate or die.

As Porter remarked: 'Just bulking up and being big and having lots of branches is not going to be any sort of advantage. Ultimately, you are going to have to deliver something distinctive.'

I agreed with a lot of what he said, after all he is a Harvard business professor and recognised guru of strategy. I particularly agreed with his conclusion that banks get it wrong because they blindly try to serve all customer segments. You cannot please all of the people all of the time. As a result, rather than investing in customer segmentation and targeting all segments with different service levels which simply confuse and distract frontline staff, banks should instead determine which particular customer segments they want to serve and excel in, and then just invest, in retail delivery to those segments with differentiation and dump the rest.

That means deciding whether you want the sceptics, the indifferents or the receptives. You cannot have them all and you cannot serve them all the same. That is a losing strategy. Whichever ones you go for, just create a compelling and unique value proposition for them and forget the rest. That may mean losing a third of today's customers or even more, but in the long term it will be worth it. After all, trying to serve all of the customers in all of the ways they want to be served all of the time, is just dumb.

Bottom-line: differentiate or die.

9

The Banks That Like to Say No

Retail banking has been around for over 400 years so it should work by now. It appears that this is not the case though because, as we increasingly automate banking services when things go wrong the cracks begin to show. The issue is that banks have forgotten or do not understand what business process re-engineering (BPR) means.

During the 1990s, there was an explosion of spending associated with BPR. Yet, as we change processes, disintegrate and reintegrate business functions, right 'source' and right 'shore' our operations, we increasingly cause fragility of people, product, process and systems. This came to mind during three unfortunate encounters I experienced with my bank. The three incidents show a bank that has misaligned people, process and technology and the visible illustrations of the results are quite telling.

Before going into the exact issues, I need to give you a little background on my deposit account – not the numbers or anything – so that the discussions are in context.

The account I use is for privileged customers who are willing to pay a small fee of $300 a year, for a few bells and whistles. The bells and whistles include a pre-authorised overdraft facility of up to $15,000 without notification, a concierge service, automatic insurance on all purchases when using the account card, travel insurance, discounts on restaurants, and so on. It is apparently targeted at the 'mass affluent' and yes, I may be one of the masses but I also like personalised service and offers, ok?

Now you know the sort of account I'm talking about, let's look at three examples where people, process and technology breakdown.

The first is an issue in process and technology that made the people providing the service box-ticking monkeys rather than intelligent humans. The error was made by a mixture of factors beginning with my account manager changing a flag on my account. The change was a short-term measure to allow an increased overdraft limit – I wanted my account manager to increase my standard facility of $15,000 to $20,000 due to some major fund transfers I had to process during a busy investment month. The problem was that the flag was set in place for a month and when it reset – a pure binary '1' and '0' part of the programming on the bank's database – instead of reverting to its original overdraft amount of $15,000, it flipped over to zero, as in no overdraft facility at all.

Now I pay quite a lot for that overdraft facility as it allows me never to have to think about my current bank balance when paying for things, and ensures that I am not penalised at all for going into credit. The facility is a standard product that this particular bank offers to their best clients. Therefore, when that flag reverted back to a zero credit limit, as in no overdraft facility, it did cause me an issue.

It happened at 17:45 on a Friday night during a bank holiday weekend, the worst possible time as, apparently, it could not be fixed until Tuesday.

At 17:45 on that fateful Friday, I was getting some groceries in my local supermarket when my payment with my bank debit card was refused. Total embarrassment of course, with lots of people behind me going 'tut, tut'. Thank the stars for credit cards.

Leaving the supermarket I was immediately on the phone to the bank call centre. The conversation went something like this:

Customer Service Representative (CSR): 'Hello'

Chris Skinner: 'Hi, I've just had my debit card refused in the local supermarket. Can you tell me why?'

CSR: 'Yes, you're $5 overdrawn. Please make a payment into your account'.

Me *(now angry, but restrained from a complete meltdown)*: 'But being overdrawn doesn't matter because I pay for a $15,000 overdraft facility'.

CSR *(trying to be helpful, but has not got a chance)*: 'Ah. I see what's happened. Your facility has been withdrawn by your account manager'.

Me *(now red-faced)*: 'WHAT?? Set it back again then'.

CSR: 'Oh no, I can't do that. You have to talk to your account manager'.

Me *(purple-faced)*: 'WHAT???? But it's a bank holiday weekend and he's not back in until Tuesday. What am I supposed to do till then?'

CSR *(sheepishly)*: 'Urmm. . .use your credit cards?'

Anyway, the conversation went on for a while longer, with two supervisors and a team manager involved. Conclusion: the database had reset my account to zero after my account manager had temporarily increased my overdraft limits (system and process error) and the call centre folks could not do anything about it because it could only be dealt with at branch level (process error).

Result: one very angry customer who was left cashless during a bank holiday. Note: that is when the banks take holidays, as does the rest of the British nation, and hence you are completely stymied if your bank messes up on the Friday night.

So I am now aware that my bank's call centre and branch systems are separated. I also know that the system does not work with the branch processes, or possibly vice versa, as it had not reminded the branch staff to reset the overdraft flag back to the previous level after a temporary change.

Well, that was a temporary setback I could live with but once bitten, twice shy. And the second incident was slightly more inconvenient.

This problem involved one of the featured 'benefits' of my all-in-one account, travel insurance. I have had this account for about 10 years and never felt the need to use the travel insurance, but always felt reassured that it was there. Therefore, when I lost an iPod, camera and about $300 in cash in a Las Vegas hotel, I thought 'aha, time to use that travel insurance' so I rang the bank from the USA at a cost of about $2 a minute. Why would I ring whilst in the USA? Because you should always register an insurance claim when it occurs shouldn't you?

The call centre number is ringing and, after about five rings, an automated voice comes on the line: 'Sorry, all of our operators are busy at the moment but we have placed you in a queue and your call will be answered shortly.'

OK, that's fine, I can wait a minute or two.

After another ten rings, the message comes on again: 'Sorry, all of our operators are busy at the moment but we have placed you in a queue and your call will be answered shortly.'

OK, keep it up.

Ten rings, 'Sorry. . .' Ten rings, 'Sorry. . .'

Ten minutes and $20 later: 'Sorry, we are all still really busy but we really want your call, you are important to us, and we do promise to be with you any second now, so please stay on the line.'

Mmmmm. . .I really should hang up, but if you think I'm important and I'm in a queue and I've been on 10 minutes, then I must be near the front of the queue by now, so OK, I'll hold a little longer.

Ten rings, 'Sorry. . .' Ten rings, 'Sorry. . .'

You eventually reach a point where you think: 'I've held on for so long now that if I hang up now it may just be at the point where I would have had an answer.' So you stay on the line, waiting.

Forty dollars and 20 minutes later we're still getting ten rings and 'sorry', but the message is at least a little bit more entertaining: 'Sorry, we may all still be busy but we wondered if you would like to play a game of i-Spy whilst you wait for us to get around to talking with you. You go first.'

By this point, I'm sorry Mr Keep-Me-on-Hold Bank, but I put the phone down.

So I land in the UK and finally get to report the loss, and the bank sends me various forms to fill in. Duly completed with all documentation, the forms are returned.

Now, as mentioned, I have spent 10 years believing that because I pay for my bank account with the free travel insurance then I will be covered by that policy. I was always confident that, should I come down with some sickness whilst overseas, the bank's insurance would pay for the hospital fees; or that, should I be abroad and some reprobate stole my wallet, the bank's insurance would pay. That's what travel insurance means to me. But no. It turns out my bank defines travel insurance as holiday insurance.

The claim was rejected because it was not a package holiday. Now, you might tell me that there's more to this than meets the eye, but the claim was rejected because I bought the flights with American Express. Apparently, the bank's insurance would only pay if a complete package of flights and hotels were booked and paid for using the bank's cards.

The reason for citing this second example is that it highlights two issues – a process issue and a product issue.

The process issue is that the travel insurance call centre never received or processed a call unless it was the third Thursday in a month with a 'y' in it.

The product issue is more fundamental. This is because the bank's marketing folks created a product – this deposit account – which has all of these bells and whistles thrown in which, in reality, customers either do not want, do not need them or do not use. I had not thought about using the travel insurance feature for the 10 years I had the account although the fact that I knew it was there meant that it provided a reassurance. In reality, what that feature achieved is a product cannibalisation whereby this add-on to the account, when triggered for use, actually proved to be worthless and, worse than this, brought into question my whole relationship with the bank and whether to keep my account with them.

Therefore, the most telling message from this story is that the tiny things the marketing department see as product features may actually be product weakeners if they do not support the relationship. Beware account cannibalisers and focus upon account stabilisers.

On to the third and final example.

I happened to move house in August 2006, the sort of mad thing you do when everyone else is away on holiday. Just to make life easy, I printed off a standard letter to all my service providers with details of the old and new address, and then wrote onto the letter the account numbers and so on, signed and posted the letters off to all my bank, insurance and related firms.

Everyone changed my details without question. . .except my bank.

They sent a letter back with a form attached.

The reason for the form, as became clear, is that the bank had implemented new procedures related to fraud and identity theft. As a result, the old way of allowing customers to send a letter with a signature saying 'I've moved' is no longer good enough. You have to fill out much more information on a standard bank form.

However, this was not what the bank's cover letter said. In fact, I have no idea who dreamt up this letter but it was pretty impressive, and read something along the lines of the following: 'Thank you for informing us of your change of address but we no longer accept those pithy little letters. Instead you have to fill in the form we enclose and, if you do not, we will continue to write to your old address until you do so.'

Now, if they had said, 'Due to new procedures to protect you from identity theft, we would like you to complete the attached form. After all, any old Tom, Dick or Harry could have sent us a letter with a signature', I might have filled in the form. Instead, I felt a little bit angry that my address change letter was not good enough. Luckily, the bank's letter finished with 'if you would rather talk to us then call our special house moving hotline number'.

Back to the trusty old telephone and house moving hotline.

Engaged.

Try again, engaged.

Try again, engaged.

After 10 minutes of redialling to an engaged hotline, a sudden realisation hits, 'I know, ring the bank's usual number for customer service' so I rang that number and got straight through to the automated menu system.

After entering my account number, sort code and password, I then pressed '0' for a customer service representative (CSR).

CSR: 'Name.'

Me: 'Yes and hello to you too. My name is Chris Skinner'.

CSR: 'Account Number'.

Me (*getting red-faced*): '12345678 and why you need that when I entered it in the first place to get through to you, I don't know'.

CSR: 'Sort Code'.

Me (*very red*): '123456, you robot'.

CSR: 'No need to be rude Mr Skinner. Now, before I can deal with your question, I need to ask you a couple of security questions. When were you born?'

Me: 'Before your time son. 1st May 1970'. (note, not my real birth date but I'm not going to reveal what a dinosaur I am now, am I?)

CSR: 'Mother's maiden name'.

Me: 'Jones, and at least mine was married'.

CSR: 'Sarcasm will get you nowhere sir. Now, what seems to be the issue?'

Me: 'Well, I've just moved house and sent the bank a letter with the new address. I then received a letter this morning saying that was not good enough so I have to fill in a long and complex form. Rather than doing that I rang the "moving house hotline" number to register my new address there, but the number has been engaged for the last ten minutes so I thought, instead, I would let you know my new address, as I don't really want to fill in the form as I've got enough to do, what with the move and everything'.

CSR: 'Sorry Mr. Skinner, I cannot do that, as you do not have the right security levels on your account to do that through our service. Now, is there anything else I can do for you today?'

Nuclear explosion at other end of phone.

This last example shows, yet again, fundamental process errors in the bank's internal operations. In particular, the lack of thought as to how all of the pieces fit together. In this case, there are a number of pieces:

- an address change form;
- how to write a covering letter that explains to customers exactly why the form is relevant;
- an address change call centre that is inoperational due to the fact that it is permanently engaged with people who do not like filling in forms; and
- a main call centre that is stripped of any empowerment to make anything happen for anyone, in particular address changes.

The bottom-line is that these three examples which all occurred within a 12-month period, demonstrate a catalogue of cracks in the processes of my bank. The cracks between the branch systems and the head office systems. The cracks between the account manager's processes and the customer service representative's processes. The cracks between the address change departments procedures and the head office procedures.

You may now be asking yourself: 'Why the hell does Chris stay with a bank that treats him this way?' I can give you two reasons why.

First, I do not believe the cracks in my banks processes are unique or even unusual. Every bank has these issues and has had them for decades. The issues today are exacerbated by pressure on cost-income ratios, shareholder returns and reward, bonus and incentive structures, which mean that banks' staff and management focus upon those areas where they get the most rewarded and banks' processes and procedures are implemented at the lowest cost possible. Hence, the cracks appear as management focus upon cross-sell and acquisition, whilst the real front-line – the people, processes and procedures – are stretched to the limits by marketing and regulatory burdens.

Second, following on from the last chapter, I am a complete indifferent when it comes to my retail bank. Business banking is different – you need a partner in your business activities who you can trust – but retail banking in the UK, where I have three major accounts with three major high street banks, is proving to be a totally homogenous market where the banks all provide similar levels of service as described.

Third, and more importantly, my bank has a secret weapon. His name is Oz and Oz is my account manager. The difference with Oz is that he knows my voice, my attitude, my demands and my demeanour. Therefore, if I ever have a problem, I just call Oz. Oh yes, and by the way, Oz is a human who actually behaves the way that bank manager's used to behave, as in talking to customers as customers, not just numbers.

This chapter builds upon the earlier discussions of process and technology touched upon in Chapters 6, 7 and 8. Therefore, although the examples are very personal, the aim is to re-ignite the debate about BPR.

That debate goes back to the essence of the lessons we should have learnt a decade ago which focused upon 'Don't Automate, Obliterate'. That was the title of Michael Hammer's seminal 1990s Harvard Business Review article that created the BPR business. The paper said that before you automate, completely rethink the process in light of the automation.

BPR had a few simple steps:

- look at the process;
- question everything about it;
- focus upon optimisation of every customer interaction; then
- rethink how it works.

Only after completion of these simple steps should technology be considered.

Then implement the right technology to make the whole thing work seamlessly, in an integrated fashion, which supports the human involvement in the process.

These simple steps are the lessons that banks seem to have forgotten in the last 10 years. Instead of implementing technology to create improved processes, banks are implementing technology and not thinking through the processes. The three incidents outlined in this chapter illustrate this point well.

BPR mandates a few other cornerstones also, such as trusting customer-facing employees with empowerment to solve the customer's issues as those issues arise; such as talking with customers as humans who have needs to be served. After all, banking should be about humans dealing with humans – the nature of service – not machines dealing with humans – the nature of self-service.

This is the other misnomer about banking.

Banking is a service and service is provided between people. People are the factor that makes the difference, not technology. People who are supported by good processes and systems will always outperform people who are not.

This is why it has been fascinating to watch the recent movement within retail banks to outsource their call centres both onshore and offshore. The reason it is fascinating is that the call centre is the primary customer touch point. For both the indifferent, the sceptic and the receptive customer, the call centre can be a make or break in the relationship with the customer because banks only keep business with the individual retail customer whilst the customer trusts them. As they outsource that trust, they are in danger of breaking that trust. That is why we are already seeing many banks taking action to bring their call centre operations back inhouse, having previously outsourced them onshore or offshore and this is a trend that, for the longer term, needs to be watched carefully and is discussed in much more depth in the next chapter.

Nevertheless, my bank would have lost my business long ago if I had to rely on their general back office people, process and systems. I am lucky enough to have an Oz, but my bank should not need an Oz if things worked properly in the first place.

Here's to the human bank where people are at the fore, supported by good processes and good technologies.

10

The Future is Video-Banking

When discussing the future, I often get a reaction I call the 'Edupyrryr Syndrome'.

Edupyrryr, pronounced phonetically as 'head-up-your-rear', occurs when people are confronted by something so obvious but so threatening that they don't want to hear about it. Therefore, they use the edupyrryr principles and blank it out. I usually get this reaction to the idea of the death of cash or the death of debit and credit cards (see Chapter 15, 'The Cashless, Cardless Society'). I got it again recently when I announced the death of something else. . .the keyboard.

The fact is that things only die when something else is born. Cash dies due to micro and contactless payments. Plastic cards die due to contactless payments, wearable computing and biometrics (all explained in Chapter 15, 'The Cashless, Cardless Society').

In fact, I was pleased to see these views corroborated by the keynote session at the EBA's payments conference in Frankfurt in June 2006 when Mark Garvin, chief administrative officer at JPMorgan Chase AG, agreed with the vision that the payments industry in 2016 would be one where paper cheques are non-existent, payment by mobile phone is commonplace and biometrics have wiped out fraud.

Therefore, it came as a shock to find an audience of technology people roundly denouncing a new vision for banking which I expounded at a recent conference. The focus of the presentation is a vision I've held for years that the biggest technology disruption for banks will be the widespread usage of video channels: video over IP, video over 3G, video over anything. As an extension of this concept, I promoted the idea that if everyone connected visually and verbally, then why would anyone type? After all, we only use keyboards because we can't see and talk with each other. Twenty years ago, the only people who used keyboards were in typing pools and secretarial roles. Now, we all type and so the typing pool has disappeared, and secretaries have found a new role as personal assistants.

Maybe it was that last bit that caused the audience to vote the presentation the worst on the agenda! And yet I presented the same idea again in Amsterdam the following week where it was voted the best presentation.

Something strange is afoot.

Let me explain the logic of the presentation.

In 1986, I was in discussions with a major UK insurance group around the theme of direct insurance operations. The radical concept was doing insurance new business on the telephone, rather than face-to-face or by post. The insurance firm in question told me that such a radical new scheme would not work. They had tried it and it failed. Firstly, it failed because consumers did not have the technology: touch-tone telephones. The clients they dealt with were impoverished types who only had rotary phones. Secondly, it failed because consumers did not like dealing with underwriters on the phone. There you have it. Point proven. Been there, done that. Move on.

The shock came a year later when Direct Line wiped out their business. As did First Direct in the banking world, when they grew at a pace of 100,000 new clients per month and soon knocked out incumbent players.

The radical concept being a touch-tone telephone, call centres and people on the phones who were not underwriters or credit risk managers, but Customer Service Agents! People who provide Customer Service, who like customers, who know how to deal with them and can talk to them on the telephone.

The result was that that insurance firm went bust in the early 1990s and was acquired. Wow, how times have moved on.

Since 1986, we have seen a massive surge in call centre operations with thousands of people employed in the industry, both in the UK and increasingly in offshore locations. Having said that, the UK call centre industry is still thriving with over 375,000 UK citizens employed in call centre and customer related jobs, representing an 8.8% growth since 2002, according to the Office of National Statistics. We even see a return to onshore call centres.

Since 1986, Direct Line and First Direct have become two of the biggest financial brands in the UK, and all banks now offer 24×7 call centre customer services, some of them even onshore.

So far so good.

However, we have also seen a proliferation of other forms of channels and communications.

From the touch-tone telephone, we have moved to the mobile telephone. From letters in the post, we have moved to instantaneous e-mail. Layer on top of this WAP, SMS and instant messaging and we have call centres that are over-burdened with an avalanche of communication.

TowerGroup estimate that US banks will be receiving over 1 billion e-mails per annum in 2010, employing 70,000 staff across America just to service those e-mails. That is good news for some, as US bank call centre numbers are on the decline so those folks can get jobs answering e-mails. For example, according to the North American Call Centre Report, the USA had over 50,600 call centres employing 2.86 million agents in 2004 but this is estimated to decline by 2008 to 47,500 call centres with 2.7 million agents because of self-service technologies, increasing use of speech recognition, the growth of offshore outsourcing and the federal 'do-not-call' list.

This means you will have to hedge your bets on call centre numbers being on the rise or the decline, but the one thing you can bet your bottom-dollar on is that you will be upgrading your call centres to the internet, generally referred to as IP-based telephony.

Skype-based telephones, Voice over Internet Protocol (VoIP), all that cheap and easy calling using wireless and internet. . . there's the future. For banks, it means that the traditional PBX switchboards are being ripped out and replaced by integrated Digital Exchanges that manage not just their telephony, but branch security services, broadband bandwidths into branch systems, CCTV and so on. All over cheap, internet lines.

Here's a few figures.

Various estimates state that VoIP line shipments increased by over 50% in 2004, while PBX-based line shipments were down almost 30%. Spending on VoIP will jump from just over $1 billion in 2004 to almost $25 billion in 2010.

I hear a few whoops and hollers from the IP camp, but this really does miss a trick.

All of this misses one fundamental.

A fundamental flaw in our short-term logic.

VoIP is not about supporting cheap telephone calls, or even placing them globally to wherever the cheapest service centres reside.

VoIP is not about Voice over Internet Protocol.

It's about video.

Real-time video.

Person-to-person video.

This is not 3G mobile video, but true, High-Definition, Broadband and Wireless Video.

Video over Internet Protocol.

If you want to see what the new generation of IP video can really do, just check out Apple's iChat AV (http://www.apple.com/macosx/features/ichat/).

The idea of high-quality person-to-person video is coming of age right now.

This is not the crude web-cammy stuff, but the real deal.

You think an HD-ready TV is hot, wait till you see HD-ready internet.

Having said that, Apple's been delivering HD-ready internet over a technology called H.264 since 2005 and Microsoft is delivering the same through Vista, the successor to Windows XP, in 2007.

Why is this critical to banks?

Because it brings back face-to-face communications.

It finally gives bankers back what they lost when the technology revolution moved us all out of branch and onto ATMs, phones and keyboards.

Add onto this the fact that you can talk with someone, see them, touch the screen and be animated, and you might get the idea that this is not just cool, but it gets us back to what 'services' is all about, as in human contact.

Services are not about products, things you can manufacture or kick. Services are about ephemeral promises, dialogues, relationships and human interaction. That is why 'Financial Services', with the emphasis on service, cannot be marketed like a box of cookies or a car. You have to focus upon the human elements to differentiate and win.

This then leads us back to the Edupyrryr Syndrome.

Whenever we talk about video telephony, the luddites say things like 'Who's gonna walk down the street staring at their phone to talk? Just look around at what people do today buddy. No-one's using Video yet. Just look at 3G and how that's failed. You're talking rot.' Is that why you can put 'videophone' into google and get millions of returns including the offer of free videoconferencing, and videophones from under £100? 'Yea, but people don't want to see who's on the other end?' Read the last paragraph. 'What about the fact that you might not look the best yourself?' Thanks, but there's always the button that says 'Only Let Me See You' isn't there?

It makes me think the Edupyrryr Syndrome sufferers are only looking up there because that is where they keep their brains.

This then leads to the seminal moment when you accept that video bank servicing is here and now.

What does that mean?

It means you have to rethink the call centre.

The call centre – whether onshore or offshore – will be your key alternative virtual channel to your physical branch. The imperative will be to have culturally and visually acceptable staff on those centres, which already leads into arguments over diversity and globalisation.

In addition, it may mean a massive increase in staff numbers, unless you automate the front-end with robotics, or 'avatars' as they are known. Avatars can either be cartoon or realistic automated agents who, like the touchtone menu systems of the traditional call centre, can handle 80% of the calls. 'What's my balance?' 'Where's my payment?' 'I need to change a regular payment order?' can all be dealt with by these automated videobots. The remainder of calls are more service oriented anyway. 'I need a mortgage – should I go fixed or variable?'

'My pension fund statement is wrong!' 'Should I build my own cross-asset class, multi-region hedged trading strategy or just use yours?' Whoops, sorry. Last one a bit of a surprise.

The core of what we get into is that the video-servicing world will mean very different service cultures and structures. It will most definitely mean that your back office and core systems will become transparent and totally visible to Joe Public. You will have to carefully rethink the way you route calls but, more importantly, the impression given once the call is routed. If your culturally and visually acceptable call centre operators are struggling with multi-screen legacy systems, it will show. Therefore, you will need to have single screen, simple systems to support the new world of visual communications, especially as many of those screens will be shared with the customer in collaborative communications online.

Now, I am jumping. This leads into all sorts of implications. For example, if I can talk and see you, why would I talk and type? In fact, why would I type at all? Most of us only type as that's our interface to the PC. If you can use voice recognition systems integrated with visual services, then drop the keyboard! Oh no, another edupyrryr moment.

There is the rub though. Why would you type if you did not need to? Why do we type? We type because we have all had to learn to use keyboards in our current internet-enabled world. But tomorrow's world will be all about connecting visually. Talk with your mom and dad through your broadband TV. Connect with your friends to plan your evening through your wireless communicator, currently called a telephone or PDA. Create a book by talking to your electronic desk system. That is the future, and that is why you don't see anyone typing in *Minority Report* or *Star Trek*.

So there's the presentation logic.

Since I started this mantra in 2003, I'm still waiting for a bank to offer me video-servicing via broadband or mobile wireless. I know that some banks are doing this for their employee communications; some banks are doing this to deliver expertise to remote branches; and some are offering video services to their high net worth clients. But the bank that offers the mass market the video channel, efficiently, appropriately, conveniently and easily will dominate the next generation of retail banking as there's no easy way to respond to this easily. You cannot just bolt a video screen onto your offshore call centre. You cannot just reinvent your core systems overnight to provide seamless servicing for collaborative commerce.

By the way, if anyone out there knows of a bank that does this today – for their mass market retail customers – I'd love to hear about it.

Anyway, back to that rubbish presentation I did. Maybe it got a poor vote as it not only foretold the end of the keyboard but the end of many retail banks. Maybe I frightened everyone so much that they had to have an edupyrryr moment. Or maybe it's because the conference organiser told me later that they scanned the feedback forms into their database incorrectly and instead of recording my scores as the best, they recorded as the worst.

Either way, the world is moving to one where we will be visually and vocally connected, 24×7, through HD-ready Internet Protocol-based systems that will feel as easy to deal with as real-life communications. That world will no longer demand that we type and dial, but that we talk and share. We already talk about collaborative commerce and IP-based communications, so this world is purely an extension of those foundations. It is a world that will command massive investments in core systems renewal and infrastructures, staff training and organisation, smart sourcing and smart services.

For the bank that gets it right, they will become the next generation of the First Direct's and Geico's. For the banks that wait for it to happen, they may well be the, urm, what was that bank's name again? Y'know, the one that went bust.

11

Call Centre of the Future

NEXT YEAR

The VideoBank is launched, but has poor processes.

Automated Bank:
Hello and welcome to Vision Bank. Please enter your 8 digit account number followed by the hash (#) key.

Beep, Beep, Beep, Beep, Beep, Beep, Beep, Beep, Beep.

Automated Bank:
Thank you. Please enter your four digit password followed by the hash (#) key.

Beep, Beep, Beep, Beep, Beep.

Automated Bank:
Thank you, Press 1 for account balance, 2 for your last five transactions, 3 for account services, 4 for money transfers, 5 for insurance services, or press zero for an operator.

Beep.

Automated Bank:
Your account balance is one thousand, three hundred and twenty two dollars and thirty five cents overdrawn. You must contact a customer service representative before we can service you further. Please press zero for an operator via voice or one for an operator via video.

Beep.

A screen pops up with a call centre operator looking hassled.

Bank Call Centre Operator on Interactive Video Screen:
Hello Mr Skinner, how can we help you?

Me:
Hi. I've just heard I'm overdrawn, can you tell me how and when this happened?

Operator starts clicking buttons and looking all around the screen.

Bank Call Centre Operator on Interactive Video Screen:
Yes, Mr Skinner, Can you please tell me your mother's maiden name?

Me:
I'm sorry, I just want to know how and when I went overdrawn – why do you need that info?

Operator looks sternly.

Bank Call Centre Operator on Interactive Video Screen:
It is for security purposes Mr Skinner. Can you please tell me your mother's maiden name?

Me:
Ok yes, it's Jones. Now how and when did I go overdrawn?

Bank Call Centre Operator on Interactive Video Screen:
Thank you Mr Skinner. I'm just checking your account details.

Operator starts clicking buttons and looking all around outside the screen, e.g. as though searching windows on their desk other than the window that I'm looking at.

Bank Call Centre Operator on Interactive Video Screen:
What was your last transaction?

Me:
I can't remember at the moment, I'm just interested in how and when I went overdrawn?

Bank Call Centre Operator on Interactive Video Screen:
I am sorry I cannot do that Mr Skinner until you have cleared our security screening. (*Operator gives big smile.*) What was your last transaction?

Me:
Come on, I've already entered my PIN and given you my mothers' maiden name – just tell me what made me overdrawn.

Bank Call Centre Operator on Interactive Video Screen:
(*Operator now stern and brusque*) As I said Mr Skinner, I cannot give you that information until you have cleared our security screening, What was your last transaction?

Me:
I brought some aspirin from Greens the Chemist for about fifteen dollars?

Operator looks away to check and then looks back with a frown and a wry smile.

Bank Call Centre Operator on Interactive Video Screen:
No you did not Mr Skinner. (*Operator breaks into a big smile.*) Thank you for calling Vision Bank. Goodbye.

A YEAR PASSES

The VideoBank is relaunched, and has replaced poor processes with automated agents called 'Avatars'.

A screen pops up and says 'calling bank'. Then a Call Centre Agent appears who looks a bit stiff and formal – a bit robotic but not too much.

Bank Avatar (in a deadpan manner):
Hello and welcome to Vision Bank. Can I please take your name and first line of your address?

Me:
Hello, my name is Chris Skinner and I live at 86 Warren Gardens in England.

On the screen, a line under the agent screen states 'voice verification in action'.

Bank Avatar (in a deadpan manner):
Thank you Mr Skinner. My name is Robert. How can we help you today Mr Skinner? (Agent has a vacuous expression.)

Me:
You can call me Chris. I was just wondering what my account balance and last few transactions were?

On the screen, a window appears by the agent showing my last five transactions.

Transaction	Date	Amount	Balance
Whisky from WalMart, London	23rd	$20.00	−$1,322.35
Aspirin form Greens, London	23rd	$15.00	−$1,307.35
Cigarettes from Shell Station, Norwich	23rd	$520.00	−$787.35
Gasoline from Shell Station, Norwich	23rd	$52.00	−$735.35
Magazines and Books from WHSmith, Norwich	23rd	$56.35	−$679.00

Bank Avatar (in a deadpan manner):
Thank you Mr Chris Skinner. Your account balance is one thousand, three hundred and twenty two dollars and thirty five cents overdrawn. Your last transaction was for twenty dollars from Wal-Mart for whisky and fifteen dollars from Greens for Aspirin.

Me:
Whoops. Overdrawn again? Can you tell me when I went overdrawn?

On the screen, a window appears showing recent transactions as follows:

Bank Avatar (in a deadpan manner):
Yes Mr Chris Skinner. You went overdrawn on the 21st after buying a shotgun from Davisons the gunsmiths for two thousand dollars.

Transaction	Date	Amount	Balance
Whisky from WalMart, London	23rd	$20.00	−$1,322.35
Aspirin form Greens, London	23rd	$15.00	−$1,307.35
Cigarettes from Shell Station, Norwich	23rd	$520.00	−$787.35
Gasoline from Shell Station, Norwich	23rd	$52.00	−$735.35
Magazines and Books from WHSmith, Norwich	23rd	$56.35	−$679.00
Shotgun from Davisons, Norwich	21st	$2,000.00	$1,321.00
Jewellery from Mappin & Webb, Norwich	21st	$1,100.00	$2,521.00

Me:
I guess I should have bought that on my loan account. Can you bring up details to transfer funds from my savings account to cover the temporary overdraft situation and equally I think I'd like to take out a loan.

Operator starts clicking buttons and a window pops up with details of the savings account and another with details of loan rates.

Bank Avatar (in a deadpan manner):
Yes Mr Chris Skinner. In order to proceed with your current transaction I need to transfer you to a specialist in savings and loans. Would that be ok?

Me:
Sure.

Bank Avatar (in a deadpan manner):
Yes, Mr Chris Skinner. I shall now transfer you to Amy, a specialist in savings and loans. Thank you for your business with Vision Bank today.

Robert, the Avatar Agent with the vacuous expression remains on screen whilst another video screen pops up with a nice smiling attractive young lady who is very bubbly and animated.

Human Agent:
Hello Mr Skinner, I'm Amy and will take your requirements onwards and upwards from here. What is it we can do you for today. . .?

Me:
Well, I'm a bit concerned about going overdrawn. I wonder if you can arrange a loan for me?

Human Agent:
Absolutely Mr Skinner. What sort of loan would you like? We have big ones and little ones (*Amy puts her index finger and thumb together to indicate 'small'*). Ones that last a few months and ones you can keep forever (*Amy raises eyes to the heavens on the latter, as in 'forever'*). Loans that cost you virtually nothing and others that make a fortune for Vision Bank. Do any of these sound like your sort of thing?

Me:
Yes. I'd like a little one for a few months.

Human Agent:
Fantastic Mr Skinner. We have a few of those as well. On your screen. . .

Amy presses a button and a PC screen pops up next to the window containing the following:

Little loans for a few months – Vision Bank's Special Offers to Mr Skinner

	Interest Rate	Amount	Period
The Little Belter	5.5%	$1–$10,000	1 day to 1 year
The Belter	5.25%	$1–$20,000	Six months
The Total Belter	5%	$1–$20,000	Long as you want

Human Agent:
. . .you can see the choices today that are offered especially for you, personally, just because it's you. Do any of these suit you sir?

Me:
Looks good Amy – can I have a total belter for $2,000?

Human Agent:
Of course you can Mr Skinner. I guess we should just give you a clue as to how that one works. . .

Amy presses another button and the PC screen that had the loan offers now zooms in to the Total Belter and illustrates the offer as follows:

The Total Belter – Vision Bank's Special Offers to Mr Skinner

	Interest Rate	Amount	Period	Total Paid
The Total Belter	5%	$2,000	1 year	$2,100 + $50 fees

. . .which shows you would be paying us $150 if you kept that money for a year. Is that ok?

Me:
I don't suppose you would do that for $100 today would you, as in drop the fees?

Human Agent:
Let me just check Mr Skinner. . .

Amy presses a button and looks hard at a screen and then and beams a big smile:

. . .we can't drop the fees Mr Skinner, but we can do that for $20 discount if you agree to the service today.

the PC screen that had the loan offers changes with a little 'ding' as the $50 drops to $30 as follows:

The Total Belter – Vision Bank's Special Offers to Mr Skinner

	Interest Rate	Amount	Period	Total Paid
The Total Belter	5%	$2,000	1 year	$2,100 + $30 fees

Me:
Great. I'll take that.

Human Agent:
Fantastic Mr Skinner. We'll get the money into your account today with details of this conversation and the loan costs. Now, is there anything else I can do for you today?

Me:
Nope. That'll do nicely and thanks.

Human Agent:
Thank you Mr Skinner. See you again soon and thank you for doing business with Vision Bank, the most attractive and friendliest bank you'll do business with.

Amy presses a button and all screens close to a little white dot on a black screen as though you've turned off an old telly.

12

The Big Issue – Fraud and Identity Theft

There is a long debate about the issue of identity theft and fraud, especially after the case of Derek Bond, the 72-year-old British tourist, who was arrested by the FBI in South Africa in 2003. Mr Bond had his identity stolen by someone in the United States, who had been using it for about 15 years to commit various crimes. Now, in the age of the online connection, identity theft is potentially much simpler, with phishing and spoofing scams propagating the issue. Is this as bad as the headlines make out?

According to figures from the U.S. Government, the major form of fraud being reported by SARs – Suspicious Activity Reports – is still money laundering with cheque fraud running a close second and computer intrusion rising rapidly since it entered the charts in 2000. SARs are completed by banks, and have been submitted to the U.S. Government since 1996 although their influence has widened since the Patriot Act of 2001 which extended the requirement to complete SARs to the capital markets, covering brokers, dealers and any other money based organisation including casinos (Figure 12.1).

Violation Type	1997	1998	1999	2000	2001	2002
Money Laundering	35,625	47,223	60,983	90,606	108,925	154,000
Bribery/Gratuity	109	92	101	150	201	411
Cheque Fraud	13,245	13,767	16,232	19,637	26,012	32,954
Cheque Kiting[1]	4,294	4,032	4,058	6,163	7,350	9,561
Commercial Loan Fraud	960	905	1,080	1,320	1348	1,879
Computer Intrusion[2]	0	0	0	65	419	2,484
Consumer Loan Fraud	2,048	2,183	2,548	3,432	4,143	4,435
Counterfeit Check	4,226	5,897	7,392	9,033	10,139	12,575
Counterfeit Credit/Debit Card	387	182	351	664	1,100	1,246
Counterfeit Instrument (Other)	294	263	320	474	769	791
Credit Card Fraud	5,075	4,377	4,936	6,275	8,393	12,780
Debit Card Fraud	612	565	721	1,210	1,437	3,741
Embezzlement	5,284	5,252	5,178	6,117	6,182	6,151
False Statement	2,200	1,970	2,376	3,051	3,232	3,685
Misuse of Position or Self Dealing	1,532	1,640	2,064	2,186	2,325	2,763
Mortgage Loan Fraud	1,720	2,269	2,934	3,515	4,696	5,387
Mysterious Disappearance	1,765	1,855	1,854	2,225	2,179	2,330
Wire Transfer Fraud	509	593	771	972	1,527	4,747
Other	6,675	8,583	8,739	11,148	18,318	31,109
Unknown/Blank	2,317	2,691	6,961	6,971	11,908	7,704
Totals	88,877	104,339	129,599	175,214	220,603	300,733

[1] Cheque kiting is the 'bouncing cheque' where there is an illegal act of writing cheques against a bank account with insufficient funds to cover the cheque.
[2] The violation of Computer Intrusion was added to Form TD F 90-22.47 in June 2000. Statistics date from this period.
Source: US Department of State

Figure 12.1 Suspicious Activity Report Filings to the U.S. Government 1997–2002

As can be seen from Figure 12.1, there were 154,000 cases of money laundering incidents during 2002. Meantime, in the same year, the Federal Trade Commission (FTC) processed 161,819 alerts from American consumers regarding identity theft, up from just over 30,000 in 2000. Of these, two-thirds related to bank fraud with 42% of incidents for credit card fraud, 17% for bank account fraud, 6% for fraudulent loans and 1% for internet account fraud.

Sounds bad doesn't it? And for banks it is pretty bad as identify theft costs US lenders about $1.5 billion a year in lost revenues. Thanks to the internet, we now have a few more issues.

THE INTERNET THEFT TIME BOMB

When the internet was just taking off there was a great cartoon used in many presentations showing two dogs on a computer, with one saying to the other 'the great thing about the internet is that no-one knows you are a dog'. Now that old joke could be slightly changed to say 'the great thing about the internet is that no-one knows you are a thief'.

The simplest level of online thievery is the pure scam. How many of you have received the e-mail that goes something like 'my father was the head of the army of fraudland and, if you give me $30,000 for administration costs, I'll give you 25% of his $2.8 million of savings'? Of course, most of us are not fooled by these scams but then the organised attacks evolved into much more sophisticated fraud through phishing and spoofing. These fool the consumer into thinking they are dealing with bona fide organisations but are dealing direct with criminals instead.

A recent survey of American consumers by TRUSTe and the US Electronic Payments Association, NACHA, found that almost seven out of 10 consumers had unintentionally visited a spoofed website, and 35% were getting phished at least once a week. The same survey estimated the financial losses of phishing and spoofing to be in the order of $500 million a year. That is half the cost of identity theft or, to put it another way, a 50% increase in losses since online financial fraud became organised criminals' flavour of the month.

And this is only set to get worse as the Anti-Phishing Working Group (APWG) finds that new phishing attacks are increasing by 50% per month with the main target being bank fraud.

Obviously, no-one is sitting back ignoring this evolutionary trend, with the average time for most banks to fix holes in their websites dropping to under a few days, but that is still a few days too long as the organised gangs can exploit the security flaws for a few days more than is acceptable.

THE REAL ISSUE HERE

The real issue here is that online banking, offline banking and especially payments, must be reliable and secure. The was illustrated at a conference I attended with the elite of America's payments industry. During this conference, a presentation from the Federal Reserve Bank of Chicago and Bank of America entitled 'Information Security in a Web-based Payments World' reviewed the latest state of online systems security. Bearing in mind that Bank of America was one of the first online banks to introduce two-level authentication of any substance, and that they run the world's largest online bank with over 13 million online users, this had all the makings of an interesting session. . .and it was.

The Federal Reserve discussed the state of payments security and described online payments as being a bit like plane crashes. If one plane in 10 million flights crashes, you do not fear flying too much. If the plane crashes every other flight, then most folks jump in the car or catch the train. That is a critical point. The fear of payment crashes online is huge and has already seen large numbers of consumers frightened away from online payments. For example, according to a press release from Visa, 24% of consumers are shopping less online because of these fears. In another recent article in Information Week, over 50 million people are believed to have had data about themselves exposed to criminal factions during 2005, at a cost of $47 billion. That cost is the pure costs of data lost to organised crime. $47 billion. No wonder we are a bit fearful.

Then the Bank of America stood up and raised the hee-bee gee-bee stakes even higher by going through the facts and figures for Bank of America.

Apparently, in 2006, every hour of every business day, Bank of America is exposed to:

- 150,000 paper pages of data being disposed of incorrectly;
- 16,000 'sniffer' intrusions on their website;
- 175 denial of service attacks; and
- three brand new phishing websites launched targeted at Bank of America.

Every hour of every day.

No wonder there is so much concern about online fraud.

SO WHAT IS THE SOLUTION?

There are some things banks are doing. One big focus is the introduction of two-level authentication.

The most common forms of two-level authentication in payments is based upon something you have – a card or computer – and something you know – a PIN or password.

Some banks have taken this further. For example, Bank of America's SiteKey is partially based upon a users' specific computer identifier, their IP address, being used as a unique identifier to allow access to their online bank services. ABN Amro, e*Trade and Lloyds TSB are using unique identifiers with randomly generated numbers on keyfobs. The idea is that to gain access online you enter your username, password and then receive a unique access code that is available for only 10 seconds to gain access online. In other words, you must have the keyfob and a smart card and PIN to access the site.

All of these layers of security serve to improve the reassurance of managing online financial servicing. But is it enough? Maybe not.

That is why country regulators are making it law to implement two-level authentication, with the USA leading the way. That is why one of the big buzzes has been the FFIEC (Federal Financial Institutions Examinations Council) introduction of mandatory rules for two-level authentication. The regulation actually does not mean that all American banks must have systems in place, just processes and procedures.

Australia has similar rules in place covered by law, although their implementation sparked a huge debate because three of the four big banks wanted to implement biometrics as the second authentication.

This brings us around to the question of what is the right authentication technique. For many, it is between using something you have (a card) and something you know (a PIN) versus something you have and something you are, as in biometrics.

BIOMETRICS

It amazes me that we go to great lengths to avoid fraud and yet, by and large, ignore the potential of biometrics. Just look at the recent examples of security efforts where financial institutions have invested heavily in anti-fraud schemes such as Chip and PIN, 128-bit PKI encryption systems, password controls with six layers of questioning to get through to websites, compared to the number of banks using biometrics.

Why is this?

Historically, it is because financial organisations have been concerned about the intrusion people might feel if they said that you had to offer up your finger or eyeball to make a payment. That is the trouble with biometrics in that everyone always talks about fingerprints and eyeballs which immediately leads to concerns around fingers being cut-off, customers being held at knife point or worse. Although what could be worse than having your finger cut-off or eye gouged out is something that most of us would prefer not to think about. For those who would like to know more, just watch the films *Minority Report* or *Saw* but, just to be clear, this is not suitable for those of a nervous disposition.

Biometrics does not have to be so dangerous, as the technology also covers voiceprints and signatures, for example. A biometric voiceprint can be stored as a digitised identification during account opening and is highly accurate, even when the customer has a cold. Biometric signatures are also non-intrusive, and register the weight of the pen during the signature entry. With digital pen and paper taking off, it is highly likely that biometric signatures will become a more common identification factor.

Equally, banks concerns about consumers' reactions to biometrics being negative has been disproved over and over again. For example, in a survey by Privacy & American Business in 2003, 85% of consumers said it would be acceptable for a private firm to ask for a biometric scan to authenticate credit card transactions. In addition, since 9/11, we have all come to accept that biometrics will be used for border controls with US Customs leading the way towards biometric passports and the rest of the world following.

So it comes as little surprise to find that there are a few more examples of banking biometrics appearing, such as the rollout of Pay-By-Touch fingerprint payments with the Discover Card in the USA and Co-operative grocery stores in the UK. There is also the interesting example of the Bank of Tokyo-Mistubishi in Japan who introduced palm print recognition at ATMs for cash withdrawals. In this instance, the bank discovered that female customers felt palm recognition far more hygienic than fingerprint recognition because you hold the palm above rather than on the biometric reader. In fact, the range of different options for biometric rollout all have pro's and con's of this type.

Specifically, what comes as a surprise is that so few banks have committed to rollout these technologies. A recent TowerGroup survey found that only 35% of banks have a biometric authentication program in place although, more encouragingly, a further 10% of firms were piloting. That is why bank spending on biometrics increased from $1.4 billion in 2004 to about $4 billion in 2007 with a Compound Annual Growth Rate of 28%.

The net result is that you should expect to see many more biometric deployments proliferating across the financial industry as we see these technologies becoming commonplace and mainstream.

After all, would you rather have someone pretending to be you or would you rather give them the finger?

Equally by using biometrics, you now have a way of tightening security by having three-level authentication: something you have (a card), something you know (a PIN) and something you are (biometric signatures or similar), as a very secure method of identification. Even then, a bank can add other forms of identification verification. For example, behaviour (what you have been doing) and location (where you are).

FIVE-LEVEL AUTHENTICATION

Many banks already do this. My bank placed a security watch on my credit card because I used my card for a single transaction in Las Vegas – a cash withdrawal (after heavy losses on the tables of course) – before turning up again in London. This was obviously one suspicious transaction, and caused my account to be placed upon a security watch because it did not fit the pattern of what I normally do.

The 'where you are' is related to this, and card companies easily track where you are when making payments at a merchant's terminal in a physical location because, obviously, to make a payment in a physical location you have to physically be there. All well and good, but this is harder on the internet because the World Wide Web is exactly that: worldwide. This means that you do not have to physically be there and the bank cannot as easily track your physical location. That is why Card Not Present (CNP) fraud is a major issue online. Going back to one of my favourite phrases, 'the beauty of the internet is that no-one knows you are a dog', the problem here is that not only does the bank not know you are a dog but they don't know where the dog is either. I could be accessing the internet over my wireless PC in Vegas as easily as London. My IP address stays the same and so authentication is harder.

This is changing though.

There are some clever technologies that show graphically where the internet user resides at any moment in time. For example, I saw a technology recently which integrates online bank security with Google Earth. As a result, any bank security officer can bring up a world map at any time of the day, and point to a user to see where they are, who they are and what they are doing.

If they are called 'Joe Brown', performing online bill payments, have passed all the normal identification checks, do not appear to be doing any unusual activities based upon past behaviours and are in New York, then that passes under the radar. On the other hand, even though all other factors might be acceptable, if this user happens to be in a town where Joe Brown would not normally be using online banking, then the alarm appears and additional security can be used to check it really is Joe.

The result is five-factor authentication for online and offline banking services. The five factors being:

- something you have, such as a card, a key or a radio frequency chip;
- something you know, such as a PIN, a password or an answer to a unique question;
- something you are, such as your unique way of signing or your voiceprint;

- your behaviours, based upon your usual transactions and whether this transaction fits that profile; and
- your location, and whether this is a place you would normally transact.

Banks' security systems will continually improve in these five areas until the integration of these five factors catches more and more crime.

In conclusion, the truth is that no-one does know whether you are a dog on the internet but the more criminals use 'sniffers' to try and commit fraudulent activities, the more banks will send out rottweilers to bite the nose of those sniffing. Banks will never eradicate crime or criminals, but minimising the $47 billion of losses to organised crime has to be an aspiration worth targeting.

13

Channel Technologies Through 2015

The end of the 20th Century saw a sudden explosion and implosion of technology, commonly referred to as the internet boom and bust. During the last decade of that century, the world changed fundamentally and banks struggled hard to keep up. Now, banks are faced with another leap forward that may be even more disruptive than the internet boom. From Web 2.0 to social networking to continuous wireless communicating.

Welcome to the dawn of the ever-ready bank. The 'ever-ready bank' is always-on, always-available, always-appropriate. . .simply ever-ready.

This is the first of two chapters reviewing the critical technologies retail banks need to consider over the next few years and their impact on current systems and structures. This chapter examines the technology trends which will most impact retailing bank services from a channel and customer perspective, especially RFID, NFC, Biometrics, Internet2, IPv6 and WiMax. The next chapter continues this examination but focuses more upon the retail bank's back office organization and infrastructure and examines Web 2.0 in depth from both a customer and bank perspective. I recommend you read these together as a single thesis, as the themes tend to overlap, but you are welcome to read as you see fit of course.

BACKGROUND

In the early 1990s, many people were still playing vinyl records and cassette tapes. The fax machine was the new technology for communication and the PC was just taking off with a few nerds. Microsoft had just released Windows 3.1 *(at that time Windows had release numbers)* and a laptop was something you found in dodgy clubs in the seedy parts of town. Then the record and cassette were replaced by the CD, and the PC boom was fuelled by the associated burst of Netscape and the internet. Suddenly, technology had moved from backwater to fashion. As a result, today, most of our technology drivers in banking come from consumer tastes rather than government and defence as it was 10 years ago even.

By the end of the 1990s, the technology boom was in full flow. AOL took over Time Warner, Amazon's Jeff Bezos and eBay's Meg Whitman were the hottest executives in town, and Google was just a fledgling. The internet was widely viewed as being representative of the next generation of businesses, connecting consumers globally and completely dismantling the traditional structures of commerce.

Retail banks began to close branches and invest everything in online, internet banking services. Security First Network Bank became hot property, as did any internet operation, and various internet-only banks were launched including the David Bowie Bank and the G&L (Gay & Lesbian) Bank. Banks that probably could not exist as physical entities but could launch online due to low-cost operations and national reach.

No sooner had an entrepreneur added dotcom to their firm's name, than they were valued with a market capitalisation in the billions. A good example was a joke that did the rounds at the time:

Two beggars are begging in San Francisco. The first one wrote 'beg' on his broken steel cup. After one day he had received ten bucks. The second one wrote 'beg.com' on his cup. After one day he had received hundreds of thousand of dollars and someone wanted to take him to NASDAQ.

The reason it became such a feeding frenzy was largely due to the ignorance of the investors piling into the market. Whilst most investors can understand and price oil, airlines and financial services firms reasonably, the internet represented the future and was an entirely new investment opportunity. Everyone was telling everyone to be in there or they would miss out. Equally, many of the firms were being led by young and unproven business people who had little knowledge or ability to develop and implement a strategy, let alone a business model.

However, investors didn't worry that these startups had no foreseeable profits in their forecasts because they saw Amazon and eBay, and focused on the massive potential for global markets and phenomenal revenue projections. Therefore, sane investors were blinded by greed and the need to cash in on the next big thing.

The result was a burst of Initial Public Offerings (IPOs) that defied business and economic logic. These IPOs, and all the internet hype associated with the boom, were in no small way supported by the Wall Street broker organisations who added to the buzz of the internet hype, and made millions themselves in the process.

The leading proponent of the hype was Frank Quattrone, the $200 million a year investment banker at Credit Suisse First Boston (CSFB) who took Amazon and Netscape through IPO's in the mid-1990s. The IPO's made billions for the firms and millions for the executives. Soon, Quattrone became the 'star' of Wall Street and all internet firms wanted his golden touch.

Then it all went wrong and the internet went bust. Money leaked out of the markets like rain. The reason is that something smelt wrong about the hype. Not every firm could be magically converted overnight into a money-making machine. Equally, the feeding frenzy ground to a halt when investors realised that not every dotcom firm was made of gold.

Suddenly, the huge swathe of venture capital disappeared and firms hailed as the new generation collapsed overnight. Webvan.com, Boo.com, Furniture.com, Kozmo.com, Pets.com...so many big names no more. A great example was eToys.com. eToys raised $166 million through an IPO in May 1999. By October 1999, eToys shares had risen to an $84 high, only to tank to just nine cents per share in February 2001. During this rollercoaster cycle eToys, like most dotcom boomers, spent millions on advertising, marketing and technology. For example, at its height, eToys had an $11 billion market capitalisation. Not bad for a firm that lost almost $2.50 for every $1.00 in sales. Similar firms existed across the net space with Boo.com spending $160 million before liquidation in May 2000, a third of which was on software and almost half on advertising, whilst Disney took a write-off of $790 million for their yahoo-styled website Go.com in January 2001. Similarly, eToys found that all that spending on advertising, marketing and technology outweighed the company's income, and investors bailed out, forcing it to fold in March 2001.

By that time, the penny had dropped with most investors with *Business Week Online* reporting that venture capital spending on the internet bubble peaked in the third quarter of 1999 at $4.8 billion. A year later, the spending had been halved to $2.4 billion.

Ever since, we have been looking for the next big thing. The next major technology surge. The next thing to make a quick buck out of.

The problem is that, from a technology viewpoint, it probably does not exist.

The reason after all, is that the whole internet boom and bust was more a reflection of investor's hopes and aspirations, rather than the reality of the internet revolution.

THE STORY OF ONLINE BANKING

The reality of the internet revolution can be seen in the story of online banking.

As already mentioned, there was a massive upsurge in startup .com banks online during this period, with new startups like the Golf Savings Bank for golf lovers, the Pet Lovers Bank for pet lovers, and the Gay & Lesbian bank for lovers of a different sort. The new banks were being launched at a rate of knots, and existing banks were struggling hard with how to understand and deploy online services.

As a result, most retail banks began to cutback on branch networks and refocus upon technology deployments. The assumption was that the branch was no longer required by customers for service, but that the customer would migrate naturally towards ATM, call centre and, specifically, online banking offers.

Figure 13.1 provides a good example of the mentality of this thinking from a European perspective. As can be seen, several countries such as the UK, Netherlands, Belgium and Germany were axing branches rapidly through the end of the 1990s. The release of funds from such closures provided enhanced technology budgets for online services.

This mentality has since reversed. By the mid-2000s, most retail banks had realised that people wanted a multi-channel service, and that the branch is a critical sales channel in that multi-channel mix. Rather than servicing within branches therefore, the focus is to sell within branches. 'Turn tellers into sellers' is a regularly heard mantra, and is the reason why many retail banks have moved away from branch closures. In fact, most are now heavily reinvesting back into the branch with renewal investments in systems and branding. A key driver in this space has been learning that the online bank provides an excellent means of

Number of Branches of Financial Institutions in the European Community

	1997	1998	1999	2000	2001
➡ **Belgium**	**7,358**	**7,129**	**6,975**	**6,610**	**6,168**
Denmark	2,283	2,291	2,294	2,365	2,376
➡ **Germany**	**63,186**	**59,929**	**58,546**	**56,936**	**53,931**
Greece	2,510	2,687	2,742	2,862	2,968
➡ **Spain**	38,039	39,039	39,376	39,311	39,024
➡ **France**	25,464	25,428	25,501	25,657	26,049
Ireland	1,180	1,076	1,083	1,007	#N/A
➡ **Italy**	25,265	26,283	27,154	28,189	29,266
Luxembourg	314	289	310	300	#N/A
➡ **Netherlands**	**6,800**	**6,787**	**6,258**	**5,983**	**5,230**
Austria	4,691	4,587	4,589	4,570	4,561
➡ **Portugal**	4,746	4,947	5,401	5,662	5,534
Finland	1,294	1,254	1,188	1,194	1,190
Sweden	2,823	2,197	2,140	#N/A	#N/A
➡ **United Kingdom**	**16,344**	**15,873**	**15,470**	**14,225**	**#N/A**

© Balatre Ltd, www.balatroltd.com

Figure 13.1   Number of Branches of Financial Institutions in the European Community
Source: EU, 2003

self-service, but it is not the way to leverage new business or provide advice. That still relies on a human touch. Figure 13.2 illustrates this well.

Figure 13.2 basically identifies that people may apply for simple products such as credit cards online, but the complex, relationship-based products such as pensions and mortgages need to be sold within branch. Why? According to most consumer surveys, because they prefer the friendly, fast and personalised service from helpful and knowledgeable employees. Something that is harder to convey through a machine. This is not to say that it will remain this way forever, as you will see, but that the transition from physical branch to online self-service and vice versa is going to be an evolution rather than the sudden revolution banks believed would occur.

Other industries have learnt similar lessons through the internet revolution with the view that the internet channel is now just a service enhancement and cost saving mechanism. For example, you cannot physically fly from London to New York on the internet, but you can make your booking, get your eticket and check in online with no human hand involved other than the customer's. That saves checkin staff and paper. Although the difference between online airline self-service and bank self-service is that you do still have to physically visit with the airline, whereas you do not with the bank. Bank services are purely based around bits and bytes, so there will be a transition over time towards potentially purely online services, as we shall see. But, for now, the point of the internet revolution today is that it is primarily for self-servicing to reduce internal service costs, whilst also being one of several channels that need to be focused upon for marketing and sales purposes.

In summary, the internet revolution was taking place all through the period from the early 1990s through to today. However, the boom and bust was a reflection of the valuations of the market capitalisation of firms involved in that revolution, which were being wildly distorted. Today, the internet is not bust but flourishing. Today, we see a maturing internet where people Blog, iPod, share and collaborate in myspace.com, and create virtual social networks and games. The internet today is still that vision of 10 years ago, but with more

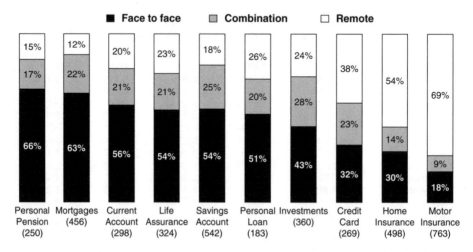

Figure 13.2 Complex Products Sell in the Branch
Source: Nationwide Building Society Survey of UK Consumers, 2002

finesse and opportunity than ever before. This is the internet referred to today as Web 2.0, which we will discuss in much more depth in the next chapter.

The focus of this chapter is to ask the question: where are we going next? Within this area, there are a range of technologies that will complement and enhance the internet of tomorrow. Of these technologies, a small number will be critical to tomorrow's retail bank, and should be the core focus of future investments. The technologies I have selected fall primarily into two major categories: Authentication and Connectivity. The rest of this chapter studies what these disruptive technologies mean to Retail Banking.

AUTHENTICATION TECHNOLOGIES

Authentication technologies relate to those technologies that provide authentication and authorisation of identity for access to financial services and for payments. For years, you may be surprised to know that such technology has been called cash and card. Cash has been a great, anonymous, payments instrument in the physical world, whilst debit and credit cards have been a convenient method of paying with a swipe and a signature or PIN.

Due to the internet revolution and technology innovations generally, these two areas are being dramatically changed.

Cash is being forced to change as a payment method because cash cannot be used on the internet. It is only accepted in a physical environment as a physical payments instrument. Debit and credit cards are also being challenged by the internet because they are not anonymous. Some of this is changing today due to the increasing use of prepaid cards. Prepaid cards, which in this context allow the user to pay cash for an anonymous card that can be used as an online payments system, are growing rapidly in usage. They are also a great innovation in the sense that this is the first time a card has been invented which can be truly anonymous. You do not have to provide a name, account number or even a signature with some of these cards, such as the Virgin 'Stash' card in the USA. For these reasons, prepaid cards should transact around \$3 trillion in 2010. However, prepaid cards are not necessarily a technology innovation, rather a banking product innovation. The two technologies which are really changing the way we think of cash and payments are actually NFC and RFID.

NFC, or Near-Field Communication, and RFID, or Radio Frequency Identification, are related technologies that focus upon a chip and terminal linkage. The system allows low-range radio signals to be sent from the chip to the receiver, and this in turn can then exchange information between the chip and the receiver. This could be anything from a marathon runner running over a measurement system that checks their time to an item of goods being purchased in Wal*Mart. The base chip technology allows for the small, cheap and flexible NFC or RFID chip to be scanned and recognised.

As a technology development area, NFC and RFID complement other technologies, such as Bluetooth and Wi-Fi, although each of these has subtle differences. For example, whilst Bluetooth is being used to connect computing and communication devices locally, such as printers and mobiles with PC's, without the use of cables; and Wi-Fi technology is again targeted towards computer connectivity; NFC and RFID are different. Specifically:

- **Near Field Communication (NFC)** is a technology chip standard for very short-range connectivity enabling consumers to initiate and perform contactless transactions and access digital content such as ringtones and downloads to mobile telephones;

- **RFID (Radio Frequency Identification)** is a chip-based identification method using tags which contain silicon chips to enable them to receive and respond to queries from an RFID reader/writer – many people consider RFID to be a replacement for barcode tags and magnetic strips because of this.

Hence, the NFC standard for contactless transactions combined with RFID chip has made these technologies particularly successful in the financial sector. This is because they can be easily integrated into a card or non-card payments device, are cheap to roll-out, increase bank volume and value of transactions, and appeal to consumer convenience.

Placing the RFID chip into a card or non-card is simple. For example, JPMorgan has incorporated RFID chips into millions of their Chase Blink cards in the USA. On the cost side, the price of these chips has been dropping continually, from around 50 cents per chip in 2003 to under 10 cents for the same chip capability in 2006. That is why the 3.2 million tickets for the World Cup in Germany 2006 each contained an RFID chip to minimise fraud and forgeries on the black market. Each ticket's small microchip contained access information, but no personal data. This was the first time that RFID tickets had been sold on such a large scale, although the experiment didn't come cheap. Each RFID chip cost 10 eurocents and with 3.2 million tickets the organisers had to cough up at least €320,000 – although that is a small price when it stopped the thugs, criminals and fraudsters exploiting the game and who might otherwise have ruined the football jamboree. Philips, the firm who provided the World Cup RFID chips, therefore expect that further to the success of this venture, RFID ticketing will be more widely accepted and the price may drop.

Consumer convenience is proven in that contactless cards allow you to 'tap and go'. No more 'swipe and sign' or 'Chip & PIN'. The fact that there is no identification or authentication involved, other than having the card in your possession, is the reason why the technologies are ideal in low-value payments environments, such as quick service restaurants, transport systems and news kiosks and vending machines. As a result, banks like JPMorgan and Royal Bank of Scotland have determined to use these technologies for extensive roll-outs across the USA and UK.

AUTHENTICATION TECHNOLOGIES: NFC, RFID AND ZIGBEE

Another technology which will prove interesting as an overlay to NFC and RFID is Zigbee. Zigbee, like NFC and RFID, allows chips to wirelessly recognise each other. The difference is that the Zigbee chips are incorporated into doors, windows and tarmac.

In context, Zigbee is the standard being developed for automated devices, such as light bulbs, to communicate with receivers such that as a person walks into a room the lights go on. Zigbee is just the technology standard for the production of chips that allows such intelligence to be built into a chip-based network. A generic example of how this might work in practice is that a car has NFC communications built-in. As it drives down the road, the Zigbee sensors recognise how central to the road the car is driving and how fast. If the car goes too fast or too near to the other side of the road, then Zigbee sensors alert the car's wireless receivers and they, in turn, trigger an alarm to the driver.

In the same way, Zigbee could be used in branches. As the customer enters the branch with a credit or debit card emitting NFC or RFID radio pulses, the Zigbee network would send a signal to the branch manager alerting who has entered the branch. Integrating such technology capability with CRM would then alert the branch management and staff as

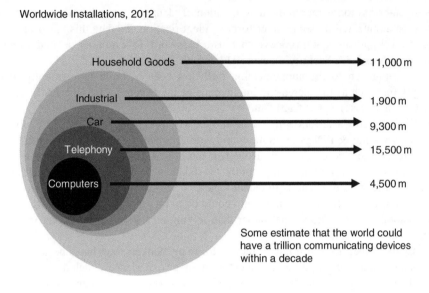

RFID & Zigbee network over 40 billion devices

Worldwide Installations, 2012

Household Goods	11,000 m
Industrial	1,900 m
Car	9,300 m
Telephony	15,500 m
Computers	4,500 m

Some estimate that the world could have a trillion communicating devices within a decade

© Balatro Ltd, www.balatroltd.com

Figure 13.3 Billions of devices communicating
Source: Sun Microsystems

to who the customer is and what they might want. So, for example, as I walk into my branch next time, having research mortgage deals the night before online, by the time I get to the service station the assistant may have already printed off a personalised brochure outlining all of the bank's mortgage offers and special rates for me.

These proximity technologies and related services are expected to become the key customer technologies of the next five years. After all, as Figure 13.3 illustrates, with over 40 billion devices emitting radio waves from chip-based intelligence, including cars, mobile phones and entertainment devices, the consumer will be connected to the network 24 × 7.

The question then is what technologies the bank deploys to connect to them? We will explore more in this area in the next chapter, which studies bank-enabling technologies.

AUTHENTICATION TECHNOLOGIES: THE QUESTION OF IDENTITY

Thus far, we have only reviewed chip-based technologies such as RFID and NFC for contactless cards and payments, and Zigbee for card recognition and customer proximity servicing. These technologies are fine as far as they go, but we have yet to find a way to authenticate the customer. All we have so far is a way to sense that a customer is there. The fact that the customer is holding a valid card then authenticates the payment. However, we have no intelligence of the customer's name or proof as to their identity. That is why the chip-based technologies discussed are only used for low-value purchases, such as cinema tickets, coffee and car parking. In order to use such technologies for higher value payments requires the authentication technology to have some form of integrated authorisation technology, such as the client's signature or a PIN number.

Where authorisation is required – a verification of identity – an authentication technology needs to be augmented by some other form of identification. To date this has been through a second level authentication process, such as a password, PIN number or random number generator such as RSA Security's SecureID keyfob.

Another approach to the authentication push has been to build more intelligent chip-based systems, such as the increasing intelligence being driven through the EMV (Europay, MasterCard and Visa) Smart Card Chip.

The EMV Smart Card, following on from the early trials with Mondex, has evolved into what is now a Chip & PIN programme worldwide. The chips can also offer more forms of stored value worldwide on the card. However, the downside of this programme is that the 'Smart' chips being used are being rapidly overtaken by other capabilities, such as those described in the form of cheap chip technologies.

However, the essence of the Smart Chip could be to incorporate the Identity Management of the customer on the chip so that rather than relying on a PIN number, other information is carried, such as, biometric data.

The use of biometrics is still fairly emotive for many bankers, but this is because the early experiments resulted in negative customer reactions or experiences, such as those of South African bankers whose biometric trial resulted in customers' fingers being amputated.

Today, many biometric experiments are being actively encouraged by governments to avoid terrorism, and fingerprint, palm and iris recognition technologies have been rapidly becoming more robust and reliable. Even so, the impact of false positives, where the real customer gets rejected due to a faulty fingerprint, makes many financial professionals nervous of these technologies. The other aspect is the nervousness of banks when it comes to the intrusion such technologies might provoke, when asking customers to present their eyeballs or hands in order to get money out of their accounts.

Therefore, the most likely biometric technologies to be used with these customer access authentication developments are biometric voiceprints and signatures. The biometric signature in particular provides a logical development for a variety of reasons:

- signatures have been used for the past 50 years as the identification method for credit cards, and are therefore the most natural method of authentication and authorisation;
- biometric signatures recognise the dynamics of each individual's signature pattern, in terms of pressure on the paper, which makes the biometric signature unique and virtually impossible to forge;
- as banks move towards digital pen and paper, digital pen technologies can easily incorporate biometric recognition; and
- a biometric signature is not something that a criminal can cut out, in the same way as a hand or eyeball.

In summary, from an authentication viewpoint, retail banks are likely to deploy many new technologies to allow customer enablement and access to financial services through chip-on-card based developments, in the forms of RFID and NFC, chip-in-branch technologies such as Zigbee, and identification technologies such as biometric signatures. The result will be much easier access to services which leads us to our second area of discussion: connectivity.

CONNECTIVITY TECHNOLOGIES

The internet revolution has led to a new generation of connection online, globally, 24 × 7. That is what is meant by the World WideWeb. However, the web is no longer just a PC-based phenomena. It is now a TV-based system, a mobile-network, a communication capability and a connectivity infrastructure. That infrastructure is changing phenomenally due to the rearchitecting of the web.

For example, in 2002 the predominant web access for most consumers was a 56 kilobits per second (kbps) modem. In 2003, it may have been a 500 kilobytes per second (500 Kbps) DSL system. Today, it is probably a 10 megabytes per second (10 Mbps) ADSL service. Tomorrow, it will be 100 or 1,000 megabytes per second.

Moore's law of computing power doubling every 18 months whilst halving in price is proving to be just as true on the internet, where the bandwidth of connectivity is more than doubling every 18 months whilst the price is halving.

This has led to a conundrum for many retail banks, where the speed of connectivity to branches was for many, until recently, limited to old leased lines with a maximum speed in many cases of no more than 56 kbps. For example, one bank gained the approval for a multimillion dollar branch renewal programme when the head of Retail Banking asked the board, 'Which of you use Broadband Internet at home?' When all the Executive team put up their hands, the response was, 'you all have ten times the speed of access at home from one PC than our branch tellers have across the whole branch to our head office systems'.

As a result of that presentation, the bank regenerated all of their branch network infrastructures from dedicated leased lines, to Internet Protocol (IP) networking. Interestingly, in so doing, their branches now have access to not only Broadband speed networking, but also all of their CCTV and telephones are using the same services, resulting in significant savings.

The point is that we have seen a proliferation of other forms of channels and communications between consumers and their banks. From the touch-tone telephone, we now have the mobile telephone. From letters in the post, we now use e-mail. TowerGroup estimate that, in total, all US banks will receive over one billion e-mails per annum by 2010.

But the nature of next generation internet is one where this changes fundamentally. For example, just look at the range of technologies involved here:

- **3G** is an International Telecommunications Union (ITU) term for the third generation of mobile communications technology.
- **4G** (or 4-G) is short for fourth-generation, the successor to 3G.
- **'Fibre to the building' (FTTB)** refers to installing optical fibre from the telephone company's office to a specific building, such as a business, or to the kerbs near homes or any business environment, as a replacement for the old telephone service.
- **IEEE** is the Institute of Electrical and Electronics Engineers, Inc., a non-profit, technical professional association.
- **IP** is Internet Protocol, the basis for using internet communications.
- **IPv6** is the operating systems for the next generation internet, and stands for Internet Protocol version 6, the successor to IPv4, which is the standard of the last decade; the main difference is that IPv6 uses a 128 bit IP-address compared to a 32-bit address in IPv4.

- **IP Multimedia Subsystem (IMS)** means an explosion of new, personalised real-time services across any network and any device, whether it's a PDA, PC, mobile phone or TV.
- **Internet2** or UCAID (University Corporation for Advanced Internet Development) is a non-profit consortium which has been developing and testing the next generation internet.
- **Voice over IP (VoIP)** refers to internet-based telephony, a set of facilities for managing the delivery of voice information using the Internet Protocol (IP).
- **WiFi** is Wireless Fidelity, a term used generically when referring to Wireless LAN standards created by IEEE 802.11, the set of standards for wireless networks.
- **WiMAX** is the next generation of IEEE standards, or IEEE 802.16, which defines high speed wireless networking across cities rather than in 'hot spots'.

Although not exhaustive, this is the list of the major technology changes that will be integrated and deployed as whole over the next five years to change the way we link and connect and communicate over the internet using fixed and mobile devices.

For example, Internet2 with IPv6 will allow gigabytes of data to be accessed instantaneously. This is to facilitate movies-on-demand, integrated entertainment platforms and high-definition TV (HDTV) over IP. That is why a movie delivered as a 1,000 Gigabyte file (90 minute, DVD quality film) would take around 12 to 24 hours to download using the best ADSL broadband speeds of 2006. Using Internet2 with IPv6, the same file would download in less than thirty seconds. That is speed. That is Moore's Law in action. And that is delivered to the consumer by the end of this decade.

Therefore, today, we talk around VoIP – Voice over Internet Protocol – which is, in essence, the idea of using Skype. VoIP is all about cheap or free telecommunications. However, using the next generation internet, VoIP becomes Video over Internet Protocol. HDTV style video communications. This will be video between people at home with their loved ones overseas, or even at home with their banker around the corner. For example, many software firms today are demonstrating a vision of the near term where you can telephone your local restaurant through your PC or mobile handset and book a table whilst talking to the *maitre d'* in real time using high definition video connections.

This connection will not only be over an internet or computing platform however, as these technologies converge with mobile communications. That is one of the big themes today. Convergence. Therefore, WiFi, WiMAX and 3G and 4G telecommunications all come together with next generation internet enabling HDTV Video communication anytime, anywhere. In all instances, this will be ubiquitous, cheap, video connectivity of a very high quality.

This connectivity can already be delivered today, but is viewed as being too poor in quality. Just think of your own web camera connections. However, as bandwidth increases, so such connectivity will gain in quality, such that the full multimedia service will soon allow you to see your banker and talk with them at the same time, with television levels of quality guaranteed.

VIDEO OVER INTERNET PROTOCOL: CRITICAL FOR RETAIL BANKING

High-quality person-to-person video is critical to retail banking because it brings back face-to-face communications. It gives bankers back what was lost when the first technology revolution occurred in the 1970s. Since that time, consumers have been educated to leave the branch and move onto using ATMs, the telephone and, for the last 10 years, the keyboard. Self-service has been the focus, alongside cost cutting, and the consumer has lost a face-to-face connection with their bank. The face-to-face connection has been a critical connection, as demonstrated by Figure 13.2. Therefore, the loss of that face-to-face relationship is a key reason as to why banks lost the 'relationship' focus.

In this new world of video over internet, the remote user can connect face-to-face once more. It may be that they have a branch manager who they know and are familiar with. Now, they can discuss their financial matters with that branch manager remotely via their home internet-enabled high-definition TV or PC, or via their next generation HD-mobile. All of their connections, 24×7, will be supported by an ability to talk with someone, to see them, to touch the screen and to be animated. This brings us back to what the essence of 'services' is all about, as in human contact. And half of the phrase 'financial services' should involve just that.

Financial *services* is not about products you manufacture but about dialogues, relationships and human interaction. That is why 'Financial Services' cannot be marketed like computers or spaghetti. You have to focus upon the human elements to differentiate.

This is why the video over internet revolution will be critical for retail banks because it will mean we will have to rethink the call centre. The call centre – whether onshore or offshore – will be the key channel to use remotely. As a result, retail banks will aim to differentiate through a focus upon hiring culturally and visually acceptable staff, which immediately creates a debate around diversity and globalisation. This issue may be overcome through the solution to the other challenge of video retail bank services, which is staff numbers.

If you provide video connectivity, it may imply a massive increase in staff numbers, unless you automate the front-end. This can be achieved and is already being tested by some organisations using video robots, or 'avatars'. Avatars are cartoon-based or realistic automated agents who, like the touchtone menu systems of the traditional call centre, can handle 80% of the calls. The standard balance and transaction requests can all be dealt with by automated videobots whilst the remainder of calls which are service oriented around complex products, such as mortgages, will be transferred to a human agent. These areas are explored in depth in Chapters 10 and 11.

The outcome is that the video-servicing world will mean a very different service culture and structure. It will mean that a retail bank's core systems and back office administrative services will become transparent and totally visible to the customer. It will mean that retail banks will have to carefully rethink the way calls are routed and, more importantly, the impression given once the call is routed. If the bank is not culturally and visually acceptable to the customer, or if the call centre operators are struggling with multi-screen legacy systems, it will be highly visible to both the customer and the competition. Therefore, retail banks will carefully consider how to deliver single screen, simple systems augmented to videobot avatars, to support the new world of visual communications.

THE DECLINE OF THE KEYBOARD

The other critical factor in the next generation of connectivity is that the keyboard will become more and more redundant as point and talk systems take over, driven by haptic technologies and reliable voice recognition.

Haptic technologies use sensors to allow users to manipulate data using touch and feel interaction and are typically based upon glove systems. A little like the way Tom Cruise moves information around in the film *Minority Report* using a pair of light emitting sensor gloves, these interfaces are in early experimentation today, but will gradually become more predominant. Combining such interface with voice commands and voice recognition will mean a gradual movement away from typing towards talking and pointing.

This sounds a little extreme, but if you think of the keyboard in context, it is not a natural interface at all. Just one we have learned to adapt to use.

For example, we all type today because we have to. You cannot live in today's digital world without being able to press the QWERTY keyboard. As long ago as 1990 however, most financial institutions had typing pools and most managers had secretaries. The typists and secretaries were there to press the QWERTY keyboard, not the professionals. Even in 1995, most bank CEO's would be PC non-literate and would delegate such activities to their assistants.

Ten years later, the world is a different place. Most bank CEO's could not survive without their Blackberry. Bank professionals at all levels rely on their laptops and PCs, and all of these are driven by keyboards. Anyone who wants to communicate these days via instant messages, email or texts has to be keyboard-literate.

However, this may be just a temporary phase.

Since the inception of the computer era, the technology vision has been to create a virtual world that is as easy to live in as our physical world. In the 1930s, telephone firms were already experimenting with video telephony. Today, the world of video telephony has arrived.

Equally, since the creation of typewriters, telex and fax, firms have tried to evolve to simple touch and point voice activated systems. Using simple point and touch systems today are mouse-based, but there are already experiments with haptic technologies, where the user wears gloves to interact with the system. Combining such systems with reliable voice commands will gradually erode the need for using keyboards and therefore, over the longer term, users will eventually dump the keyboard.

A little like the CEOs of 15 years ago who never thought they would be using a PC, the CEOs of today will be amazed to think that 15 years from now they will not be using a keyboard.

This is already being seen in early form as a trend as the mouse evolves to digital pen and paper. As digital pen and paper becomes more predominant, combined with behavioural biometrics as mentioned earlier, this form of writing and pointing, combined with voice activation, will start to override the keyboard as an interface.

Screens you can write upon, point at, touch buttons and talk to, will become predominant, rather than screens you stare at and key into. The result will be an overhaul of bank communication channels. As the customers evolve towards video connections and digital pens, the bank will find they receive less e-mails. Eventually, e-mails may even disappear.

This sounds like heresy today, but children are already shunning e-mails for text messaging on their cellphones. A survey of USA teenagers in 2005 found that their e-mail usage declined by 8% whilst their text and instant messaging increased. As one young 16-year-old stated: 'If I want to talk with my friends I text them. E-mail is for work and school.'

In summary, from a connectivity viewpoint, retail banks will find the continuing doubling of bandwidth and halving of cost will deliver the truly virtual online experience. Driven by new standards and infrastructures, such as WiMAx, IPv6, Internet2 and 4G, real-time, non-stop video communications and point and talk applications will be common.

The result will be a major challenge to deliver high quality services through online channels, which meet customers' expectations.

SUMMARY

The pace of technological change is ever increasing and did not end when the stock prices of the internet boom burst. It just took a slight pause. Retail banks have used this pause to return to the renewal of branch services. As a result, branches are thriving and are complemented well by other channels such as their internet self-service facilities for billing and payments, call centres for remote services and ATM for fast withdrawals and deposits.

However, this period of relatively stability is about to change because the internet itself never boomed or busted, it just kept evolving and developing on a path towards ever-connected consumers. We will explore these developments in the next chapter. This chapter has demonstrated however that, at the front-end channel level for authentication and connection, banks will be challenged by a revolution in products, services and delivery. This challenge ranges from chip-based technologies allowing customers to gain authentication more easily, to biometrics to provide improved security and identification and through to high speed networking to facilitate face-to-face video connectivity. The result will be the always-on bank and only the ever-ready bank will survive. The 'ever-ready' bank operates 24×7, intimately understands their customers, delivers proactive proximity services and is brilliant in the back office services to their customers offered through both branch-based and video-based banking.

Some banks will find this a relatively simple change, as they have trialled and tested such concepts regularly and keep pace with the speed of change; others will find themselves subsumed by the speed at which customers adapt and adopt these new technologies and will fail to be flexible or agile enough to keep pace.

KEY DEVELOPMENTS IN FRONT-OFFICE BANKING

- The internet boom of the 1990s and bust of 2000 did no more than represent the hopes and aspirations of investors.
- The internet itself has never boomed or busted, but has kept evolving and developing on a path towards ever-connected consumers.
- Authentication and connectivity technologies will deliver the next generation of the ever-connected consumer and the always-on bank.
- Authentication and connectivity technologies include RFID, NFC, Biometrics, Internet2, Ipv6, WiMax, 3G, 4G and many more.
- The result of these waves of new technology standards will be the always-on bank and only the ever-ready bank will survive.

14

Web 2.0 and Online Banking Technologies Through 2015

In the last chapter, we reviewed some of the base technologies, such as RFID, NFC, Biometrics, Internet2, IPv6, and WiMax. This was in the context of how these technologies may impact the front office retail experience for the customer, from payments to online. This chapter reviews the impact from both the customer's perspective and from the other side – the bank operations – by focusing upon how a retail bank must use Web 2.0 to structure their operations to keep up with today's internet and exploit customer delivery through these new channels and services in the future.

THE ARRIVAL OF THE 'ALWAYS-ON SOCIETY'

As we all witnessed the internet boom of the 1990s and bust of the 2000s, what we actually saw was an explosion of technological change. The boom and bust was based upon the wave and hype of investment without thought for the returns on investment. Underlying all of this investment was still the fundamentals of change.

The creation of a technological revolution.

The arrival of the 'always-on society'.

Now that the internet investment cycle has busted, the always-on society is still here. The always-on society wants instant access to services, instant gratification for their needs, total online experiences, anywhere, anytime, $24 \times 7 \times 365$.

We used to talk about the 'Martini Bank' – anytime, anywhere, anyplace. Today, Martini servicing is the only way you can work with the always-on society.

Amazon, eBay, Skype, iTunes, and a few others are burning strong as the leaders in this new wave society. However, there are some other attributes to this new world that are causing organisations to sit up and wake up to the fact that we are entering another fundamental wave of change.

A vast range of technologies are disrupting the way in which banks connect to their customers and the way that their customers are identified and authenticated. This is not an overnight phenomena, but has been a slowly building change process, based upon simple technologies that are now working effectively to redefine online access and experience.

At the front-end, a range of authentication technologies such as RFID, NFC and Biometrics, alongside a range of connectivity technologies, such as Internet2, IPv6 and Wireless, are combining to revolutionise retail services.

Combined, these technologies will deliver the next generation of the internet and this was reviewed in depth in Chapter 13.

This version of the internet will be device-agnostic, with consumers connecting from home entertainment devices, workstations, mobile and wireless devices. It will be an internet enriched by unlimited bandwidth, storage and speed, so that high definition video connectivity will be simple and easy. It will be an internet that will provide the always-on consumer with access to services $24 \times 7 \times 365$. An internet where customers will expect to access the always-available organisation, and only the ever-ready bank will survive. It will be an internet based on online servicing experiences, not access availability.

What survival tools are required for the ever-ready bank?

PRINCIPLES OF THE 'ALWAYS-ON SOCIETY'

We are entering a transition period in the online world today, where banks are challenged by a range of new words, concepts and ideas. Rich media, interactive marketing, personalisation were the buzz words that were popular in 2000. Search engine optimisation, viral marketing, podcasting, RSS and blogging were the words of 2005. Today, mash-ups, Web 2.0, vidcasting and blogvertising are the major focus for marketing in the online world.

Various other maxims are appearing, such as Chris Anderson's *Long Tail*. Chris is the editor of Wired magazine, and he describes the internet as a world of inordinate niches rather than homogenous masses. The Long Tail therefore focuses upon how you reach all of those niches, rather than just the core. The best illustration he gives of this is the way in which Amazon, iTunes and similar services find that between 20% and 40% of sales are from books and songs that fall outside the top 100. Even the 100,000th or 500,000th or millionth book on Amazon or tune on iTunes gets purchased and makes money. The reason such books and songs get purchased and make money is because there is no cost to retail them. These books and songs are purely data files that can be stored cheaply online through unlimited bytes of speed and storage until a customer accesses them. Compare this to Borders Books or Tower Records, who cannot stock such items because they take up expensive real estate.

The message of the Long Tail is that success in the online world is through appealing to the millions of niche communities in the online world by having breadth and depth. In other words, the complete catalogue. This is the opposite of the physical world of retailing, where you only appeal to mass markets by stocking today's popular hits due to limited shelf space.

Running through all of these lessons, messages and changes is one mantra: if you stand still, you get run over.

IF YOU STAND STILL, YOU GET RUN OVER

New words, new ways and new ideas for reaching and marketing to the consumer are appearing every single day. In fact, just to put it into context, we live in a world today where technology is converging fast, and all of those technologies are internet-enabled. PCs, TVs, Nintendos, Sonys, iPods and cellphones, are all becoming one. We no longer think of our PC as a workstation, our Sony as a playstation, or our television as a videostation. They have all become one – a digital station.

The speed at which such change has occurred has been like lightning, even though the seeds for such change have taken 20 years. And the only way to manage such speed of change is to get wired or, should I say, wireless, through the new world of Web 2.0.

Let's look at what Web 2.0 means, as this is the label that really expresses the way to understand today's digital world.

WEB 2.0

Web 2.0 is a term originally coined by Tim O'Reilly, CEO of O'Reilly Media, and is based upon the fact that the internet has evolved into a pervasive technology that is now ubiquitous.

During that metamorphosis, certain companies, such as Amazon and eBay, had specific attributes they shared in common in becoming online powerhouses. Web 2.0 therefore laid to rest the first generation internet and started talking about the new generation as Web 2.0. A little like Internet2 is the technology of the next generation internet, Web 2.0 focuses upon the commerce – the business – of the next generation internet. It focuses upon what businesses should do to win online.

Here's a few of the differences perceived to exist between the old web and the new.

Application versus Platform

The old web was based upon strong Microsoft domination. The combination and predominance of the Microsoft Operating Systems and Microsoft Windows meant that Microsoft were the only platform to base your solutions. Hence, if Microsoft offered a competitive solution, they normally won.

However, Web 2.0 is not about a battle between applications on the Microsoft Platform, but a battle *between* platforms. There is no owner of the internet architecture, infrastructure, standards or agreements. They all just work as one through open connectivity, open standards and open access.

Therefore, it's a battle between who wins on the servers, rather than who wins on the client workstation.

Browsers versus Services

The old web was similarly based upon who delivered the web browser, similar to the way in which Netscape sold their product based upon APIs and licenses. The focus was still on desktop applications.

Web 2.0 does not work that way, in that it offers web-based services rather than web-based products you need to download. Google is a native web application. It does not need to be downloaded, sold or packaged. It does not need continuous upgrades, software releases and enhancements. It just sits there, getting bigger and better, every hour of every day.

That is the nature of web-based services.

Computers versus Devices

Most traditional web thinking worked on the basis that a website would be viewed using a web browser. Therefore, the sites were designed for single channel access via a computer. However, devices are now converging. An iPod is a TV, radio and walkman. A cellphone is an iPod, telephone and camera. A laptop is a cellphone, wireless access device, entertainment system and filing cabinet. A TV is a laptop with high definition. You cannot differentiate between devices today as nearly everything has 'intel inside' or a chip of some sort, as in 'intelligence inside'. The result is that web services cannot be built for web browsers, but must be built for access by any device: a playstation, a workstation, a desktop, a laptop, a cellphone, an iPod.

Language versus Interface

Old web firms talk about Java, XML and similar development tools as their core focus. These are valid, but redesigning core systems using J2EE and XML is only half the story.

Google, for example, is developed as rich user experience web service based around a collation of many technologies that, collectively, are known as Ajax. Ajax is the potential of the web to deliver full scale applications which hit the headlines when Google introduced Gmail, Google Maps, and other services

These web services are web-based applications with extremely rich user interactivity and interface, and the underlying technologies Google used to deliver such richness was christened Ajax by the web design firm Adaptive Path. The real difference therefore is that although XML is the language of the internet, Ajax is the interface.

Ajax incorporates the following web-based standards:

- XHTML and CSS for presentation;
- the Document Object Model for dynamic display and interaction;
- XML and XSLT for data interchange and manipulation;
- XMLHttpRequest for asynchronous data retrieval; and
- JavaScript as the glue to integrated all of these online.

It is not an area we need to delve into in-depth here, unless we want to get really technical, but this conglomeration of technologies is a far cry from base discussions of how XML integrates things together. The bottom-line is that today's online bank services must be managed by those who really know their web from their glue.

Data versus Data Management

Another feature is that Web 2.0 companies succeed because they are the best at organising data for usage. Turning data into information, in other words. The internet firms that succeed are the ones who invest in the best data collation, aggregation and management. There is one feature that they then add that makes them even better. They enrich their data and enhance it. The best example is the way in which Amazon take the raw data – the book title, author and ISBN (International Standard Book Numbering) reference – and then enhance it through user reviews, cross-references, preference links and related data enrichment. As a result, the Amazon ASIN (Amazon Standard Identification Number) is now being used more commonly than the traditional ISBN.

Users versus Participants

Old web firms always took the view that they were creating websites for users. They built things and people used them. They built software and people would pay for it, license it and use it. They built databases and people use them. Yahoo! paid their staff to get their original database and information service up and running, but today's powerhouse Web 2.0 services are built by the users. Wikipedia, BitTorrent, Amazon and eBay are all strong user endorsed and owned businesses because the users are included in the business. The business would not exist without user participation.

Take Wikipedia. Wikipedia provides the infrastructure, the model and data structure, and then Wikipedia's users build the data and enrich it. Take MySpace, Flickr, YouTube or any other emerging web services that are causing a disruption. They all involve user participation. Participation is critical in the Web 2.0 world.

Mass Marketing versus Collaborative Commerce

Web 2.0 focuses upon participation, but it goes further than this. The organisations succeeding in today's world use the collective power of their users to improve, enhance, enrich and gain traction. This is because they focus upon enabling their users to express themselves. As individuals provide their views and input, it builds into a collective view. This collective aggregation of self-expression can be seen in many areas of today's internet world:

- Yahoo! – the collective's portal;
- Google – the collective's index, based on popularity;
- eBay – the collective's trading system;
- Amazon – the collective's views on entertainment;
- Wikipedia – the collective's encyclopedia;
- Linux, Apache, MySQL, Perl, PHP, Python – the collective's programming languages;
- RSS and permalinks – the collective's voice for blogging.

The bottom-line is that today's web enables people to engage, express and dialogue. To succeed in such a collaborative and engaged peer-to-peer, person-to-person environment means avoiding the old tenants of 'mass marketing' 'high volume' products and focusing upon supporting users to deliver 'collaborative commerce' through 'social networking'.

Figure 14.1 summarises the lessons of moving from Web 1.0 to Web 2.0.

WHAT DOES THIS MEAN FOR RETAIL BANKS?

What this means for retail banks is that they need to shift from centralised marketing and client strategies, to distributed and heuristic client strategies, and build their Web 2.0 services very differently to their old web services, which constrain themselves to traditional bank services online.

Old web services started in the late 1990s, when most banks were still using websites that announced they existed. 'Hello, look here, we've got a website.com' was the typical style of a bank website, with general information about the bank and its services, but very little interaction. The website, in other words, was a pure marketing brochure.

By 2006, most banks had achieved the transition of their online brochure into the launch of full online bank services. These new enhanced bank websites offer online interaction and

Web 1.0 to Web 2.0

Web 1.0	Web 2.0
– Application-based	– Platform-based
– Browser-based	– Services-based
– Computers	– Devices
– Languages	– Interfaces
– Data	– Data Management
– Mass Marketing	– Collaborative Commerce
– Networks	– Social Networks

© Balatro Ltd, www.balatroltd.com

Figure 14.1   Web 1.0 to Web 2.0

focus upon the automation of traditional services into the online world, such as, statement and balance checking, online billing and payments, ordering services and changing address, etc.

However, many bank websites have still been built using old web thinking. This is why:

- online statements are a dull replica of the old printed statements;
- online billing, if offered at all, involves the user navigating a nightmare of numbers and confirmation checks;
- most websites are only accessible using a PC or laptop; and
- many services still require some form of physical identification, which usually means the transactions cannot be completed online.

The new bank web service sites need to be built using Web 2.0 thinking. This means building bank websites that:

- manage all of the security within your domain, rather relying on the customer's firewalls, antivirus and spyware, which is inevitably flawed;
- appeal to access $24 \times 7 \times 365$ using any device anywhere, not just the PC user;
- get your customers engaged by getting them to participate in your web services; and
- appeal to all of the web, the niches, the specific, the long tail, not just your traditional markets.

This may sound difficult, but the best examples have been and gone in early web experimentations and are starting to reappear in new forms.

For example, the David Bowie Bank and Gay & Lesbian Bank appealed to the niches and appeared and disappeared in the early 2000s. They disappeared primarily because of flawed design, but these banks could not have existed before the internet, in a branch-based world. Such niche banks will reappear and some did survive, like the Golf Savings Bank of Washington, which is themed for golfers.

Equally, new online exchanges, such as Zopa and Prosper, offer online person-to-person loans systems. Such systems appeal to the long tail. After all, how many bank websites have the line, 'Say goodbye to your bank manager and come join basil365, milkmongoose and CowgirlJo, on their home page?

Bearing in mind the niches, the long tail, this is the sort of approach that is likely to work. That is why Zopa secured a further $5m financing from Silicon Valley venture capitalist Tim Draper and the UK's Rowland Family in July 2006. This is on top of the $26 million previously raised from Bessemer Venture Partners, Benchmark Capital and Wellington Partners. It is worth noting that Tim Draper knows a little about the internet as he was heavily involved in other internet start-ups, funding firms such as Skype, Overture.com and Hotmail.

Web 2.0 is all about catching up and keeping up with today's internet world. However, to really get to grips with the always-on society, banks need to understand tomorrow's world, as discussed in depth in the previous chapter.

The main conclusion of that discussion is that the base infrastructures of Internet2, combined with the redesign of the web architecture through Internet Protocol version 6 (IPv6), will provide unlimited bandwidth and, in so doing, will inspire a new way of connecting to service organisations through video communications with 'point and talk' applications.

This will be an always-on society that will now be able to see and hear their always-available service providers. That is why the only successful providers will be those who are ever-ready.

That concludes the critical things we need to consider to deliver in today's internet world for the always-on society. Let's look now at delivering banking services in tomorrow's world.

BUILDING THE 'EVER-READY BANK'

For a bank, the underlying technologies which create verbal *and* visual connections to the bank systems and services will be a challenge.

In this new world of video over internet, the customer will be connecting face-to-face once more to discuss financial matters. Now, they will be doing so remotely via their home internet-enabled High-Definition (HD) TV or PC, or via their next generation HD-mobile. All of their connections will be supported by an ability to see someone, to point and talk, to touch the screen, to be animated, $24 \times 7 \times 365$.

From the bank's back office viewpoint, this raises many questions:

- how do you route the call to the most appropriate individual?
- does that individual have the knowledge, customer service skills and visual manners to be appropriate to the call?
- how do you deal with the angry customer who you can now see gesticulating?
- should the bank provide visual connectivity $24 \times 7 \times 365$?
- what is the impact upon offshore outsourcing and scripting?
- how do you protect the privacy of employees from having their images used to create a fake passport or drivers licence?

What this means for a retail banker is thinking very differently about delivering services virtually. Bearing in mind that the customer now has remote authentication tools, easy visual connectivity, point and talk interfaces, $24 \times 7 \times 365$, it means thinking very carefully through the process and structure of how you deliver services through digital media.

It means building the 'ever-ready bank' for the 'always-on society'.

Figure 14.2 illustrates the architecture for the ever-ready bank.

This architecture is structured around three main platforms:

(a) The Connectivity and Authentication Hub;
(b) The Information Routing Hub; and
(c) The Applications Hub.

The Connectivity and Authentication Hub

The Connectivity and Authentication Hub is based around a single connectivity platform to access the bank's services online and offline for both staff and customers.

All connections to the bank will be through this single connectivity platform: customers using home and mobile devices such as TVs and cellphones, and internal connections from branch and call centre. It's called the internet, and just as VoIP in the mid-2000s is providing the critical backbone for bank's internal networking, over the next five years the internet backbone will deliver all connections.

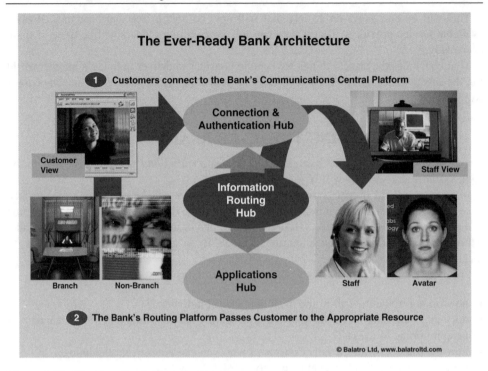

Figure 14.2 The Ever-Ready Bank Architecture
Source: Balatro Ltd, images courtesy of ABN AMRO and AT&T

This is what makes the Connectivity and Authentication Hub non-device specific, because all devices use the same underlying standards. As a result, the Connectivity and Authentication Hub serves two primary purposes:

(a) recognising the device being used to access and how to present information to that device; and
(b) authenticating the customer accessing the bank's services, and ensuring their identity is valid.

The first area, device recognition, is based around the protocols of access where the base technology is still the internet – Internet2 and IPv6 – but the devices are all High Definition video connections to TV's, telephones as well as laptops and other digital devices.

The second area, authentication, will be based upon whichever authentication and authorisation systems are used by the bank, which will be biometric, information and/or chip based.

Equally, the Connectivity and Authentication Hub will recognise customer locations through the signals emitting from the chips embedded in their bank card or other chip-based devices. As a result, the always-on consumer will accept proactive services from the ever-ready bank, and the bank's hub may often contact the customer with automatic alerts, proactive offers and servicing calls to explain complex financial matters or loan issues, based upon the bank's records and the customers location. The example that amuses me the most is the one of the customer leaving the casino and being offered an instant loan so they can go back in again. This is the intelligence we are talking about here. Therefore, proximity marketing of mortgages to customers entering an estate agent or car loans to customers going into a car dealership are not just likely, but inevitable.

Once authenticated, the Connectivity and Authentication Hub will hand-over to the Information Routing Hub.

The Information Routing Hub

This hub will take the authentication data and device information and, based upon the customer's latest profile of interactions with the bank – whether they be through proximity services or otherwise – will route the customer to the appropriate agent: whether that be an automated agent (an 'avatar' or 'videobot') or human agent.

The agent will see the customer and they will both share a single screen of data. That single screen of data is serviced through all of the applications within the bank across all of the bank's systems, via the Applications Hub. The Information Routing Hub also gathers all of the information relating to the customer's connections, transations, activities and interactions, and integrates this information onto the agent's screen as part of the routing. All of this information is private to the agent's screen and is designed to assist in cross-selling, marketing and servicing the client's needs during that moment of connection. Everything is designed to assist the agent in their service and dialogue with the customer.

The same process is being used in the previous example of proactive, proximity-based marketing services. In this instance, the Applications, Connectivity and Marketing services all come together to deliver an automated or human proactive exchange with the customer, based upon their proximity to relevant services or requirements. For example, if the customer has given permissions for marketing of loans, the bank may proactively call the customer as they leave a casino to offer them a loan.

The Applications Hub

The Applications Hub will access objects throughout the bank and hence can pull in information from any data sources: deposit account, credit or debit cards, loans, mortgages, investments. You name it.

At the device level, both the agent and the customer will see the same screen of information, except for those areas partitioned for purely agent usage, such as credit scores, marketing programmes and other internal bank information. The screen will be voice-activated and touch sensitive so that both the customer and the agent will be able to point and talk to the screen with the whole conversation, including the screen discussions, recorded and stored as part of the customer records for future reference and audit purposes.

Although applications may reside on different servers, with data and database management held in different applications and programs, all of the information on-screen will be seamlessly integrated and accessed as though delivered through one application service. The information will show enhanced pictorial imagery, moving images, graphical interfaces, touch and voice response areas, as though dealing with a television programme rather than a computer interface.

As a result, the bank's applications and information will be as easy to understand and use as a television remote control.

The Hub Foundations

The ability for a bank to deliver the hubs described above does not require a major systems redesign, as many banks are building exactly this structure today through Service Oriented Architecture (SOA). SOA allows existing software applications within the bank to be redeveloped piece by piece into objects and components. These objects and components can then be reused wherever required as they are completely reusable without any further developments. This is due to today's standards using open systems. However, the interfaces and front-end systems related to these components will be heavily impacted by all of these changes.

Today's end-points – ATMs, POS, Terminals, Screens – are all going to be radically overhauled over the next 10 years as we move to touch and talk rather than text and type. It is for these reasons that banks will find that they are challenged as they will be required to achieve a number of major changes in organisation and interface, rather than back office applications and technology.

The back office technologies, based upon consolidated server farms providing application objects and applets through SOA to front-end interfaces, are already being developed. The front-office technologies of RFID, NFC, proximity marketing, biometrics, touch and talk screens and interfaces are yet to be engineered and deployed.

This will be the challenge from a *technology* viewpoint, in terms of how a retail bank appears at the front-end, not the back-end. However, the real challenge at the 'back-end' is the organisation.

As a retail bank becomes more transparent, and as accessible online as they are in the branch, the bank will need new skills, services and products. The bank will need to consider location of contact centre agents versus branch agents versus automated agents. Potentially, all human agents will be specialists with the co-location of specialists in onshore centres. Then the question will be what to do with the offshore centres that, by and large, may be replaced by automated avatars and videobots.

SUMMARY

Today's world of $24 \times 7 \times 365$ connectivity means that we find ourselves living in an always-on society. The always-on society expects organisations to be ever-ready. They expect service anytime, anywhere, anyplace. They do not expect to wait.

As a result, retail banks are evolving into always-on, ever-ready online services. These services incorporate and evolve towards what is now known as Web 2.0. Web 2.0 focuses upon web-services being delivered to any device, rather than applications being built for PC access. Equally, Web 2.0 focuses upon using collaborative commerce techniques, such as participation, to enable users to define and build the products and services that suit them, rather than the bank defining how users use their service.

The real challenge lies with the fact that, just as retail bankers catch up with the wave of change of Web 2.0, new front-end technologies – RFID, NFC, Biometrics – combined with new high-speed services through Internet2 and IPv6 are creating another sea change. This one is focused upon connecting to tomorrow's bank through high-definition video.

High-definition bank services evolve access to another lever, where you are visually and verbally connected. Such visual connections, where you feel as though you are almost in the same room together, mandates communicating online as easily as we do offline, through all devices. This change to the front-end will radically challenge today's retail bank back office operations.

For a retail bank that is already building tomorrow's back office technologies, using Web 2.0 and SOA through consolidated servers representing connection, authentication, application, and routing hubs, they will be ready technologically. The challenge then will be to create the organisation to be ready culturally, to be ready in terms of products and services...in other words, to be 'ever-ready'.

KEY DEVELOPMENTS IN BACK-OFFICE BANKING

- We live in an always-on society, connected 24×7, who expect service providers to be ever-ready.
- Retail banks must rearchitect their current internet services to exploit the lessons of Web 2.0.
- Web 2.0 requires new thinking, where retail banks define a role in collaborative commerce and social networking before others build alternative ways of banking in these new forms.
- Retail banks will succeed in this process because they are already building Web 2.0 architectures using SOA and server farms based around connectivity, routing and applications hubs.
- The challenge for retail banks who do succeed will be in creating the ever-ready organisational structures to provide effective online services through these hubs to new interfaces based upon voice, video and touch channels.

Part 3
Payments Challenges

I had a realisation sometime in the mid-2000s, that payments is the area that is experiencing the most change in banking overall, from retail through wholesale. On the retail side, we see a range of issues:

- new kids on the block, especially PayPal, threaten traditional bank payments providers;
- iTunes and ringtones are increasing the volume of micropayments and the use of mobile telephones for making payments;
- MasterCard and Visa are now commercial payments operators rather than co-operative bank-owned infrastructures, further to IPO's in the mid-2000s; whilst
- new technologies, especially chip and biometrics, are changing the landscape of payments away from cash and cards and towards touch and pay.

There are many more such changes in retail, but these are the headline news items.
Meanwhile, on the wholesale side:

- increasingly faster, real-time payments are being demanded by governments, citizens and corporations;
- corporations are demanding more access and control over payments and are creating their own groups to enable this;
- corporations and governments are demanding more standardisation of payments, especially standards that cover the end-to-end flow of the supply chain through electronic invoicing and billing automation;
- SWIFT, the bank-owned wholesale payments network, strives to grow the franchise they operate for global payments infrastructures through expansion into new economies, products and services, and by enabling corporations to achieve their aims of supply chain control; whilst
- big changes are occurring due to regulatory reform, such as the Payment Services Directive in Europe, and the banks' response which is the Single Euro Payments Area (SEPA).

These are the most critical areas of change reviewed in this section.

Some of these changes, such as the evolution of retail payments through chip technologies, have been alluded to in the last section, especially Chapter 13 which focuses upon the technologies underlying these payment systems. However, this is delved into in-depth in Chapter 15 in what is considered to be one of the most impactful presentations and areas I discuss: the cashless, cardless society.

Most of the bankers I deal with are keen to create a cashless society – even though their customers are less enthusiastic – but have rarely considered the idea of a cardless society. This is possible today as Chapter 15 details.

Chapter 16 then moves focus from the retail client to the corporate client, and discusses the supply chain from purchase orders to invoices and everything therein, including payments.

The reason this is important is that due to the cost of poor supply chains. For example, the EU generates 27 billion invoices per annum, around 85% of which are on paper. Paper invoices cost an average €5 to process, if nothing goes wrong, but increases to €50 for an incorrect invoice. Similarly, the USA sends out around 29 billion invoices per annum, with 90% of them on paper.

An electronic invoice only costs $0.26 ¢ or €0.21 ¢ to process. That is why corporations could save upwards of $100 billion per annum through supply chain automation, and banks play a critical role in this process by providing the invoicing and billing standards for automation.

Chapter 17 takes an in-depth tour of SWIFT through the last few years. This chapter is an amalgam of two articles that appeared around SIBOS 2005 and 2006.

Every year, SWIFT hold an annual bankers' jamboree called SIBOS, the SWIFT International Bank Operations Seminar. This is the largest banking networking, conferencing and exhibiting opportunity in the world and is the only place to see the world's global banking community in one place. This can be corroborated by the tongue-in-cheek blogs, replicated in full at the end of this book, which provide a true insight into the whys and wherefores, ups and downs of the SIBOS weekly affair.

Chapter 17 therefore picks up in the first half of the article with a review of Heidi Miller's comments at SIBOS 2004 in Atlanta. Ms Miller, who was newly appointed as head of treasury and security services when she made these comments, took the banking industry to task and asked a number of challenging questions around why banks make it so difficult for their customers to communicate. One year later, the industry still had not addressed all of her questions but then, in 2006, the SWIFT2010 strategy was released. The second half of the article reviews this in light of Ms Miller's comments, with the conclusion that Heidi, Chris Skinner and many others may well be working for SWIFT before we know it.

The final chapter in this section then places a spotlight on the most important change in the payments world for most of Europe's banks: SEPA, the Single Euro Payments Area. This chapter is a twin chapter with Chapter 20, Make or Break for Europe's Equities Markets, as they both discuss key European regulatory agendas on the forms of the Payment Services Directive in Chapter 18 and the Markets in Financial Instruments Directive (MiFID) in Chapter 20.

If you decide to read Chapters 18 and 20 together, as twin chapters, then that makes sense. Alternatively, you may read these chapters in page order including the intervening chapter which opens the investment banking section. This chapter discusses the similarities and relationship between MiFID and the RegNMS, which is a related regulatory change for the USA. In that case, I would also recommend that you read Chapters 4 and 5 at the same time, as these chapters provide further backdrop to the theme of the bankers' greatest global challenges: regulations and compliance.

Chapter 4 studies the frictions between politicians and bankers, along with Chapter 5 which reviews the implications of the European Union or lack of union.

These five chapters are recommended as a group together, but can also be digested easily individually. It's up to you as to what works best.

15

The Cashless, Cardless Society

During the last decades we have seen several technology revolutions. The 1980s introduced the personal computer, the 1990s the internet and the 2000s the iPod. What can we expect in the next 10 years and how will this impact banks?

The speed at which revolutions take place is collapsing. The television took three decades to become accessible whilst the iPod took about three months. The digital generation is rapidly and radically re-landscaping markets from music to travel to fashion to entertainment to banking. All of which is made viable by the internet and mobile connections.

These days, in our constantly connected global society, new ideas and innovations can spark new ways of doing business within months. The result is that we are living in a state of flux which is leading to a cashless, cardless society. Now, many of you will stop reading at this point because of that phrase. 'A cashless, cardless society.' I know you will stop reading because you think a cashless, let alone cardless, society is a fallacy. A cashless society is like a clothless suit – it is the Emperor's new clothes. Everyone can talk about the idea of a cashless society but, in reality, there's nothing there.

THE CASHLESS SOCIETY

There are often wild predictions of things disappearing that never do. Like paper. Many would claim that the idea of the paperless office is about as realistic as a paperless toilet. Yet, the Japanese do have just such a device – a paperless toilet – for your derriere today, and digital pen and paper is making strong inroads into the traditional usage of pen and paper.

Therefore, the idea of a cashless society is also tenable. Cash, as in coins and notes, is passé in the world of wireless and digital life and cash will be displaced by other forms of payments, specifically chip-based payments, including contactless and prepaid cards.

Banks in particular will drive this change, as they recognise that they must overhaul their cash management and treasury operations if they are to deliver efficiencies and achieve profitable margins. The main barrier to achieving this is that there historically has been no viable alternative to cash.

Although debit cards and related debit instruments offer a substitute for cash, they lack one essential quality: anonymity. The fact that existing credit and debit card payments can always be traced back to the individual or company making such payments means that most of us prefer cash for its anonymity.

Cash is used not just for low-value payments but as a favoured form to avoid paying taxes and to engage in other unregulated or illicit commercial activities. Cash usage is particularly high in Ireland, Spain, and Italy, with up to 70% of total payments made via coins and banknotes. In the other extreme, cash represents less than 5% of payments in Finland, thanks to a culture of open exchange combined with innovative electronic services using electronic wallets and online payments and invoicing.

However, banks' success with electronic payments will be elusive as long as use of cash remains as high as it is today. Therefore, they need a true debit-based and anonymous alternative that does not include identity recognition as part of the electronic payment. These factors, along with cost, convenience, availability and, of course, regulation, are driving banks toward the deployment of prepaid cards.

Prepay cards can replace cash over time because, unlike chip-based credit and debit cards, prepay cards can be anonymous for online and offline payments. Banks will therefore fully support the delivery of prepaid cards to overcome the cost of cash and to further encourage customers to make the transition across to electronic payment schemes.

Banks will also seek to use prepaid cards to achieve the efficiency gains and new markets that these programmes can offer and are attracted to prepaid cards for a variety of reasons: the increasingly successful use of prepaid services in the United States; within Europe, the issues of new payments regulations, such as the Single Euro Payments Area (SEPA) and the Payment Services Directive (PSD); the overall benefits to retailers, corporates, government, and consumers; and the ability prepaid cards offer to gain new markets and customers.

Alongside this trend, retailers are recognising the marketing opportunities, while corporates and governments are beginning to identify the cost savings prepaid cards could deliver. For example, corporates have long recognised that the significant inefficiencies in cash usage and cash movements impact working capital and liquidity. Finding a way to overcome such inefficiencies has historically been a challenge for them because there has been no truly viable alternative to cash.

The consequence of all of these factors will see banks using prepaid cards as a way to reach out to new consumer segments, to attract the unbanked to bank, and to displace cash by providing anonymity and increasing convenience. That is why the combined market for all prepaid cards is estimated to be $3 trillion by 2010 in the United States whilst Europe, which is behind in this area, is around $75 billion.

That leads to a brief discussion of another revolution in payments that has just started – contactless payments. Rather than signing or entering a PIN to pay, you just wave your card over the payments terminal and the payment is made. These payments use Radio Frequency Identification (RFID) and/or Near Field Communication (NFC) chips to pay, and are already commonly in use in systems such as PayPass from MasterCard, and subway cards such as Oyster in the UK and Octopus in Hong Kong. These chips are discussed in more depth later but the real question is how long it will take prepaid contactless cards to take over from cash. After all, the UK payments associations APACS found that it was only in 2005 that plastic payments overtook cash payments, so the erosion of cash must be several years away from now.

The real answer is dependent upon the attitude of each nation towards money. The Irish have recently seen a massive upsurge in ATM deployment as banks see access to cash on every street corner as a differentiation. But then the Irish nation has one of the highest usages of cash, more than four times the amount of cash in circulation and usage as compared to the UK or Finland. Meanwhile, Finland has almost all payments made electronically and abhors cheques or non-electronic forms of payments.

And this is a key point. You have to track the experiments that are working around the world of payments and then identify and deploy the ones that make sense for specific businesses in specific markets. You cannot expect that the familiar notes and coins will disappear overnight. The erosion of cash by other forms of online, mobile and contactless payment will take decades rather than years. Although it may be sooner than we think for some.

For example, in 2002, I walked into a major high street store in the UK and asked for an MP3 player and the assistant said they had stopped stocking them as 'who would want download music off the internet?' By 2005, the same store was the biggest seller of iPods, closed their high street stores and moved to being a pure internet retailer, and you would now be hard-pressed to find a CD player anywhere in a typical electrical shop.

That is another point. For each new technology innovation, something has to become obsolete or what is the point? If you buy an iPod, do you still want a cassette or CD-Walkman? If you have a laptop with DVD in your teenager's room, do you still buy them a TV and DVD player? If you buy a mobile telephone with three megapixel camera, do you still use your 35mm or digital camera?

These technology innovations are easy to accept in our personal lives, and it is the reason why each wave of change that moves cash to credit card, cash to debit card, cash to contactless card, cash to online, cash to mobile, erodes the dominance of cash.

That is why there will eventually be a cashless society and, if we can believe in the idea of a cashless society, what about a cardless society?

THE CARDLESS SOCIETY

We were living in a cardless society only 50 years ago.

It was not until 1958 that the credit card revolution occurred with the immortal 'Fresno Drop'. The Fresno Drop was conceived by a middle manager at the Bank of America named Joe Williams. Mr Williams mailed out 60,000 credit cards to nearly every household in Fresno in 1958. The result was that the BankAmericard became a success and the credit card became part of all of our daily lives.

So it took about three decades for the credit card to become accepted and another two for it to become the major retail payment mechanism in most countries. How long for it to disappear? Maybe a decade? And the same goes for cash too.

What are the signs that this may happen?

The first is the increasing use of mobile telephones for small value payments. The mobile telephone is not a telephone anymore. It is a stereo music player, a digital camera, an entertainment console and a payments mechanism. Throughout many countries, the ability to make payments using SMS text messaging is as natural as using cash. In many countries you can see people walking around today and texting from their phones at vending machines or bus ticket machines, and the payment is made. The result is that mobiles are paying for lots of things from car parking meters to taxi fares to drinks and snacks from vending machines. Telephone payments through texting however, are already outmoded as we move towards payment chips integrated into the telephone. In particular, Japan's NTT DoCoMo is leading the way. Initially, DoCoMo made a business out of mobile payments through the i-mode mobile entertainment system, which gives access to internet, 3G and other services. By increasing functionality on the phone, DoCoMo's i-mode created a massive upsurge in spending on games, ringtones and other services through the phone. i-mode is now available in Japan, Germany, the Netherlands, Taiwan, Belgium, France, Spain, Italy, Greece, Australia, the UK, Israel and Russia and services are being continually enhanced in terms of range and functionality. The result is that mobile payments are a standard for not just ringtones and games, but music, internet orders and a variety of other payments.

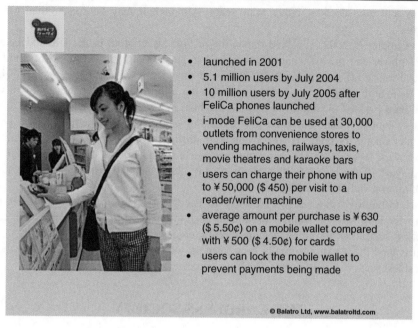

- launched in 2001
- 5.1 million users by July 2004
- 10 million users by July 2005 after FeliCa phones launched
- i-mode FeliCa can be used at 30,000 outlets from convenience stores to vending machines, railways, taxis, movie theatres and karaoke bars
- users can charge their phone with up to ¥ 50,000 ($ 450) per visit to a reader/writer machine
- average amount per purchase is ¥ 630 ($ 5.50¢) on a mobile wallet compared with ¥ 500 ($ 4.50¢) for cards
- users can lock the mobile wallet to prevent payments being made

© Balatro Ltd, www.balatroltd.com

Figure 15.1   NTT DoCoMo, Japan

NTT DoCoMo then launched the Edy mobile wallet (See Figure 15.1). Edy is a mobile payment system integrated into a contactless chip on DoCoMo's mobile telephones, branded as FeliCa and manufactured by Sony. The phones are accepted as payment in over 30,000 outlets, including shops, convenience stores, restaurants and even – as of April 2006 – by the taxi drivers in Tokyo. As a further demonstration of the increasing domination of mobile payments in Japan, the same FeliCa telephones can now be used to make Suica payments. Suica is a contactless scheme similar to Oyster and Octopus for Japanese Railways East Japan, JR East. The significance of having both Edy and Suica on your telephone in one, is like having your MasterCard and Transport Card on your mobile handset. It just makes life simple.

The chip is the next sign of change.

Over the next five years, we will see increasing numbers of technologies being delivered that will revolutionise the business of consumer payments based upon chip-based technologies, from SIM chips in telephones to RFID and NFC chips in Credit and Debit Cards. RFID enables contactless payments where you wave the chip over a reader; NFC chips enable contactless payments but do not involve passing the chip over a reader but just reading the chip's microwave signal as you pass by a receiving station.

RFID and NFC chips are wafer-thin, and can be placed into almost any object invisibly. For example, in textiles to track stock movements and sales of clothes in retail stores. RFID and NFC chips can be used in cans and cartons to track sales and stock in grocery stores. Within financial services, RFID is being used to develop contactless payment mechanisms, such as PayPass from MasterCard, and NFC is being used primarily for entering stadiums and ticketed events.

Contactless payment cards, such as the Oyster Card in London, MasterCard PayPass and JPMorgan's Blink in the USA, and E.Sun Bank's mixed credit and contactless payment card in Taiwan, are springing up everywhere around the world and taking off rapidly.

One of the most ambitious contactless payment programmes is JPMorgan's US rollout of the 'Blink' card. In technology trials, JPMorgan found that the typical card user's

- speed of paying improved by 15%–20%;
- number of payments increased by an average 12%;
- amount spent increased by 20%–30%.

compared to cash payments. It is interesting to note the increase in amount spent and number of payments, which can be largely attributed to the fact that people spend more when they are unconstrained by the coins and notes in their pockets or purses. This is why JPMorgan. This is why JPMorgan is aiming to issue over 100 million such cards to US consumers over the next few years. Contactless payments are fast and easy, convenient and cheap; they also get rid of cash.

For example, going onto the London Underground used to involve heaving around mounds of coins in your pocket or purse if you did not want to queue for hours to change a note. Now, thanks to the Oyster Card, blink and you have paid. The same is true in Hong Kong with the Octopus Card or Tokyo with the Suica Card. And all sorts of other destinations for contactless payments are popping up overnight. For example, McDonald's now takes contactless payments across all of its US stores and Bossini in Hong Kong accepts the Octopus Card for buying clothes.

Then you have the big three card providers – MasterCard, Visa and Amex – each with massive contactless payments deployments. All three are making rapid inroads by partnering with cash-friendly franchises – cinemas, 7-Eleven convenience stores, gas stations, fast-food outlets, etc.

If contactless payments grow such that you can pay for all of the things you currently buy with notes and coins, then why do you need cash at all? If you do not need cash, why do you need cash machines? If you do not need cash machines, then what is the ATM for?

The ATM has to find a new role in life. That might be depositing cheques, accepting payments, paying bills, offering advertising, dispensing tickets, topping up contactless payment devices or even downloading bank statements to PDAs. . .but it won't be dispensing cash.

That leads to the next sign of change – the fact that payments are now sliced and diced. It used to be that we would only pay for things if they were 1.99, 11.99, 99.99 or any other amount with a 0.99. The fact is that the amount today is just the 0.99. Everything from iTunes to i-mode price at a fraction of a cent and can support that micropayment transaction level because the amounts are being treated like airtime on the mobile. Just as you pay a fraction of a cent for a fraction of a phone call, so you can now pay a fraction of a cent for a fraction of a tune. As a result, TowerGroup estimates the total market for micropayments in the USA to be $11.5 billion in 2009, with almost $5 billion being made by mobile phones. The future is one of pay-as-you-go for the bits you want-as-you-go wherever-you-go. Therefore, the mobile, internet and micropayment world will not be fuelled by cards and cash but by mobile contactless low value payments.

Banks worldwide are now taking these developments seriously, although they were not a few years ago. Until the mid-2000s, most banks viewed mobile and micropayments as 'wait and see' pilots and trials, whilst many of the mobile and micropayment leaders are telco's such as NTT DoCoMo or innovators like PayPal. The same is true with the innovations in contactless payments.

For example, the Oyster card was introduced to London as a rechargeable contactless prepaid card in 2003. It originally targeted London's rail and subway users with lower cost fares and, as a result, has been a runaway success with over two million users today. The use of the card is now extending to pay for traffic meters, newspapers, burgers and chewing gum. In fact, it will soon become a real substitute for cash and therefore the use of cash will decline further whilst the use of the card will increase. But the vision for this type of contactless card does not stop there. The Oyster card is likely in fact to follow the example of the Octopus card in Hong Kong. The Octopus card was launched back in 1997 and has over 12.5 million users today. Not only can the card be used for payments across a broad spectrum of retailers, but it is even usable in Bossini. Bossini is the equivalent of a Marks & Spencer or LL Bean agreeing to accept the card. Now, you have a real alternative to both cash and credit and debit cards – the contactless rechargeable payments card from the local transport system.

Mobile, micro and contactless payments are in fact disruptive technologies in the payments world. Disruptive technologies were identified specifically by Clayton Christensen in his book, *The Innovator's Dilemma*. Mr Christensen talks about disruptive technologies as often being a cheap alternative to an existing product. The alternative is often a no-frills, stripped-down, basic option to the incumbent product which, as a result, is dismissed as cheap rubbish by the existing providers. However, as the cheaper alternatives gain market demand, they also gain investment dollars and use those investment dollars to upscale until they challenge the incumbent providers.

One of the examples Mr Christensen uses to illustrate this is the Japanese car manufacturers. When Japan entered the US car market in the 1950s, the cars were dismissed as irrelevant by Chrysler and Ford as they were cheap, rusty, poor quality and unfashionable. However, for people with a limited budget who just wanted a car to go from A to B, these new cars were just what they wanted; affordable, comfortable and nowhere near as hard to acquire as a car made in America. Over the years, Honda and Toyota garnered more demand and upscaled until they became the most popular cars in the USA.

That is a disruption and we are seeing these disruptions in the payments world. There are many simple methods of making low value payments which have been launched in the last few years that could, over time, upscale to higher value payments. These include telecommunications firms focusing on mobile payments; online organisations such as PayPal taking a large slice of internet payments and in 2006 launching into mobile payments too; alongside payment providers from the transport systems, such as Octopus and Oyster, offering electronic cash systems that are slowly upscaling from paying a fare to buying a burger to purchasing clothing.

Now you start to think laterally and you can see a range of other ways in which RFID and NFC can change our payments processes. For example, what about the idea of using jewellery – rings, bracelets – or even clothes as payment cards? Sounds ridiculous? Well, it is not and one card processor already offers this functionality. JCB – the Japanese credit card provider – has teamed up with Casio to create an RFID-based Wristwatch. This watch allows you to wave your wrist over the contactless payment terminal and credit your card with payment. So be prepared for the 'fashion' cards of the future – rather than have gold, platinum and black card, I'll have a gold, platinum or black ring, bracelet or watch. For example, Figure 15.2 demonstrates one of the first of these sorts of watches. Launched in 2006, to promote the Football World Cup in Germany, Chinatrust Commercial Bank teamed up with Laks watches and Mastercard PayPass to create this Swatch-style watch. The fashion statement is obvious and led to a major surge of new account openings. Oh, and by the way, the watch also happens to be a contactless payments method for low value payments across transport, fast food and other outlets.

- Chinatrust Commercial Bank and MasterCard PayPass working with Austrian watchmaker LAKS and On Track Innovations introduced the contactless payment watch as part of a promotion tied to the 2006 FIFA World Cup.
- The watch allows wearers to simply tap their watch on a contactless reader to pay for their purchases.
- The watch is called 'the LAKS SmartTransaction Watch' and is the world's first watch equipped with MasterCard PayPass.
- The watch has a sporty exterior with soccer ball images on its face, and is offered in green, blue or orange.

© Balatro Ltd, www.balatroltd.com

Figure 15.2   Chinatrust Commercial Bank introduces a watch as a payment device
Source: https://www.laks.com/index.php?lang=en&laks_s=off&land=&nameB=PressRoom

All of these mobile, micro and contactless payments are convenient and easy for consumers and have the potential, over time, to upscale. But upscale to what? This leads me to the major misnomer with mobile and contactless payments, which is that banks believe this is just for low value payments.

Currently, most mobile payments are for items under $10 and contactless payments for items under $100. The thing that prevents these systems offering payments for higher value items is that there is no authentication of the payment. Unlike card-based payments where you need to carry something you have – the card – you also need to present something you know – the PIN or signature. It is the second piece that allows higher value retail payments today. Without a second authentication mechanism, mobile and contactless payments will be restricted and yet adding these verification mechanisms – PIN or signature – would defeat the reason for using these payment processes which is speed. The fact that contactless payments take 20 seconds off traditional payment times is the reason for its success in fast food restaurants, cinemas and subway stations. Add extra time onto the transaction and that defeats the purpose.

However, you would expect to take longer over a $1,000 transaction than you would over a $1 transaction. Therefore, if you could bring in a second level authentication to the payment instrument then it could easily replace existing Chip and PIN and signature systems. That is where the importance of biometrics comes into focus.

Biometric payments will maintain the speed of transaction whilst allowing high value payments based upon something you are, which is more secure than something you have or something you know. At present, biometric payment systems are few and far between but that could all be about to change.

The very fact that governments have focused upon tightening border security through biometric programmes is the key to unlocking this potential authentication tool. As you pass through US Customs today, you give your fingerprints and have your face scanned for biometric authentication. Soon, in the UK, all citizens will be issued with biometric identification cards if the government achieves its aims. Meanwhile, many airports are introducing iris recognition in place of a passport. Such systems are typically voluntary for citizens, but are very popular as they allow people to jump the customs queues and walk straight through.

As governments force biometric programmes into their countries, so will banking and payments piggy-back on this change. The reason, if for no other, will be to address the challenges of fraud in banking today.

For example, the major inhibitor to online transactions is the fact that many consumers feel threatened by identity theft and online fraud. This is not surprising when the UK government reported there were over 100,000 victims of identify theft in the UK in 2004 costing a total of £1.3 billion in losses. It takes up to six months for an identity theft victim to sort out the issues and nine out of 10 victims think the fear the theft created for them will never end. On the other hand, one in five people throw out their bank statements and utility bills without any concern over the fact that they might be picked up and used by those with evil intent.

In particular, many of us know that usernames and passwords do not work. Many of us write passwords down on post-it notes that are left on the desk or in drawers, and one in five of us use the same password for everything. So how secure is online banking when people use the same password to access their account as they do to order a book from Amazon?

The result is that almost half of the customers of banks would actually claim to think about switching to an alternative financial services provider if they offered stronger authentication. In other words, usernames and passwords do not work, signatures do not work and Chip and PIN does not work. None of these systems are that secure because they depend upon traditional means of authentication based upon something you have and something you know, both of which can easily be usurped or stolen.

This culminates in a wicked concoction of internet fraud and identity theft, aligned with government concerns over terror and money laundering, which are all creating the need to introduce new and improved levels of authentication. That is why many see the future of authentication being based upon something you are – your face, iris, finger or palm. That is why governments are introducing biometric border controls and, as a result, banks will do the same.

Many folks still argue that biometrics is a long way away. Customers do not like the idea of having their fingerprints or eyeballs scanned. Just go and see the film *Minority Report* if you want to see the impact biometrics can have on your vision. Nevertheless, biometric authentication combined with RFID embedded in our jewellery is inevitable. And, in a survey of 2,000 Americans in 2003 performed by the United States Department of Justice, most American citizens believed that a fingerprint biometric authentication would be more acceptable to them than a signature at the point of sale. How can this be? Well, with over 10 million Americans suffering identity theft every year, consumers are just as keen to get systems in place that protect them from identify theft and fraud as the banks.

There are many fingerprint-based biometric systems in use already. One of the largest is the Pay-by-Touch rollout with the Discover card in the USA. This system does not actually store the fingerprint but instead keeps forty data points unique to each finger which are verified each time you pay. The result is that transaction times have been reduced by a third for payments.

Another significant biometric programme is the rollout of Biometric debit cards to eight million customers of Banco Azteca in Mexico. The reason is that most of their customers cannot present a viable form of identification, because they do not have passports or driving licences, and so this is a much more reliable means of authentication. The bank processes over 200,000 biometric transactions a day, accurately and smoothly. As does ICICI Bank in India, who provide biometric cards to their rural base of farmers, who are often illiterate and therefore cannot sign their names.

In all three cases – the Discover Card, Banco Azteca and ICICI Bank – payments are speeded by biometric fingerprint recognition with a variety of reasons driving the move to such programmes, specifically unique identification, speed, convenience and security.

Of course, there are also other ways to use biometrics, such as the users of the Bank of Tokyo-Mitsubishi in Japan use palmprints, rather than fingerprints, because it is more hygienic and reliable. Equally, ABN AMRO in the Netherlands uses voiceprint recognition as a biometric for their call centres. These examples are discussed in more depth in Chapters 12 and 13.

The bottom-line is that contactless chips integrated with jewellery and supported by biometric authentication and identification will allow a cashless and cardless society to exist. In this vision, you can tap your watch on the counter, or even just use a fingerprint without a card or watch, to make payments.

There is one more evolution of these systems that can be introduced here though: an evolution which will create the ultimate form of customer relationship management. An evolution that is a logical extension of all of the above. An evolution that can be seen in action today. This trend is the big one. The next big thing. And brings all of the cash replacement and new chip technologies into focus.

What is the next big thing?

Precognition.

Yes, as you walk into your bank they will know who you are before you walk through the door. As customers come into contact with their bank, the bank will know whether it is Mr Big Spender of Grand Mansions and worth that extra smile of service or Mrs Notwortha Sausage of Tenements who they might ignore.

How?

Because the RFID/NFC chip in his watch or her purse will be picked up by the sensors in the walls, floors and windows of their local bank branch. The result will be pre-identification and tracking of customer's movements physically and virtually. This revolutionary evolution in service is already available in some US stores. For example, the 'Shopping Buddy' screen has been rolled out in the Stop & Shop Supermarkets. The Buddy is a DVD style screen built into the grocery store's shopping trolleys. As you arrive at the supermarket you swipe your loyalty card – in the future, you wave your watch – and the Buddy now tells you all you need to know. Instant personalised offers are made as you walk around the store. The Buddy guides you to your regular items of purchase, tells you if they have moved and even works out that the can of soup you need is on the bottom shelf and hidden behind two other cans.

Imagine that you can now track all of these things through the air, real-time, online, 24×7. That is where chips are going. The near future is one where you pay by a wave, authenticate with your finger and have full-time service tailored to your every need through the bank continually analysing, monitoring and offering services based on your location and likely needs. Some may worry about the privacy in all this, but many will trade privacy for the benefits of improved service with decreased chance of fraud or identity theft.

The day of banking with a physical card and signature is long gone.

There's one more twist to this story, as illustrated by Figure 15.3. The future is actually one where the contactless watch is not needed at all. The final form of payments is purely going to use a chip. All of today's payments are chip-based and the chip is getting more powerful and more capable. Just as today's mobile telephones are as powerful as yesterday's personal computers, today's silicon chips are as powerful as yesterday's smartphones.

As chip-based products become more powerful, the chip of the future will be offered to citizens as an implant for a variety of applications. For example, as a health system to monitor blood pressure, cholesterol, brain activity and heart rate, and wirelessly report any

Now we can start paying by chip in skin

AMONG the bikini-clad pole dancers at a Spanish nightclub, a quiet consumer revolution has begun which could soon arrive in Britain.

Customers in the VIP lounge at The Baja Beach Club in Barcelona have microchips implanted into their bodies to allow them to pay more easily.

Instead of fumbling with credit cards in the dimly lit club, they can wave their arm over a scanner to gain entry or order drinks.

The idea has caught on because the chip provides a convenient way to bypass queues and is a quirky fashion

GRAHAM KEELEY
in Barcelona

item. But it is not just a gimmick for Spanish clubbers or drunken tourists on a night out, according to the Institute for Grocery Distribution.

It found that almost one in 10 British teenagers and one in 20 adults would not mind having a chip implanted.

The tiny glass chip, the size of a grain of rice, is inserted by a nurse under the left arm of club visitors at a cost of €125 (£84.50). Each one carries a 10-digit personal number

which can be linked to the clubber's bank account. The chip can be easily removed too.

In the past two years, 100 people have had a chip put under their skin at the Baja Beach Club. Among them is Juanjo, who won Operación Triunfo, the Spanish version of TV's Big Brother.

Steve Van Soest, the club's marketing manager, said: 'We started it because we saw what was happening in the US, where workers and children were having chips put in.

'We want to extend it so people can go through certain doors in the club without

having to wait.' He insisted Spanish health authorities backed the idea and no clubbers had complained of a reaction after having a chip inserted.

The institute found one in five teenagers was happy to pay for shopping using biometric methods.

Geraldine Padbury, senior business analyst with the institute, said: 'With teenagers happy to use MySpace and blogs to share details of their private lives, there may be less concern surrounding privacy than for other generations.'

Bar coded: this implanted clubgoer is cleared to enter

Figure 15.3   From the UK's Evening Standard, October 2006, reproduced by permission

unusual activity to your doctor. This guarantees that early indications of anything like a stroke or heart attack are caught before you would ever have known. Or implanted because governments promoting chips as fast and convenient travel services:

> No more heavy duty and intrusive searches at airports, ports and terminals, just turn up and go. For citizens who have the National Chip ID, you can just go through the wireless fast track station and hop on your boat, plane or train . . . meanwhile, for the rest of you, please join the thirty minute queue for the security scan, take off your shoes, belts and jewellery and ensure that your pacemaker is switched off.

I know many folks would jump at the chance of such a fast track system, even if it meant having a small chip implanted in your arm. If chip implants provide us with guaranteed health, security and ease of travel, why not use the same chip for payments?

An implanted chip would enable people to pay in exactly the same way as we are thinking of payments for mobile and contactless today. And this future is not that far away for, as Figure 15.3 demonstrates, it is already here.

The vision of the future of retail payments is one where your payment mechanism is built into a watch that your bank gave you or implanted into your skin. The chip inside provide wireless payments capabilities combined with unique biometric authentication, and is supported by bank's existing infrastructures at the merchant front-end and money transmissions back-end. The retail consumer can therefore go into any store and pay by holding their hand over a biometric palm reader which also reads their chip-intelligence in their watch or hand or arm. No card or cash involved.

We are almost there today. The near term world of retail payments will be one of a cashless and cardless society. A society based upon micro and macro contactless payments with biometric secure authentication through bank provided mobile and wearable and implanted devices.

The focus will be convenience and cool. Give your customers trend-setting payments devices rather than coloured cards. Deliver cashless solutions and infrastructures rather than notes and coins. Dump the gold or platinum card for the gold or platinum ring. Develop the mobile wallet with free phone, iPod, 8 megapixel camera and 3G.

The winners will be the ones who disrupt payments because they have a vision of the long term. The losers will be those who think these innovations are meaningless.

16
Corporates Demand Access

Over the last 10 years, corporations have been requesting more and more direct access to banking operations and infrastructures. The reasons are many, and have specifically grown out of the internet age where customers and staff need to have access to information worldwide in real-time. Corporate customers recognise this, but are keen to do so securely and electronically, with their banking partners' support. This move is demonstrated well by groups such as the European Association of Corporate Treasurers (EACT) and the Transaction Workflow Innovation Standards Team (TWIST). In particular, in terms of automation, TWIST has been very active in the area of technology standards.

What is interesting is that TWIST has been trying to gain agreement between corporations and banks around standards for treasury automation, working capital management and commercial payments since 2001, and yet there is still a battle taking place to achieve these ambitions.

The reason for the battle is that there is no standard in linking treasury operations with banks. Sure, there's SWIFT for post-trade settlement, but TWIST is frustrated because SWIFT is only one piece of the payments process whilst TWIST is looking at the end-to-end trade process between governments, corporations and banks. In that context, there are many standards from FIX for pre-trade to SWIFT for post-trade and from FpML for trading in complex financial instruments to MDDL for market data.

TWIST's stated mission is to deliver 'non-proprietary XML-based standards' that enable organisations to implement 'effective straight through processing' through 'single points of data entry, from end to end of the relevant processes'.

This means that organisations such as TWIST are trying to bring groups pick up key standards and technologies that are widely accepted, such as FIX, FpML and SWIFT, and then leveraging these through the relevant authorities, such as the International Standards Organisation (ISO) to agree single standards for key areas of the supply process. This is becoming easier to achieve through XML – the eXtensible Markup Language – which allows for easier integration of complex systems, but XML on its own is not enough. Nor do they deliver common sense as the issue is not just around technology but, more importantly, around process. And it is the process issues in the supply chain where standards break down.

That is why treasurers, corporations and banks are concentrating efforts to create new standards in the areas of processes rather than technologies. Processes in the supply chain include areas such as invoices and remittances, as well as standards for identity management.

The issue with identity management is that it crosses over the boundaries of the supply chain – between governments, corporate and banks – and none of the parties have had a burning requirement to change things.

For example, governments will not enforce identity management standards as it would cause issues with other governments. Corporates should be the enforcers of a single identity management standard, but they have historically been uncoordinated in their activities. Meanwhile, banks are considered to be excellent issuers of identity keys, but corporates do not feel comfortable with the idea that banks become the managers of identity in the supply chain cycle. A bank's role is perceived to be purely for the payments element of the process, not the whole end-to-end process.

In addition, banks have compounded identities by issuing multiple standards and multiple identity keys. Historically, every country in Europe had its own identification system but, following regulation from the European Commission in 2001, banks have now standardised upon IBAN (International Bank Account Numbers) and BIC (Bank Identification Codes) for all cross-border transactions. Even then, IBANs and BICs are non-standard, as the USA uses UPIC (the Universal Payments Identification Code) and corporates use IBEIs (International Business Entity Identifiers).

The reason why this is something that needs to be resolved is due to a variety of pressures that are creating the impetus for corporates to work closely with banks and governments.

The first pressure is that it is no longer acceptable for individuals to have multiple identity signatures in today's world of 24×7 electronic communications; pervasive connectivity; low-cost global airlines encouraging continuous movements of economic migrants; and extreme terrorism.

The second is that banks and corporates believe the time is right to create a global standard for identity management due to regulatory change. The significant changes in corporate processes demanded by Sarbanes Oxley, combined with similar changes to payment processes demanded by Europe's Payments Directive and related global Anti-Money Laundering and Anti-Terrorism regulations, means that banks and corporates are willing to look at working together for standardisation. This is for no other reason than cost efficiency and effectiveness. For example, corporates estimate the bill to implement Section 404 of SOX is around $35 billion whilst banks estimate the bill for Europe's Payments Directive to be around $40 billion. Such astronomical costs have made both parties come to the table to consider how to make globally interoperable standards between corporations, countries, banks and businesses a reality.

Regulatory change and global connectivity are forces working together to drive banks and corporates to rethink their connections. There are also other factors driving the banks to listen to their corporate customers too.

'I'M AS MAD AS HELL, AND I'M NOT GOING TO TAKE IT ANYMORE!'

The corporate voice wants to be heard, and this is no more obvious than when we discuss the idea of direct corporate access to SWIFT. Even at SIBOS 2004, the annual SWIFT networking event, the banking community was saying that direct access needed to be avoided. The view then was that corporates should only access SWIFT via MA-CUGs (Member-Administered Closed User Groups), i.e. via a bank-sponsored link.

This long-held resistance to including the customer in the settlements process has always been irksome to the large corporates. The customer's view has been that banks have maintained this exclusion as a method of keeping customers locked-in to their proprietary services.

The customer no longer believes they should be locked-in to proprietary connections when we live in an age of internet connectivity and global communications. So the lack of direct access to SWIFT is making them mad as hell.

The mantra – first bellowed by Peter Finch in the 1976 movie *Network* – has become a slogan for the corporate treasury movement. They are as mad as hell and they are not going to take it anymore. Take what? You name it: being locked into proprietary bank connections and systems that are unresponsive; being kept at bay from direct access to the bank networks; paying extortionate charges for cross-border processing fees and related transactions. . .

Corporates also get mad when they hear other corporates discussing their treasury processes and banking partnerships. For example, one corporate treasurer from a major technology firm said the following at a public conference I recently chaired:

> Our firm has rationalised systems globally to allow us to process our treasury operations on a global basis with just two banks. As a result, our quarterly financial numbers are available within two days of the close date for the whole corporation. Most companies take at least six weeks. In addition, we saved over $1 billion by digitalising the supply chain and collapsing our global bank relationships down to just two providers.

That's enough to make me as mad as hell and not take it anymore. Especially if I have banks in every country processing transactions that cause me to take two months to reconcile, consolidate, validate and produce my quarterly results. . .at 10 times the cost of my competitors.

Therefore, SWIFT is working extensively to ensure Direct Corporate Access to the co-operative network, SWIFTNet. For example, part of SWIFT's Strategy for 2010 is SCORE, the SWIFT Corporate Environment, which was announced in late 2006 for rollout in 2007. SCORE allows large corporations listed on the major stock exchanges around the world to gain direct access to SWIFTNet. The fact that SCORE was overwhelmingly voted into place by the SWIFT community is one of the most notable features of this move as, only a few years earlier, the same proposal was overwhelmingly rejected. This is a clear sign as to how the bank community are changing, and demonstrates that banks finally appear to have overcome their fear of disintermediation by allowing their corporate customers to have this type of direct access to historically exclusive bank infrastructures.

Even so, SWIFT represents a community of over 8,100 financial institutions around the world and the problem with a community, where every bank has a vote, is that the co-operative moves at a glacial pace. This is why SWIFT is directing things more aggressively from the top because the danger for the banks is that if SWIFT does not deliver direct access for all in the near future, then the corporates may just do it themselves.

For example, the European Association of Corporate Treasurers (EACT) began working on a range of activities in 2007, collectively known as CAST which stands for Corporate Action on Standards. The aim of CAST is to deliver recommendations on existing standards and requirements for new ones in areas such as the Supply Chain and Trade Financing. This is being delivered through a range of projects studying business models, best practices and standardisation in the areas of remittances, digital identities, e-invoicing and e-reconciliation. The objective of these projects is to define end-user requirements, compare them with existing standards and identify best-of-breed solutions.

What is interesting here is that the EACT, TWIST and SWIFT are all working together on these programmes.

SEE ME, HEAR ME. . .

In conclusion, banks, corporates, infrastructure providers, regulators and others are all working together improve global commerce and standards across the financial supply chain. You may be asking who's involved and the list, which is non-exhaustive, includes banks such as JPMorgan Chase, HSBC, Nordea, Standard Chartered, Deutsche, Citigroup, Barclays and SEB; corporates such as ICI, ABB, IKEA, General Electric, Nokia and Royal Dutch Shell; and other firms including clearing house infrastructures, such as Voca and Equens, to service providers including IBM, SAP, Oracle, Reuters and many more.

The real point is that all of these firms are trying to work together to agree common standards for linking corporations and banks. Whether they can get agreement or not is the next challenge. After all, after many years of lobbying there still does not seem to have been any new agreements or standards that work. However, that does not stop the customer demanding change and, if the corporate clients involved in these projects have anything to do with it, then they will achieve it.

SWIFT Changes in Wholesale Payments

SWIFT, the Society for Worldwide Interbank Financial Telecommunication, was created over thirty years ago to provide a secure electronic network to manage payments information between banks. The primary focus during inception was to create a secure, private information exchange to replace telex machines. These origins have grown such that, thirty years later, the co-operative community represent 8,100 financial instructions in over 200 countries. During this period, the community has also evolved and extended their role into new areas including securities clearing and corporate actions, as well as new markets and geographies. In particular, the network went through its biggest change recently by converting from a proprietary private network to an open internet network. This was the point of SWIFT's last strategic vision, SWIFT2006, which implemented SWIFTNet. Having said that, SWIFT is still being challenged as demonstrated in 2004 when Heidi Miller, head of the treasury and securities services businesses at JPMorgan Chase, challenged the industry to change. The challenge was delivered at SWIFT's annual conference, SIBOS, where she delivered the keynote speech and said that the industry was making it too difficult for customers to achieve their business aims. The question remained, did her comments kickstart change and, if so, what happened?

Her first question was: **'Why do we make things so complicated for our clients?'**

Miller raised the question as to why it takes six weeks to make a simple international payment. The reason is that an international payment is never simple, especially when that payment requires retail and commercial, domestic and international co-operation and processing.

There has been some movement in the right direction with regulatory changes forcing banks to move into simplified cross-border payments. EU Regulation 2560/2001 eliminated the mark-up for cross border credit transfers in Europe whilst standardising payments through the mandatory usage of the IBAN (International Bank Account Number) and BIC (Bank Identification Code). This is supported by standardising payments infrastructures using current and emerging standards, such as SWIFTNet and TWIST. In addition, industry bodies such as the European Payments Council (EPC) are driving the SEPA (Single Euro Payment Area) initiative; and there are significant international efforts to standardise ACHs by NACHA (the National Automated Clearing House Association) in the USA through the CBC (Cross-Border Council).

Banks have also recognised the inefficiencies of their infrastructures and are implementing an enterprise approach to tackle the issue. Cash and cards have been distinctly separate lines of business to corporate clearing and settlement historically, as has electronic versus paper payments processing. The result has been separate skills, knowledge, expertise and systems across these functions. These legacy systems, compounded by mergers and acquisitions, have created a payments spaghetti that even the banks cannot fathom.

Many institutions are therefore creating a single line of business in payments, to implement straight-through processing from retail cash management through to international settlements.

The industry's response to Miller's challenge Part One – the quest to deliver simplified payments solution to bank clients – is underway, so let's look at Part Two.

'How can we help our customers become more efficient and productive, when our own back offices are so expensive, fragmented, outdated and non-interoperable?'

In her speech, Miller cited several examples of the industry's lack of movement in simplification such as the USA's introduction of Check 21 which forces banks to keep two copies of a cheque – a cheque image and an Image Replacement Document (IRD).

This lack of standardisation and inter-operability is an issue, but is one that cannot be solved just by a bank. As SWIFT's CEO at the time stated, the only way these issues can be addressed is from the top. That means getting the leading banks of the world into a room to commit to new standards and adopt those standards. In other words, an industry agreement to transform the payments business.

That challenge is bigger than individual councils and internal structures, and comes back to industry associations and committees, such as the European Payments Council (EPC), the Financial Services Technology Consortium (FSTC) and BITS, working together with SWIFT and their US counterparts the Depository Trust and Clearing Corporation (DTCC) and Fedwire, to ensure that the payments structure can be truly standardised and interoperable.

Although there are individual signs of such industry-wide initiatives, there has been little to show for it. Even with more initiatives in play, it would still require institutions to renew legacy operations and technology. In other words, it requires transforming core systems which is a task that is still far too daunting for most institutions, especially the large ones.

However, it is only after those renewals that the industry can work together to effectively exploit standards and infrastructures. The issue is the chicken and the egg. Do you transform internal infrastructures when standards are not in place or do you wait for the standards to be fully agreed and then renew systems? The problem is that the standard cannot be agreed because the systems are not in place to make them the standard.

This brings us back to Heidi Miller. It takes more than a few leading banks **or** SWIFT to make this change. It takes a few leading banks **and** SWIFT to force the change through – to create interoperable industry-wide standards.

The only example of movement in this direction is SWIFT's recently introduced member concentration programme, designed to get the large financial institutions to help the smaller ones onto SWIFTNet. But that is only one example of the way in which the industry can work together to become more efficient and productive. There needs to be more.

Which leads us to Miller's challenge Part Three: **'If we truly aspire to be leaders in the payments and securities industries, why is it that so many innovations in this business are pioneered by non-banks?'**

At this point, Miller cited the efforts of companies such as PayPal, CheckFree, First Data and (BT) Radianz in creating financial innovations. She went on to point out that the financial industry itself does little to innovate and the few examples – Equilend, CLS, TARGET and SEPA – are driven by regulations or to reduce costs.

After a lot of thinking, there has been little innovation in wholesale payments. SWIFT's cost reductions, traffic incentives and CIO outreach programmes are all initiatives but they are not innovations. The nearest example of a SWIFT innovation is the corporate access programme, SCORE, which is reviewed later. Contactless payments, wireless payments, mobile payments and so on are all innovations, but they have been underway for a number of years. Sure, there are changes afoot but they are, in many instances, still either regulatory or client-created rather than fashioned by the financial industry.

There is a very good reason for that however. First, banks are there to provide secure management of their clients' money and to avoid risks. Therefore why should they innovate as innovation implies taking risks? Second, the financial industry has had to deal with Sarbanes Oxley, IAS39, Basel II, the European Financial Services Action Plan and countless other regulatory changes. Therefore, the honest response of the banks is that they would love to innovate if they had the time and money to do so – but only after dealing with the burden of compliance and regulation.

And so, the industry fails that challenge but with a good excuse.

So, to the final question Ms Miller raised: **'If we can send a secure message to any company over the internet, why should we pay SWIFT to do it for us?'**

This was the surprise moment where Miller wagged her finger at SWIFT and asked 'what have you done for me lately?' Essentially, she was looking at SWIFT to see how it was shaping the future, rather than the past. Yes, SWIFT had replaced telex machines with X25 wiring, but what about the fact that we now live in an age of free messaging over the internet?

SWIFT's response pointed to SIPN (Secure IP Network) as a value-add, but some would say that SIPN is only needed whilst the internet is unsafe and unreliable. SWIFT would say that on top of SIPN, there is the added value of SWIFTNet's InterAct, FileAct, Browse, and FIN; service and support; and, of course, SWIFT's security, interfaces, archiving and non-repudiation capabilities. These are all fine in context, but other players offer some of these services too, such as Omgeo, BT Radianz, GL TRADE and company.

And this is where SWIFT's real challenge comes into play: what is its vision for the rest of the decade and beyond? Can it truly be a messaging standard, an industry infrastructure and a technology provider? Should it really just be one of those?

This is the challenge and SWIFT is working hard to deliver. In fact, that is what the industry looked for with SWIFT's vision through 2010. This vision is articulated by the re-vamped mission statement to become the global financial services industry's 'foremost transaction management infrastructure' by 2010. Note, the focus is on transactions, not payments or messaging which is SWIFT's historical space, so this is quite a big change in positioning.

SWIFT carved out this new vision through 2005 and presented it at SIBOS 2006. The SWIFT2010 Strategy that supports this vision focuses upon growing the corporate userbase, getting into derivatives and grabbing a slice of China, India and other emerging market economies. How effective is this strategy and does it resolve the challenges Heidi Miller raised?

SWIFT2010 STRATEGY

Unlike the previous strategies, the new programme is designed to grow the organisation outside the banking domain and into the corporate community. This is very different to the previous versions which focused upon changing the operational footprint into securities (SWIFT2001) and then rearchitected the network for the 21st Century through SWIFTNet (SWIFT2006).

The essence of SWIFT2010 is about growing the business.

Growth is sought in four key areas:

(1) Europe through facilitation and close involvement in standards for SEPA and Giovannini;
(2) the corporate community by capturing 500 of the 2,000 largest corporations in the world as Corporate Participants on the network by 2010;
(3) extending SWIFT's representation in the derivatives and capital markets arena by carrying FpML messages over the network; and
(4) gaining a stronger presence in the BRIC (Brazil, Russia, India and China), African and other emerging market economies.

These are aggressive targets and potentially stretch SWIFT away from its core founding base of correspondent banking and into the end-to-end messaging space of supply chain automation. This 21st Century version of SWIFT envisages a transactional network enabling everything from the buying and selling of goods in large corporations through to investing and trading all sorts of instruments in the investment markets.

All of this sounds fine on paper but in practice will cause friction between the core community, who can exercise a vote on the direction of the company, and newer classes of participants, from the Merrill Lynch's and Goldman Sachs to the General Motors and Exxon's. Equally, new constituencies will be created as China Construction Bank, the Bank of Baroda, Alfa Bank and others from the BRIC and emerging market communities join.

At this point, one question pops into the head as a fundamental area of concern in this expansion: what will be the structure and nature of SWIFT's corporate governance 10 years from now?

The question arises because SWIFT's Board today has a few major league players, but lacks the total global reach it seeks, especially from US bankers like Chuck Prince, CEO of CitiGroup, or Jamie Dimon, CEO of JPMorgan Chase. Equally, SWIFT is putting a great deal of effort and emphasis on growing its franchise into the emerging BRIC – Brazil, Russia, India and China – economies, but currently has no base in these countries and little representation of their banks on the Board. Finally, the consortium wants multinational corporations on board and, in so doing, will have to seek to have these firms represented in the decision-marking process. Imagine a board comprising a few more Americans, a smattering of Brazilians, Russians, Chinese and Indians, and a few corporate CEO's such as Michael Dell, Richard Branson and Donatella Versace. Now that would be interesting.

What does that mean for today's bankers and bank community? Not much actually. If anything it should be good news. Good news in having a broader range of global bankers represented, and good news for including a few of the banking community's key customers.

However, there are some other questions raised. For example, part of SWIFT's 2010 strategy aims to plant the co-operative firmly into the capital markets by carrying FpML messaging over the SWIFTNet network. That is OK, but what happened to ISO20022, the standard that was being jointly developed to unify the FIX standard (from FIX Protocol Ltd, FPL) for pre-trade processing with SWIFT's standards for post-trade processing? Although SWIFT might want to engage with FPL, there are questions as to whether FPL want to engage with SWIFT and, until such questions are resolved this is a potential gap if SWIFT really wants to get into derivatives.

Equally, if the Society expands into new geographies: the BRIC's; new customers: the corporates; and new products: derivatives; is it a stretch too far? Some would question the breadth of SWIFT's ambitions, especially as the organisation lacks depth in some of these areas, such as capital markets. However, SWIFT would brush off such critique as purely a matter of investment. As a mutual community owned by its members, the last thing SWIFT's Board wants to hear is that they made a profit, so the organisation will be investing big time in hiring capital markets expertise.

The new strategic plan really plays into expanding the breadth and depth of SWIFT across a diverse field of players and will stretch the community and the organisation further than ever before. Therefore, unlike the previous strategies, the real challenge for SWIFT lies with salesmanship. Selling SWIFT to the Merrill's and Goldman's, as well as to all of the other broker-dealers, asset managers, fund and hedge fund managers out there. Selling SWIFT to the Huaxia Bank in China and Canara Bank in India who may think it is some strange European internet network provider. And selling SWIFT to the Coca-Cola's and Nokia's of this world, who probably know as much as about bank clearing and settlement as SWIFT does about making fizzy drinks or mobile telephones.

This is a big challenge, but not insurmountable. For SWIFT it means getting feet on the street. After all, people buy from people so, to sell something, you need sales people. That is why SWIFT will be hiring hot-shot Wall Street and City brokers to sell to the Merrill's and Goldman's; influential native Indians to sell to the payments decision makers in Mumbai, Chennai and Delhi; and major league corporate financiers who can go and talk to the Richard Branson's, Michael Dell's and Donatalla Versace's in their language.

That only leaves one question.

If SWIFT's governance expands to include the full range of stakeholders in the financial community – corporates, banks, fund managers and so on – what role do governments have in their governance? This question is critically important due to the storm of anger that erupted when the New York Times discovered that SWIFT had been supporting the US Government by providing analysis of SWIFT's messages, in order to track activities that could contribute towards global terrorism after 9/11. The reason for the storm of protest is that SWIFT's messages are meant to be private. In addition, SWIFT is not an American firm, but a global community, and the fact that SWIFT did not even tell or consult their members compounded the issue.

SWIFT, in response, stated that they were subpoenaed by the US Government for information related to messages through their US office, and had to comply therefore with the information relevant to US operations. This, they say, is the same issue that other banks have faced and that other banks would have complied the same way.

The problem is that SWIFT's network is meant to be unassailable and is global, not American. If anything, SWIFT is European. That is why the issue prompted a vote in the European Parliament in February 2007 which resulted in a resolution to make it more difficult for European firms to store crucial data in the USA. This response by Europe's legislators was a direct action in response to the US Treasury Department program. The result is that, after the issues of the US government tracking SWIFT messages for indications of terrorism, SWIFT's biggest challenge for the next few years is not investing in headcount, but keeping its' head below government sightlines. Should the world's governments ever get their paws on SWIFT's messaging to target money laundering, espionage or other criminal activities, then SWIFT's role really will have been compromised away from being a trusted and secure financial messaging service to just being another network.

Regardless of all these questions, SWIFT has risen to major challenges before: the rise of the internet, the increase in terrorism, the impact of 9/11, the demands of correspondent banks and corporate clients. . .the list is long and has always been addressed by the very nature of SWIFT's open communications, inclusive strategy and dialogue, and supportive network and community.

Therefore, the real bottom-line of SWIFT's 2010 strategy is headcount. Lots of headcount. SWIFT needs feet on the street across the world's capital markets, emerging economies and corporate treasurers. Champions who will pound down the doors and the barriers in these markets and bring them on board as new markets and new users. That is why SWIFT's strategy is all about hiring big guns and, as SWIFT invests in getting guns for hire, I recommend all of you brush up your CV.

You never know. Soon, you might be working for them.

18

The Future of European Payments

The 21st century has been a revolutionary period in the European financial services markets. The legislative agendas of the European Commission certainly hit the radar in the late 2000s due to the major regulatory drivers of the Markets in Financial Instruments Directive (MiFID) and the Payment Services Directive. The latter in particular, with the implementation of the Single Euro Payments Area (SEPA) by Europe's banks, was a significant change as Europe removed national Automated Clearing Houses (ACH's) and replaced them with Pan-European ACH's, or PEACHs. With over 230 billion payments transactions made every year across the European Community, worth over €50 trillion, these are critical changes. What is the logic?

WHY FORCE THE CHANGE?

The euro had a lengthy gestation period and then hit the markets in 1999 with a whoop, circulated as a currency in 2002 with a bang and is now creating a fairly large explosion in the European financial markets. Throughout this process, banks have been responsive but not proactive to the changes implied by European Monetary Union, particularly when it comes to integrating infrastructures across the Eurozone. The result is that the European Commission has forced change through the European financial markets.

Specifically, when the euro was first discussed everyone anticipated dramatic change in European business. The rationale for this change is at the core of the commitment of the European Union countries to achieve economic reform and their aim to transform the region into 'the most competitive economy in the world'.

In order to achieve this, Europe's politicians got together in 1992 to sign the Maastricht Treaty which created European Economic and Monetary Union (EMU).

Since 1992, there have been many debates, discussions, arguments and even displacements of Europe's political leaders, but the drive towards Union continues at a pace. The reason for EMU's existence is the vision to create a European economy that can compete on an equal footing with the USA and other global markets. However, the vision is continually challenged by the hiccups of political and commercial agendas which seek to change it from being an Economic and Monetary Union to either being a federated Europe at one extreme or an abandoned Europe at the other.

This is why, within this debate, the financial markets of Europe have such a key role in either supporting or blocking the Union. Kicked around like a political football, Europe's financial markets are at the core of the Economic and Monetary Union, because it is the financial markets that provide the capillaries and arteries to allow the trade to flow without clots or blocks across Europe's borders. That is why Europe's political leaders have focused so heavily on driving change into the financial arena.

The first outcome of the political changes to financial services was a variety of Directives which laid the foundation for the introduction of the euro currency in 1999. These Directives worked to an extent, but had flaws. As a result, Europe's political leaders gathered again in 2000 and signed the Lisbon Agreement which introduced a second phase of change. A cornerstone of this second phase of change has been the drive to create a single, integrated and free-flowing European financial marketplace through the Financial Services Action Plan (FSAP).

The FSAP comprises a variety of directives, most of which have already been implemented by the member states of the European Union. These include Savings Directives, Risk and Capital Directives, Fraud and Money Laundering Directives, Insurance and Pension Fund Directives, Solvency and Mergers & Acquisitions Directives and so on. Name almost any area of financial services and there is a Directive that relates to it.

As mentioned, most of these Directives have already been debated and translated into national laws, although two of them caused a significant discussion because they required massive changes to Europe's financial markets. The two Directives in question are the Directive for Payment Services in the Internal Market, or the Payment Services Directive (PSD) for short; and the Markets in Financial Instruments Directive, or MiFID. The former aims to create a single European payments area across the Eurozone in 2010, whilst the latter is creating a single European capital market and is discussed in depth in Chapter 20. This chapter focuses on the PSD and what this means for Europe's payments providers.

THE PAYMENT SERVICES DIRECTIVE (PSD)

When the euro was launched in 1999, the surprising factor was the lack of change within the European banking community to harmonise their payments processes in preparation for its introduction. Most banks implemented the currency facilities, but did not integrate their payments facilities across borders.

This lack of integration has been a major barrier to creating a seamlessly integrated euro payments structure and so, bearing in mind that this is a critical part of building Europe's future competitiveness on the global economic stage, it is not surprising that the governments of the Eurozone nations have been totally behind legislating to make it happen.

The result is that the Commission has created a raft of rules and regulations to restructure the way payments are made throughout Europe, with the objective to create 'a Single Payment Area, in which citizens and businesses can make cross-border payments as easily, safely and efficiently as they can within their own countries and subject to identical charges'. This is the intent of SEPA and the PSD.

The start of this process was the introduction of the EU Regulation 2560/2001. This Regulation was announced in 2001 and implemented in July 2002 for cash withdrawals and card payments, and extended to credit transfers in July 2003. The nature of the Regulation is that all electronic transactions within the Eurozone of €12,500 or less have to be charged at the same level as an equivalent domestic transaction. This limit rose to €50,000 in January 2006.

Within EU Regulation 2560/2001 there were other nuances which were specifically intended to harmonise and standardise cross-border payments. For example, all credit transfers must be denominated in euros, and need to include the IBAN (International Bank Account Number) and the BIC (Bank Identification Code).

This may sound like small beans, but for some of Europe's banks it involves massive change.

First, there is the loss of revenues from cross-border credit transfers and cash withdrawals. For example, pre-2560/2001 a bank customer withdrawing €100 from an ATM outside their domestic European country in 2001 would have been charged €4 on average. Overall, these charges were making healthy margins for the banks and involved little investment. After this regulation the banks could no longer make profitably high margins for such cross-border withdrawals.

Secondly, there is the pressing requirement to create new infrastructures and clearing systems. After all, you could not have ACHs (Automated Clearing House) and central bank RTGS (Real-Time Gross Settlement) systems operating as national systems in all European countries efficiently and at a cost-base to support zero-margin transaction structures under this new charging regime.

As a result, the banks all got together in 2002 and created the European Payments Council (EPC) to oversee the launch of a Single Euro Payments Area (SEPA), and the EPC has since focused upon creating a PE-ACH (Pan-European Automated Clearing House) and a PE-DD (Pan-European Direct Debit). The achievement of the launch of these ACH-based systems by 2008 is primarily designed to ensure minimal or zero charging structures across the Eurozone.[1]

HOW IS IT GOING?

Since the endorsement of the European Commission's Financial Services Action Plan (FSAP) in March 2000, most of the Directives required to be implemented have been adopted in the EU nations. That is pretty impressive when you consider that this is a complex and massive change programme, operating across so many countries: the 15 original European Union nations plus the 10 accession countries that joined in 2004 and Bulgaria and Romania in 2007. Even more so when you consider that Turkey, Macedonia, Albania and many other countries are also seeking to join and will follow suit. However, adopted by the nations versus implemented by the banks are rather different statements.

For Europe's banks, the FSAP is a major headache. For example, banks face new payments rules (Regulation 2560/2001, SEPA and the Payment Services Directive), new accounting rules (IAS), new securities trading rules (MiFID) and new capital adequacy rules (Basel II). Add into the mix other regulatory requirements – such as European banks listed in the USA who need to comply with Sarbanes-Oxley – and you can see why some bankers feel blown away by a melting pot of change.

SO HOW HAVE EUROPE'S BANKS RESPONDED?

As discussed earlier, a major impact of the euro regulation has been the change to bank charging structures on low-value cross-border payments, whereby all cross-border ATM withdrawals and credit transfers under €50,000 must now be charged at the same rate as domestic ATM withdrawals and credit transfers whilst within the euro zone. These charging structures were introduced through EU Regulation 2560/2001, announced in 2001.

---

[1] Countries using the Euro began with twelve countries in 1999: Austria, Belgium, Finland, France, Germany, Greece, Ireland, Italy, Luxembourg, Netherlands, Portugal and Spain; this increased to thirteen in 2007 with the inclusion of Slovenia; Cyprus, Malta and Slovakia join in 2008; Bulgaria, Estonia, Hungary, Latvia, Lithuania, Poland and Romania are expected to join between 2010 and 2014.

The disappearance of such a rich vein of cross-border payments charges, margins and profits, for the banks is a big loss. According to a survey by ABN AMRO with EFMA and Cap Gemini, about €29 billion a year will be lost in bank margins for cross-border payments once the PSD is fully in place. At the same time, the cost of converting systems to comply with new legislation and new initiatives is a major cost. My estimate is around €10 billion of additional investment is being made by banks from 2006 through 2010 as the cost to replace all the interfaces to traditional clearing systems with new pan-European infrastructures. Nevertheless, that change is underway and has been critical to banks being able to continue operations with the blessing of the European Commission, rather than their wrath. How have the banks managed such a massive change programme?.

The change programme began in earnest with a meeting of Europe's key financial market players in Brussels in March 2002. The meeting included key personnel from 42 European banks, three Credit Sector Associations – EACB (European Association of Co-operative Banks), ESBG (European Savings Banks Group), FBE (European Banking Federation) – and the EBA (Euro Banking Association).

The reason this meeting was critical was that it resulted in the financial markets agreeing the plan for the creation of a Single Euro Payments Area (SEPA) with the vision to ensure that 'by 2010, Euroland payments will be treated like domestic payments'. The meeting also created the European Payments Council (EPC), to provide the governance structure to guide and implement SEPA.

The implementation of that vision covers a wide variety of changes to low value cross-border payments. First there is the standardization of bank account numbers using the International Bank Account Number (IBAN) and Branch Identification Code (BIC) standards. There is then the introduction of a Pan-European Direct Debit (PE-DD) scheme and the replacement of national clearing houses with Pan-European Automated Clearing Houses (PE-ACH). Originally, the intention was to have a single PEACH under the EBA's STEP2 system but, after lengthy negotiations, there will now be a number of PEACHs which are likely to include the UK's Voca (formerly BACS), the Netherlands' Equens (formerly Interpay) and France's STET (formerly SIT). Equally, there are other changes, with procedures, guidelines, frameworks and rulebooks for the four key areas SEPA impacts: Credit Transfers (PEACH), Direct Debits (PEDD), Cards (Credit and Debit Cards) and Cash (Cash Handling and Cash Management).

STEP2: THE PAN-EUROPEAN AUTOMATED CLEARING HOUSE (PE-ACH)

With the announcement of SEPA, the EBA began development of the new generation of ACH, the PEACH, targeted to provide a simple cross-border euro processing ACH. The PEACH was called STEP2, based upon the first STEP – which stands for Straight Through Euro Processing – that had been introduced to support the original introduction of the euro in 1999.

STEP2 was launched in April 2003 in cooperation with SIA of Italy as a technology partner and SWIFT as a messaging partner, using the latest technologies and XML standards. The intent is to supersede the national ACH's with STEP2 and, sure enough, the system is slowly growing in stature processing almost 400,000 transactions per day on average at the start of 2007, up from 145,000 transactions on average per day two years earlier.

In January 2007, STEP2 counts more than 107 direct participants and 1,600 indirect participants (indirect participants are banks that are known to the system but send and receive their payment messages through a direct participant) compared to 87 direct and 1,350 indirect two years earlier.

All very worthy but there is an awful long way to go. The biggest issue is that the EBA can launch many initiatives using new technologies but most of the banks are still grappling with their own proprietary ACH's. Over thirty national and domestic ACH's were operating across Europe processing euros at the start of 2007, and any pan-European player already has to interface with these.

There are also many larger ACH processing infrastructures in existence that could have more weight than STEP2. For example, the UK's Voca, formerly BACS, processes an average daily volume of around 20 million transactions, peaking at 100 million a day, compared to STEP2's 320,000 average daily volume.

THE MELTING POT BOILS

Then you have a number of other critical euro initiatives.

TARGET2 is consolidating high value payments infrastructures and is being driven by the European Central Bank in conjunction with the National Central Banks. SWIFT is driving change through SWIFTNet and its mandate under the Giovannini Committee to create a common clearing and settlement protocol.

Add on to this the rapid pace of change of retail payments with EBPP, EIPP, micro-payments, epurses, contactless payments. Then throw in the raft of other standards bodies influencing the markets and you really have a complex spaghetti of systems and standards that needs addressing fast if the European Commission's objective is to be achieved. Remember, that objective is a 'Single Payment Area, in which citizens and businesses can make cross-border payments as easily, safely and efficiently as they can within their own countries and subject to identical charges.'

To achieve that objective, European bankers need to have clarity. Clarity can only be driven if someone unstrings the spaghetti of systems and standards.

The spaghetti comprises:

- legacy infrastructures that cost billions to maintain (banks spend about $14 billion per year on payment technologies);
- governments and central banks that invest in domestic payments infrastructures at the possible expense of the pan-European objectives;
- new technologies that are displacing existing operations and infrastructures as rapidly as they appear;
- a range of standards bodies who want to be the owners of the standard to secure their own futures; and
- global players who can muscle their own structure at the expense of the small players who cannot keep up.

Unless the spaghetti is unraveled, most banks will be between a rock and a hard place, with many of the smaller banks only able to cope with cross-border payments by outsourcing this capability. Equally, losing profitability and margins on cross-border euro activities whilst having to invest heavily in new infrastructures and systems, leads to the same conclusion.

And the most likely people to outsource to will be the big global players – Citibank, HSBC, JPMorgan, Deutsche Bank – who have the breadth of scope and depth of pockets to sustain this forced change programme across the Eurozone.

Thank goodness Charlie McCreevy, the European Commissioner for Internal Market and Services, promised us in December 2004 that we could 'rest assured, there won't be another (Financial Services) Action Plan'. He possibly made this statement in light of the issues there have been in pushing forward the agenda with the Markets in Financial Instruments Directive (MiFID, as discussed in Chapter 20) and the Payment Services Directive (PSD).

THE HIGHS AND LOWS OF THE PAYMENT SERVICES DIRECTIVE

The Payment Services Directive first draft was released in December 2005, and became a pan-European legislative structure by January 2008 as SEPA was implemented.[2]

The Directive has two main objectives. First, to generate more competition in payment markets by removing the barriers to market entry, such as access to payments infrastructures. Currently, the diverging legal rules in the different Member States of Europe create major barriers to entry for new payment service providers, such as supermarkets and telecoms firms. Second, to provide a simplified and fully harmonised set of rules across all of the European geography, with regard to the information requirements and the rights and obligations linked to the provision and use of payment services. This included making it mandatory to clear payments within 24 hours of close of business, known as D+1, for all credit transfers without any currency conversion and as a default for all other payments, as well as a whole load of other rulings on revocability, refunding and legal liabilities.

Charlie McCreevy – the European Commissioner for the Internal Markets of Europe and the man who owns the Plan, the Financial Services Action Plan (FSAP) that is – released the Directive on 1 December 2005, and made a number of specific statements about its implications.

For example he said: 'I count on the banking industry, which is responsible for removing the technical barriers which stand in the way of a Single Euro Payment Area, to accelerate its work.'

Reading between the lines, that loosely translates as: 'I count on the banking industry who are focusing upon the Eurozone to pull their finger out and start working out how to make Europe's payments work.'

This is apparent because the release makes it clear that the Directive includes the Swedish Krona, the British Pound, the Polish Zloty and the Hungarian Forint. As a result, all the work done to date on creating a Single Euro Payments Area has to be extended from a Euro area to a European Area. In other words, a Pan-European ACH and Pan-European Direct Debit, not a Eurozone PE-ACH and PE-DD.

Another point made in the release is that the 'Single Payment Area will benefit each and every European and bring big-money savings to the EU economy to the tune of €50–€100 billion a year.'

Reading between the lines, that means: 'The banks have been making huge amounts of money at European citizens expense and so we are going to get rid of their margins on payments.'

---

[2] At the time of publication this Directive had not been ratified by the European Parliament, but is expected to pass into law in January 2008 when SEPA is implemented by Europe's banks.

This too is clear because the cost of the SPA to Europe's banks will be in excess of €40 billion. That figure is based on two calculations. The first is that at least €29 billion of revenue will be lost, which is the figure ABN Amro identified as the top-side of a single payment area for just the euro. Bear in mind this is now for all European countries, not just the Eurozone, and that number will increase. Second, my own estimates based upon extensive discussions with Europe's bankers is that there will be at least an additional €10 billion investment in new European payments infrastructures between 2006 and 2009, to create the new PE-ACHs, PE-DDs, RTGSs and so on. This is why, in total, at least €40 billion will be lost to the banking industry and transferred as benefits for the citizens and businesses of Europe.

As can be seen, these statements, the PSD itself and the SEPA project is a massive change to European banking and payments. As a result, the first draft of the PSD was hotly contested and argued by the banks and the Commission during 2006, with subsequent papers produced such as the SEPA Incentives Paper in February 2006 by the European Commission. This Paper tried to introduce some half-way measures to encourage banks to implement all of the requirements for the PSD and SEPA.

The Payment Services Directive was then redrafted in February 2007 to address a number of political issues that had been discussed during 2006 including issues on:

- the scope of the PSD;
- how to deal with micropayments;
- agreement as to when a payment order starts, e.g. upon receipt or acceptance;
- the overall execution times (D+1 or longer);
- the scope of the responsibilities of payment service providers;
- the scope of liability of payment service providers;
- value dating and the availability of funds;

and many other related issues.

The fundamental issues arise from the treatment of banks versus other payment providers, such as PayPal and First Data, as well as ACHs who can now offer commercial payment processing services, such as Voca and Equens. Other issues included the fact that different products for different countries work in different ways. For example, direct debits in France and Italy are very different to those in the UK and Finland. In Italy, each direct debit transaction is authorised before payment is taken from the account whilst, in the UK, payment is taken without individual transaction authorisations. In addition, issues related to time to process severely challenged other countries, such as Germany, where D+1 processing – a 24-hour turnaround – is mandated when Germany currently runs five day processing cycles on most credit transfers.

The criticality of all of this discussion being that until the PSD passed into law, none of the requirements of SEPA for a PEDD (Direct Debits) or PEACH (Credit Transfers) are legally recognised as cross-border instruments. That is why the PSD is so critical to SEPA's two critical dates:

- 1st January 2008, when the PEACH and PEDD must be in place; and
- 31st December 2010, when national ACHs need to be dismantled and closed down.

Neither date can be implemented whilst the legal framework does not exist.

Nevertheless, the European Parliament have pushed hard to get this through and it would be surprising if the PSD were not ratified before the end of 2007.[3]

SEPA AND THE PSD: THE BOTTOM-LINE FOR EUROPEAN BANKS

The point about what this means to Europe's banks is perhaps best summed up in this abridged statement from the release: 'The price to provide a basic payment service is €34 a year for the average customer in the Netherlands compared to €252 in Italy. Price is not the only difference. In some member states payments are executed the same day or even in real time, whereas in other Member States the same payment can take three days or longer.'

This means that many banks in Europe will lose revenues whilst many others will get out of payments altogether. For the latter, they will have to ask the question: 'What do we do now?' Deliver improved and differentiated client service through integrating outsourced payment services might be one answer.

For a small few – the ABN Amros, INGs, BNPs, Citigroups and JPMorgans of this world – SPA brings into play a new era of mega pan-European bank payment services. These payment gorillas will take over from the small players, will bear the brunt of the investment costs and reap the bulk of the commercial rewards.

In fact, what it really means is that if you are in the payments business and you have not worked out your strategy for SEPA and the PSD yet, you are probably too late. Banks, payments processors and others need to work out fast whether they are going to be a payments gorilla, a payments service provider to the gorillas, a payments client of the gorillas or a non-payments provider of financial services.

---

[3] These issues were unresolved at the time of publication, but we suspect the pain of the changes required by SEPA and the PSD will rage through 2007 and onwards.

Part 4
Investment Banker's Challenges

The first two chapters of this section follow on naturally from Chapter 18, which reviewed Europe's regulatory agenda for payments.

The opening chapter looks at two investment market changes which are critical to the USA and Europe, RegNMS (Regulation National Market Systems) and MiFID (the Markets in Financial Instruments Directive). The latter is the subject of another book I have recently pulled together through contributions from friends and colleagues across the European Commission and European financial markets entitled, *The Future of Investing: In Europe's Markets after MiFID*. This leads nicely into Chapter 20 which specifically overviews MiFID in depth, and is a twin chapter to Chapter 18, in terms of being a review of the two key pillars of the European legislative drive to reform Europe's securities markets.

But first to RegNMS and MiFID. Europe's agenda is one of trying to achieve a single securities and trading infrastructure with simple, straight-through processing from order to execution to clearing or settlement. This is far removed from today's European operations of multiple national exchanges, market-makers, clearing and settlement infrastructures. The aim is to create a market that looks and behaves like the US markets. Meanwhile, the US market is also reforming to increase transparancy and therefore liquidity by stamping down on pass-through networking, where electronic cross networks (ECNs) automatically pass orders to preferred execution venues.

In both cases, the key underlying factor is best execution: creating the ideal trading environment for the investor to feel confident they are getting the best price for their investment at the time of the trade being made. All very laudable objectives but proving difficult to achieve in practice.

The second chapter in this section is a twin chapter with Chapter 18, the Future of European payments, as they both discuss key European regulatory agendas in the form of the Payment Services Directive in Chapter 18 and the Markets in Financial Instruments Directive (MiFID) in Chapter 20. You might therefore find it useful to read Chapters 18 and 20 together.

Alternatively, you may read the three chapters – 18, 19 and 20 – together, in which case I would recommend you read Chapters 4 and 5 beforehand as a reminder, as these chapters provide further backdrop to the theme of regulation and compliance.

Alongside these regulatory drivers however are many other factors affecting the global financial markets, not the least of which is the drive towards ever more sophisticated trading and complex financial instruments. This forms the focus of the final two chapters in this section.

Chapter 21 in particular looks at the impact of algorithmic trading models and how they have changed the investment markets globally. As more and more business moves onto automated platforms, human traders have to engage in more and more complex and sophisticated Over-The-Counter (OTC) trading strategies, such as credit derivatives and even more complex derivatives of derivatives. As the markets move in this direction, they also build in more risk. After all, the more complex the trading instrument, the more difficult it is to understand and the more difficult it is to understand, the more likely it is to be risky. That is the conclusion of Chapter 22, which recounts some of the most lurid stories of financial greed in the 20th and 21st Centuries, ranging from the IPO internet boom and bust hype cycle of trading in the late 1990s through to the collapse of Enron, Worldcom and Parmalat in the early 2000s.

Some would say these are all accredited to derivatives risk; others would say it is just investors' stupidity. Make up your own mind, but governments are determined to ensure that markets behave in the investor's best interests, so there is a heavy friction and trade-off between high risk, high return strategies and best execution and transparency.

It will be interesting to see who wins.

19

Best Execution with Best Intentions

Europe and America are introducing a wave of regulatory changes that are creating as much commotion as Basel II. For the world's capital markets, two regulations are really creating a stir namely: Europe's Markets in Financial Instruments Directive, MiFID, and America's Regulation National Market System, RegNMS. Both changes came into effect in 2007 and both regulations are similar in principle, but differ in fundamental areas. Their similarity is that both regulations aim to ensure best price execution, and the concern for securities players is how these legislative changes will impact their margins, pricing and competitiveness.

For example, under Regulation NMS, a market centre must 'establish, maintain, and enforce policies and procedures reasonably designed to prevent "trade-throughs" – the execution of an order in its market at a price that is inferior to a price displayed in another market'. The Regulation goes on to argue that a national market system which is run in an efficient manner should guarantee the 'best execution' for each and every transaction within an order.

MiFID has a raft of statements with a similar intent. A specific example is detailed in Article 21 which deals with 'best execution' at the most favourable terms to the client. Within Article 21 are statements such as 'the order execution policy shall include those venues that enable the investment firm to obtain on a consistent basis, the best possible results for the execution of client orders'.

But MiFID goes a step further than Regulation NMS with Article 27, which states that dealers 'shall make public their quotes on a regular and continuous basis during normal trading hours – the quote shall be made public in a manner which is easily accessible to other market participants on a reasonable commercial basis'.

This is specifically targeted at the off-exchange trading and the unregulated dealings of brokers trading off their own book of business, defined as 'systematic internalisers'.

That means European broker-dealers, who previously could compete from a private book of business at competitive rates, must now publish their prices publicly and be able to prove that their price is better than their competitors' best price at the time of the trade.

However, as managing director and international general counsel of Morgan Stanley, Keith Clark, stated in the International Financial Law Review Banking Yearbook of 2004:

> Article 27 of MiFID, which deals with pre-trade transparency, is a political compromise driven by all the worst elements of European lawmaking. It is quite difficult to reconcile the requirements of France and Italy, which have historically had difficulties with off-exchange trading, with the internalisation approach that has worked well in the US and which we would have preferred to have been the model in Europe.

What he means by this is that CESR – the Committee of European Securities Regulators who are responsible for writing the MiFID Regulations – has created a Directive based upon every possibility of variance to the Nth degree of detail. CESR have basically tried to take into account all aspects of all markets in Europe, and documented all possible nuances of how these markets operate, to ensure that every nuance of every market now offers best price execution. It might have been better just to extend the principles of the intentions of what MiFID is meant to achieve rather than battening down every detail. That is why the Directive became a can of worms and involved lengthy debates from mid-2004 to the end of 2006 in order to tone down the original wordings of the MiFID into something that could actually be implemented, as outlined in the next chapter.

The net result of these two regulatory drivers, RegNMS and the MiFID, is that America's and Europe's capital markets are feeling an immense sense of loss of competitiveness because margins are squeezed due to market transparency, whilst costs are increased due to increased regulatory overheads.

And these Regulations do imply significant cost overheads. For example, the implication of MiFID Articles 21 and 27 – publicly issuing prices to ensure best execution – is that a European dealer now has to track and store every price movement for each and every financial instrument from every market player at every micro-second of market trading. They then have to store that information for as long as the regulators require, in proving that they executed at the best price for all equities, bonds and derivatives they trade across the spread of their portfolio. Considering the volume and value of trading in the marketplace, that implies one heck of a lot of data storage.

Mind you, the impact upon brokers is nowhere near as great as the impact upon Europe's exchanges. Before the MiFID, Europe's regulations were based upon concentration rules which tried to force all trading through Europe's national exchanges. This failed as broker-dealers were trading extensively off their own book of business through internalisation. The result is that the MiFID removes those concentration rules and so Europe's exchanges are now facing open and direct competition with ECNs, such as Instinet's Chi-x, and brokers' internal price matching systems, known as 'dark pools', such as JP Morgan Chase's Aqua and Arid.

This is making some markets more competitive in Europe though, with London being the most dynamic of Europe's markets due to the skill sets in the City, as well as the dominance of London as a global bridge to liquidity. In fact, in January 2007, McKinsey issued a report, commissioned by New York Mayor Michael Bloomberg, which estimated up to 7% of Wall Street workers – 60,000 workers – would lose their jobs by 2012. The reasons cited were the overwhelming burden of U.S. regulations, especially Sarbanes-Oxley, compared to the ease of operating in London's capital markets.

The cost burdens and constraints of have become a major cause for concern in the USA a result. For example, at a 2005 SEC open meeting regarding RegNMS, dissenting Commissioner Cynthia Glassman made the following point: 'The cost savings to investors from the rule is estimated at a mere $321 million. . .given that dollar value of trading totalled $18.7 trillion in 2003, $321 million is only a rounding error. . .the cost-benefit analysis estimates start-up costs at $143.8 million, with average annual ongoing costs of approximately $22 million.'

Whatever the pros and cons of regulatory changes, the implications for the securities industry is heightened transparency, reduced margins, increased onus upon data integrity and storage, and an honesty that has had to be forced into the marketplace due to the lack of trust of off-exchange trading in the past. And maybe that is where we should learn our lessons in that it was the dealings of the few that has created the problems for the many.

20

Make or Break for Europe's Equities Markets

In the last two chapters, we have discussed various market factors related to European and American regulatory regimes. In this chapter, we look specifically at the major implications of Europe's Markets in Financial Instruments Directive, MiFID, which I have been tracking since its release.

THE MARKETS IN FINANCIAL INSTRUMENTS DIRECTIVE (MIFID)

MiFID came into being in early 2004 although it was actually dreamt up back in the early 1990s when the European Commission released the Investment Services Directive (ISD). In that first Directive, the Commission tried to force concentration rules into the European equities markets, which actually meant concentrating all trading activities through the national exchanges such as the Deutsche Börse, the Bourse de Paris and the London Stock Exchange. After a decade, those concentration rules were clearly not working as many broker-dealers were trading off-exchange using their own book of business. This is a generally recognised activity called 'internalisation', and commonly takes the form of Over-The-Counter (OTC) trading.

In practice, OTC internalisation means that you hold large blocks of trading instruments internally and buy and sell them in a 'virtual exchange' internally. Don't get me wrong though, this Directive does not apply to all OTC trading but only to those firms who do this on an 'organised, frequent and systematic basis'. The firms that fall into this category are then called 'systematic internalisers' which is a critical part of understanding the MiFID because it is new.

Part of the issue with the MiFID, referred to in the previous chapter, is that it did not define what 'organised, frequent and systematic' actually meant. In fact, the definition changed as the MiFID was being drafted and finalised. For example, the original definition in the MiFID's first wordings was that a systematic internaliser would apply to those firms who traded 15% or more of their business through internalisation. This criteria was dropped when it was realised it was too difficult to measure and enforce. Now, it is left with the national regulators – the UK's FSA, Germany's BaFIN, France's AMF and so forth – to determine which firms are and are not internalisers. Most regulators have taken the approach that the brokers themselves need to declare whether they do this on an 'organised, frequent and systematic basis'. In other words, 'systematic internalisers' are those broker-dealers who declare themselves as firms that trade internally regularly; and the MiFID is specifically targeted towards those internalisers rather than to all firms trading internally.

So what is the problem with trading internally regularly?

The problem the European Commission had with the regular OTC trading firms, who are typically market-makers, is that these firms determine many of Europe's key share movements – about 80% of shares are traded by 20% of the firms – and all of that trading can be hidden within the trading firm. In other words, it is share trading that is not made available to general investors or exposed to the regulator's touch.

Nevertheless, the impact upon internalisers is minimal when compared to the impact upon Europe's exchanges. This is due to the fact that, before the MiFID, Europe's exchanges were defined as the preferred trading venues through concentration rules, which aimed to force all trading through the national stock exchange. These rules were encapsulated in the Investment Services Directive (ISD) of 1993 which the MiFID replaced. The fact is that the ISD's concentration rules failed, as broker-dealers were trading extensively off their own book of business. The result is that the MiFID removes those concentration rules and so Europe's exchanges are now facing open and direct competition with what are termed Multilateral Trading Facilities, such as virt-x and Chi-x, as well as brokers' internal price matching systems, known as 'dark pools', such as JPMorgan Chase's Aqua and Arid.

Another little quirk occurred as MiFID was born which was that a certain gentleman from Belgium known as Alexandre Lamfalussy, had just delivered his principles for better regulation of the securities markets. The European Commission had asked Baron Lamfalussy – the respected former president of the European Monetary Institute – to investigate how their regulatory process affected Europe's financial institutions as a requirement of the Lisbon meeting of 2000 when the Financial Services Action Plan (FSAP) was first created.

Baron Lamfalussy and his Committee of Wise Men, known as the Lamfalussy Committee, came back with a four-level process as follows:

Level 1 European Commission State the Principles of the Directive through a new body known as the EU Securities Committee (ESC) whilst another new body, the Committee of European Securities Regulators (CESR), develop the detailed wordings of the Directive.

Level 2 Consultation Period with industry representatives, governments and regulators of the Member States of the EU, before the Directive is endorsed by the European Parliament.

Level 3 The Directive is ratified by the European Parliament and passed into member states' governments and regulators to implement national legislation.

Level 4 The Directive is Law.

These four levels were proudly presented by Baron Lamfalussy to the European Commission in February 2001. Once agreed, the new process of regulation awaited its first test and the first securities regulation to really stretch the Lamfalussy process was . . . yes, you've guessed it . . . MiFID.

So, the European Commission began Level 1 with the idea of redrafting the ISD of 1993. At that point, the underlying principles of what the Directive should cover were being developed, which were that concentration rules did not work and the Directive aimed to increase transparency and best execution by focusing on internalisation issues.

Everything seemed fine in the rose garden of Europe's better regulation process.

That was until CESR (the Committee of European Securities Regulators) got their quill pens out and began to draft the detailed wordings for MiFID which were released in April 2004. That date set the milestone as the process moved from principles to consultation, as in from Lamfalussy Level 1 to Level 2. Now it gets interesting.

During the process thus far, most of the discussions had been between regulators, compliance departments of securities firms and some industry leaders. Once the consultation period started, a slow burn began. Upon release of the draft Directive, the European Commission had set the date for MiFID implementation, as in Level 4, to be April 2006 – two years after Level 1's principles came into force.

The Level 4 implementation of the Directive actually ended up being pushed back twice before it passed into country laws, and ended up being split between pan-European regulation and national codes of conduct. The pan-European regulatory areas covered transparency rules for price publishing and were implemented in November 2007, whilst specific country-based conduct of business rules were introduced at a varying rate by member states from November 2007 through to the summer of 2008. These conduct of business rules covered client handling requirements, such as KYC (Know Your Customer) and Client Classifications and contracts, as well as organisational requirements such as outsourcing rules and investment research.

The slippages were not the result of the European Commission being tardy or wayward. In fact, the Commission was surprisingly accommodating in their consultative approach. That is the spirit of Level 2, which has proven to be even more consultative than expected due to massive amounts of pressure to change. Pressure from sell-side firms in particular, as well as some exchanges, buy-side firms, industry regulators, treasury departments, even vendors, consultants and others.

This pressure built during 2004 like a slow-burning pressure cooker and exploded during 2005. The explosion was that MiFID was wrong. What was wrong? A lot.

To start with, much of MiFID's detailed wordings released in April 2004 were ambiguous or did not represent the actuality of how the markets worked.

For example, Article 29 focused upon pre-trade transparency requirements for Multilateral Trading Facilities (MTFs). MTFs are typically electronic networking venues such as an ECN (Electronic Cross Network) or ATS (Alternative Trading System). Article 29 in the original MiFID wordings read as follows:

All MTFs must '. . .make public current bid and offer prices and the depth of trading interests at these prices. . .on reasonable commercial terms and on a continuous basis during normal trading hours'.

Now this may seem picky, but some folks wondered what 'normal trading hours' meant. Nine till five? When the markets opened and closed? When all of Europe's exchanges were open? Equally, this is fine for MTFs but what about the systematic internalisers? What do they have to make public in terms of their 'depth of trading interests'?

That is just but one example of a thousand questions raised as broker-dealers, exchanges and vendors picked through the detail of MiFID. Most of the issues were also related to changes to IT Systems. For example, MiFID had words about being able to reconstitute a trade in its entirety for a period of five years. That raised fundamental questions around what does 'reconstitution' mean because if it included all data and voice transactions, as in telephone calls, then the implications for data storage and retrieval were horrendous.

None of these questions were raised initially because the interface between MiFID's wordsmiths and the industry were the compliance people, who were not technologists. It was only when the technologists read MiFID that they realised it could be a nightmare. In particular, a few people in London realised the full extent of the havoc MiFID might create in the technology rooms and began championing the campaign to change it.

One particular catalyst in this campaign was the launch of the MiFID Joint Working Group (JWG) in May 2005. The MiFID JWG mobilised the key industry associations of FIX

Protocol Ltd, ISITC Europe, the Reference Data User Group (RDUG) and SIIA/FISD to work together to analyse MiFID's true costs. The JWG was followed by the formation of another group, known as MiFID Connect, in November 2005. MiFID Connect combined the forces of the major UK Financial Market Trade Associations, including the Association of British Insurers (ABI), the Association of Private Client Investment Managers and Stockbrokers (APCIMS), the Association of Foreign Banks (AFB), the Bond Market Association, the British Bankers' Association (BBA), the Building Societies Association (BSA), the Futures and Options Association (FOA), the International Capital Market Association (ICMA), the Investment Management Association (IMA), the International Swaps and Derivatives Association (ISDA) and the London Investment Banking Association (LIBA). The purpose of this group was to establish a programme for reducing the legal risk and simplifying the implementation of MiFID.

The MiFID JWG and MiFID Connect groups lobbied the European Commission heavily throughout 2005 and 2006, as well as other bodies involved in the investment markets including the regulators and treasury departments of governments of Europe's Member States. That is one of the reasons why the final form of MiFID is viewed as being much less onerous to the markets than the original April 2004 draft. Key sections were cut back and redrafted and, in its final form, the biggest impact appears to be upon Europe's exchanges.

THE END OF EUROPE'S EXCHANGES?

As mentioned in the opening paragraphs, MiFID replaces the Investment Services Directive, which tried to force concentration rules for trading activities to take place through the national exchanges. Because this did not work, MiFID aims to make trading on or off exchanges transparent. However, in that process, the Deutsche Börse, Euronext and the London Stock Exchange all become pure trading venues. This means that you could just as easily use other trading venues under MiFID, including systematic internalisers and multilateral trading facilities.

That is why late 2006 saw some interesting developments with the launch of Project Boat, Project Turquoise, and Equiduct.

Project Boat was formed in October 2006 by a group of leading investments banks. These banks, including ABN AMRO, Citigroup, Credit Suisse, Deutsche Bank, Goldman Sachs, HSBC, Merrill Lynch, Morgan Stanley and UBS, formed a consortium to aggregate European trade data and market data in competition with the traditional Exchanges. The aim was to take advantage of the MiFID regulations that allow trade reporting to any compliant entity, rather than forcing participants to report to the relevant Exchanges – the concentration rules. Those rules meant that market participants were meant to report OTC trades to Exchanges, who charged fees to receive this information, then generate further revenue from collating and selling this information. The Project Boat approach will allow members to retain the fees for themselves and create opportunities for revenue generation. Another interesting feature of Project Boat is that any qualified market participant can use the platform.

This was rapidly followed in November 2006 by the announcement of Project Turquoise. Project Turquoise combines the focused efforts of seven leading investment banks to run their own exchange, in competition with other European Exchanges which they claim are too expensive. In particular, the seven banks involved – Citigroup, Credit Suisse, Deutsche Bank, Goldman Sachs, Merrill Lynch, Morgan Stanley and UBS – generate half of the volume of trading on the London Stock Exchange (LSE). LSE's share price dropped 10% on the day of the announcement.

Similarly, in November 2006, Equiduct was launched. Equiduct is based upon a revamped version of EASDAQ, the European exchange that disappeared in the internet bust. The service became available in April 2007 offering a pan-European pre- and post-trade reporting service with best execution for equities trading, again taking advantage of the opportunities presented by MiFID.

The result of these services is that a Frankfurt based trader might have a direct connection to the Deutsche Bourse and then use Equiduct or Project Boat to access the other exchanges and equity prices. This ensures that they avoid the high costs of having to build infrastructures to connect to all of the internalisers, MTFs and national exchanges if they were trying to build a pan-European trading service, and is particularly relevant to smaller trading firms, which is one of the key intents of MiFID: to make Europe's trading venues more liquid and transparent.

The issue for the traditional exchanges however is how to compete. As Charlie McCreevy, the Commissioner in charge of the Internal Market and Services responsible for MiFID, stated in an address to the British Bankers Association in October 2006, 'We believe the scope for competition and innovation that the MiFID will generate will be significant and lasting. We are already seeing consolidation moves by exchanges, and new transaction platforms for market players. I look forward to seeing even more creative developments in the wake of the MiFID revolution.'

This referred to the bottom-line of consolidation of the national exchanges which is part of the outcome of MiFID and other moves. This was illustrated by the rapid growth of Euronext. Euronext was formed in September 2000 when the national exchanges of Amsterdam, Brussels and Paris merged. From there, various other exchanges consolidated into Euronext, including LIFFE (London International Financial Futures and Options Exchange) and the Portuguese exchange BVLP (Bolsa de Valores de Lisboa e Porto) in 2002.

It is this style of consolidation that MiFID seeks to deliver, and certainly the huge debate over the future of the London Stock Exchange (LSE) in 2006 illustrated this well. LSE became a target in a three-way battle between the New York Stock Exchange and NASDAQ of the USA, along with Macquarie Bank of Australia. The result was that LSE's share price tripled in value from a lowly £4.53 in April 2005 to a peak of £12.76 one year later, in May 2006.

In addition, the value of national exchanges is also challenged in the post-MiFID world as MiFID introduces 'liquid shares'. Liquid shares are defined using a number of factors, including the idea that they have a free float of more than €500 million and more than €2 million and 500 transactions traded. In other words, they are the most popular shares in each of Europe's markets.

The big question here is that there is currently a range of market indices, such as the FTSE100, DAX 40, CAC 40, MIB 30, IBEX 35, not forgetting the Euronext100 and 150 and DJ Stoxx. These indices are run by and dependent upon member states' national exchanges. Well, all of that may well disappear under the post-MiFID world of trading as MiFID defines a Euro500. These are the 500 or more liquid shares defined under MiFID which market-making internalisers must now publish as transparent share pricing and trading. Bang goes the FTSE, Euronext and other indices and, potentially, the exchanges that go with them.

There will no doubt be a major war over Europe's exchanges for the next few years as more exchange services and MTFs appear, and more merger and consolidation occurs.

WHAT WILL MIFID COST?

Now to the rub. What will MiFID cost?

There are figures ranging from €1 billion to €20 billion touted around. For individual firms, you hear numbers ranging from €5 million to €150 million. The fact is that few will know the real cost of MiFID until early in the next decade. However, some are investing heavily to gain advantages from MiFID. By way of example, one large internalising European market-maker told me they budgeted €120 million in 2007 for MiFID implementation; €80 million for the investment bank; and €40 million for the private bank and other investment-related areas of their corporation.

My own estimate is that the average broker-dealer firm who deals regularly over the counter and is categorised as a systematic internaliser, has spent an average €20 million on reorganisation of organisation, systems and structures, to comply.

Half of that spend was on a broad range of technologies including data storage and retrieval, networking overhaul to exploit IP-technologies, algorithmic trading and order management and routing applications to improve straight through processing, and so on. This was a considerable investment with the bulk of it going into data warehousing and interoperability. Interoperability is driven through conformance with standards, with the FIX Protocol being a winner in setting the standards for the pre-trade and trade area. Meantime, most OTC firms also underwent extensive business process change to enable best execution compliance, and so a radical shake-up of most firms occurred.

This was not just for the systematic internalisers though, as buy-side to sell-side networking, linkage and operations all changed too. This was due to other factors, in addition to MiFID, coming into play such as the stripping of bundled services by brokers. This is another regulatory driver emerging across the markets towards the end of the 2000s. Known as 'unbundling', these regulations take the view that brokers should no longer generate commission by 'hiding' commissions in their client billing. For example, brokers tradition-ally have provided billing statements to their institutional investors and fund managers which bundle all services – connectivity, trade execution, research, market data and so forth – into a same statement. Under unbundled regulations, each component of the trade lifecycle has to be itemised with all charges shown explicitly for each time.

The result is that the trade lifecycle will be challenged as costs become transparent.

The outcome is that asset managers are paying some firms for trade execution only, whilst research and connectivity they have insourced. Some sell-side firms have spun-off services to be sold separately, such as research, and no longer offer this as part of their core operations. Connectivity has been overhauled with lower-cost connections demanded by using internet-based networking instead of the traditional proprietary fixed and leased lines.

One of the market areas that changed the most as a result is connectivity between the buy- and sell- side operators. The sell-side was no longer able to sustain paying for buy-side connectivity due to transparent pricing strategies where all of their trading costs of became visible to the buy-side. As connectivity pricing was outside the control of sell-side players, and relied on firms like TNS and BT Radianz, the sell-side gradually let the buy-side determine their own cost of connectivity with many asset managers and investors contracting directly with the network providers.

The more you think about it, the more extreme the implications of change in the European securities markets as national exchanges are opened to direct competition and sell-side firms pricing is stripped bare. The result is that all securities firms involved in trading equities, options, derivatives, bonds and foreign exchange have had to overhaul their operations to avoid being railroaded by the Directive. And yes, you heard correctly, MiFID does include all trading instruments not, as most people misperceived, just equities.

This is why Merrill Lynch and Citigroup recently moved to develop their own exchange platforms which led to the creation of Project Boat. As such, they became electronic trading venues or MTFs and so take advantage of the differing rules for MTFs as compared to systematic internalisers.

Therefore, although individual costs of MiFID for the average systematic internaliser is around the €20 million mark, there is no way to estimate the total cost of MiFID for European securities firms because there are questions as to how many systematic internalisers there will be.

Estimates ranged from 50 to 500 systematic internalisers across Europe's securities markets. The actual final number will depend upon how many internalisers convert to MTFs, how many firms declare themselves to be internalisers, and how many regulators determine that their national securities firms are trading as internalisers.

OTC firms and regulators determine whether firms are systematic internalisers by using the definition that it is those firms who trade in an 'organised, frequent and systematic' manner off their own book of business. That definition is still very loose and hence some EU states may have three systematic internalisers, whilst others might have thirty.

Therefore, estimating the total costs of MiFID is pretty much impossible. All we can say is: a lot!

IS THAT IT?

That pretty completes the review of Europe's most critical Directive, MiFID. Combined with Chapter 17, which reviewd the Payment Services Directive (PSD) and SEPA, this gives you a comprehensive view of the major changes in Europe's financial markets.

The MiFID and the PSD are two central pillars of the Financial Services Action Plan (FSAP). There are also other activities such as the Mortgage Credit White Paper, revised Banking and Insurance Directives relating to Mergers and Acquisitions, Giovannini's Clearing and Settlement standards, the Retail Financial Services Expert Group, the eMoney Directive. . .the list goes on and on. In fact, there is a virtually a never-ending list of committees, conferences, councils, commentaries, conclusions, conversations and more, that are debating, discussing, developing, delivering and driving the FSAP.

The FSAP itself is still only half-way through its cycle of development and implementation, but it now has the basic pillars and foundations built. The brickwork and roofing is still to be built by Europe's banks.

Europe's biggest pan-European operators – ABN AMRO, ING, Deutsche Bank, BNP Paribas, Société Generale, and so on – as well as the other banks in Europe with pan-European capabilities – CitiGroup, Bank of America, JPMorgan Chase – see the Financial Services Action Plan as a great opportunity. An opportunity to create an integrated pan-European banking operation. One which could compete across Europe for the business of the world's largest organisations. In cash and treasury management operations therefore, the FSAP has to be great news for both corporates and pan-European banks.

For the corporate, it means they can potentially run their complete European business through a single account, rather than having an account in every nation. That should mean considerable cost savings. Even if they do not go to a single European account, they will get considerable cost savings anyway as the FSAP wipes out banks' cross-border margins.

For the pan-European bank, it means they can finally consolidate and create a competitive European financial zone. One that competes on equal status with any geography in the world. One where the biggest banks can only get bigger and where they can truly leverage the economies of scale that a harmonised and integrated European market offers.

Meantime, for the central banks and national exchanges, clearing houses and infrastructures across Europe that support these activities, there will be blood on the floor when the inevitable fall-out from these changes hits.

In the time left to implement the FSAP, and the years that follow as banks, clearing houses, brokers, asset managers, insurers, intermediaries and the rest fight for position, there will be a great battle. A battle for Economic and Monetary Union supremacy and survival. The equivalent in the financial markets of Tolkien's epic battles in *The Lord of the Rings*. Only in this battle, there is room for more than one ring and the question is which firms will have a hand left in the markets to wear them once the battle is concluded.

It should be fun to watch.

This article is part of a series of articles published by Wiley in the book, 'The Future of Investing: In Europe's Markets after MiFID'. The book has contributions from leading figures in the European industry including the European Commission, MiFID Connect, the MiFID Joint Working Group, the British Bankers' Association and the European Business School. In addition, there are specific viewpoints collected from leading market players such as SWIFT, Reuters and Equiduct, as well as critical industry observers and suppliers, including Barlow Lyde & Gilbert, Atos Consulting, Bearing Point, Capco, IBM, Intel and SunGard.

21
To Trade or Not to Trade?

In these times of increasing automation and regulation, how can an honest broker-dealer make a dollar or euro? Some would consider chucking it in and keeping it simple, whilst others are moving towards complexity. Which trading options will work and how do you play the markets for advantage in the future?

The issue these days is that there are few market areas where you can really buck the system. By 'buck the system', I mean find alternative trading strategies to really gain competitive advantage. The last real move in this direction was the creation of the credit derivatives market 10 years ago by JPMorgan. Credit derivatives are now a $12 trillion market – about the size of America's annual GDP – but even that is becoming a commodity.

There appear to be three profitable directions for trading strategies in the future. The first is to create much more complex trading strategies; the second is to create much more complex products; the third is to move simplify and outsource the trading operation to those who can afford the technological capabilities to manage this on your behalf. All three directions are totally reliant upon high-cost technology tools to win.

These strategies are not mutually exclusive but can be mutually inclusive, depending on your overall market objectives. Let's look at what each of these strategies mean in practice.

The first focuses upon creating much more complex trading systems using algorithmic trading. Algorithmic trading has historically been the domain of engineers and scientists. By way of example, of the key players involved in creating the credit derivatives markets, most were either science or mathematics graduates. In the words of the leader of the JPMorgan credit derivatives team at the time: 'I wanted to be a rocket scientist and ended up working on Wall Street.' Actually, the real leader of the team – Peter Hancock now of Integrated Finance Ltd – was a science student at Oxford University who wanted to be an inventor. . .you get the drift.

These rocket scientists started the market towards more automated trading back in the late 1990s using quantitative trading strategies and highly automated systems. This market began with buy-side hedge funds and sell-side brokers looking to find arbitrage and other complex plays in the equities and FX markets. The original tools, referred to then as program trading, would have allowed an investor to find micro-opportunities in real-time and make trading wins of a reasonable size. For example, if the value of Microsoft (MFT) shares increase by more than 0.5% and the value of IBM (IBM) shares decrease by more than 0.5% at the same time, then buy MFT and sell IBM.

Today, the tools are being used more and more to create cross-asset class plays in all markets and are getting really clever. For example, if the value of MFT shares increase by more than 0.5% within a 30 minute window during which IBM shares decrease by more than 0.5%, then buy MFT and sell IBM whilst taking a futures option on IBM purchase and MFT sale for one month. In addition, if Oracle shares rise whilst SAP fall during the same 30 minute window, follow with Oracle buy and SAP sell with a hedged futures option.

Finally, if these movements occur after a three-point rise in the NASDAQ, then shift FX strategy from euro to US dollars, with a sales option on the dollar.

In fact, you could add as many parameters as you wanted until you were happy you had played all the different criteria that might be required during that period. But it doesn't end there.

I was at a recent conference where one key algorithmic firm discussed two new concepts of algo trading using the concepts of 'TiVo playback' and 'graphic equalisers'. What they were getting at is the idea of placing all of your complicated ideas and strategies for trading into the system, and then seeing how they would have played out over the past 30 day trading cycle. To do this, the system stores all the trade and market data for the last month and then allows you to fast forward, reverse, pause and stop the market activities during that cycle in a style similar to using a TiVo player.

Now the incredibly clever bit. Whilst you are playing your TiVo market simulations, you can see what works and does not work as a trading strategy through a sort of graphic equaliser. The system, in other words, shows you green for good stuff and red for bad.

The more you find trading strategies that work, the more you store those in the good stuff and they become embedded into the software algorithms. Equally, if your strategies didn't work, you highlight those and that also becomes embedded into the software algorithms as the bad stuff. The result is that the software learns what works and doesn't work and builds that into future trading patterns.

The impact of this is that it provides asset managers the ability to test strategies and moves their trading advice away from their brokers and onto their systems. So, you may well ask, what's the point of active trading when the software tools are getting so good that they will ultimately always know the best trades to make with perfect timing?

In other words, if we create a 'perfect' market where all trading is so sophisticated using algo tools that you can only keep up if you use algorithmic trading, then those without algo tools are dead meat.

Well, not necessarily. And this leads to the second phase of market development which, as mentioned, is complementary to algorithmic trading.

If everyone has algo tools that learn trading strategies and always strike perfect trades with perfect timing, then those in the human world have to go and find something else to do, such as more complex credit derivatives.

When the JPMorgan team created credit derivatives in the late 1990s, they were looking for a way to create something that would be hard to copy. A bit like swaps, arbitrage and other futures and options, it was really a way to find another market.

Sounds easy, but if it was then every bank's investment team would be winners. What the JPMorgan team succeeded in doing is creating something that was hard to copy because, by the time others knew what it was, they had taken the lion's share of the market.

By way of a brief explanation. The way credit derivatives work is like an insurance policy for a bank's credit risk. For example, the bank takes a basket of loans that covers, for example, $1 billions lent to Panama, $5 billion to Mexico and $2.5 billion to Columbia, and then offers the option on the possibility that these loans may not be paid back, as in defaulting, as a credit derivative. The investor only has to pay on the derivative if the borrowers default. Meanwhile, if the loans are paid off, then the investor has made a packet of cash from the premiums the banks pays to offset their credit risk.

This has contributed to an acceleration in lending, and rising exposures. For example, of General Motors' stated losses of over $10 billion in 2005, over $2 billion were hidden in the finance arm GMAC as a result of an exposure to over $200 billion in credit derivatives. Similarly, in March 2006, Austria's BAWAG Bank announced that it had used offshore companies to mask almost €1 billion of losses for similar investments that almost turned the bank insolvent in 2000.

Even with such risks, banks love credit derivatives because it takes possibilities of substantial loan losses off their balance sheet and onto someone else's, such as General Motors. That is why it is a market that has ballooned over the past decade from nothing to $12 trillion – bigger than the USA's GDP – but is also now a market that has become commoditised.

Like any great trading initiative – swaps, structured finance, arbitrage – the more popular the initiative, the more money it makes, the more others want to get in on the action, the more competitors start to buy the people who make the money, the more commoditised the market becomes. After 10 years, credit derivatives has reached market maturity and so the next big play is now being looked for. That big play is likely to be around complex cross-asset class trading strategies that combine equities, bonds, options, derivatives and FX.

There are huge dangers in this of course, and successful execution demands deep technological know-how. However, the only way in which markets can operate is to seek out and trade off risks against rewards, and the greater the risks, the greater the rewards.

Perhaps the approach is best summed up from a line out of Michael Lewis's book *Liar's Poker*, which described life in Salomon Brothers in the late 1980s. In the book, Salomon's head of law, Donald Feuerstein, took great delight in finding 'chinks in the regulator's armour' which he could use in ways to buck the markets and make greater returns. In other words, to get real returns requires taking greater risks by seeking out unregulated markets and products that are new, innovative and completely different to the general products available. These products are likely to be incredibly complex and sophisticated, using turbo-charged algorithmic cross-asset class trading strategies. Products that can only be delivered through massive investments in technological know-how, globally networked, massively scalable systems.

Which brings us to our third strategy.

The technological turbo-charging of the investment markets has meant that you have to have a huge information technology budget and infrastructure to be a player these days. Those firms that cannot afford to enter the game as a player in their own right will end up giving their trading to a third party to manage. After all, if you can outsource your customer service centre to Mumbai, why not do the same with your investment banking division?

Therefore, there will be a range of firms who find algo trading and derivatives beyond their reach. These firms will ditch their trading desks and get someone else to do it for them. By way of example, Acme Trading Desk Services Ltd offers outsourced trading desk facilities and soon finds that Acme provides the trading screens, networking infrastructure, connectivity and technology to support Hedge Fund A, Fund Manager B, Investment Manager C and Insurance Group D. Currently, Hedge Fund A, Fund Manager B, Investment Manager C and Insurance Group D use a broker-dealer to do this on their behalf as licenced dealers on the world's exchanges. In a post-MiFID and RegNMS, technologically charged world, there is no reason why these buy-side firms will not be doing it themselves through DMA (Direct Market Access) and technology provider outsourced services.

This vision is not too far away, and is in fact becoming even more likely thanks to legislation such as MiFID in Europe and the rules and regulations relating to unbundling brokers services, commissions and billing.

The combination of regulatory drivers, technology chargers and market makers' margins, will deliver a future world in financial trading that will only be played by those who have the depth of pocket and technological know-how to be a player.

22

Rising Risks in Options and Derivatives

Options and derivatives trading has led to a number of major corporate disasters, from Barings Bank to Long-Term Capital Management and from Enron to WorldCom. Is technology a help or a hindrance in pre-empting future corporate collapses?

. We all know the story of Barings Bank and Nick Leeson. The lesson from that debacle is that you must not let your front-office run the back-office as the risk it carries is that your salesperson can book orders, pay commission and run the accounts whilst fiddling with the risk controls, compliance and accountabilities. In other words, your sales people can create the sales on the systems and pay their commission because they own both the sales and the administration – the front and the back office. This is an explosive mixture that will blow up in the face of management when, not if, the volatility is exposed.

Now, we all know that Barings Bank should never have happened again don't we? Yet in 2002, AIB announced the rogue trader dealings of John Rusnak who lost the bank almost $700 million by writing non-existent options sales and booking the fictitious premiums from them as revenue. Another individual running both front and back office and causing major operational risk.

However, that could never happen again could it? Yet, Australia had a similar case in March 2005 when the former head of National Australia Bank's FX options desk, Luke Duffy, made an appearance in court to plead guilty to making $360 million in losses.

The charges were brought after an investigation by the Australian Securities and Investments Commission (ASIC) into the trading by Duffy and his team in foreign exchange and foreign exchange options. The ASIC brought the charges after discovering that the FX desk entered false information into the bank's accounting systems so that they could create imaginary profits. Wow! That sounds like the same crime as Rusnak and Leeson. You would have thought that after a decade of knowing the operational risks of front office running the back office we could have avoided this happening again, so how did it happen?

One answer is poor management control. It is pretty obvious that sales people (traders) should not be allowed to pay their own commissions and run the back office order book (operations). There needs to be some control in place and the management controls can be addressed through effective internal structuring combined with decent operational risk strategies, but there is a more fundamental issue at stake here.

John Rusnak, Luke Duffy and company in the 2000s are all in a position where they are dealing with increasing complexity fuelled by technology. The more complex the operation, the easier it is to falsify and the harder it is to catch. In particular, it seems obvious that the front office should not run the back office but, if the operation is so complex that management find it hard to see the separation of the front and back office then, in theory, you could almost get away with anything...until the volatility of the operation exposes itself.

This is because we live in a complex world turbo-charged by hi-tech and inordinately convoluted trading strategies. So let's go back to a simpler world of 20 years ago.

Back in 1987, Oliver Stone released the movie *Wall Street*. In the film, Michael Douglas makes an interesting speech about greed:

> The point is, ladies and gentleman, is that greed – for lack of a better word – is good. Greed is right. Greed works. Greed clarifies, cuts through, and captures the essence of the evolutionary spirit. Greed, in all of its forms – greed for life, for money, for love, knowledge – has marked the upward surge of mankind.

OK, so greed is good.

But, back in 1987, there were not that many ways to be greedy without being caught. In 1987, we lived in a simpler world. A world where Microsoft was not really known and the leading technologies were called DEC VAX's. Gigabytes were something you heard about in science fiction movies and people thought the internet was something to do with a passion for fishing.

Back in 1987, almost everything that was being traded was written down and could be tracked and, if it was not written down, it was probably illegal.

This has all changed twenty years later. Today, we live in a world of technologically created options and derivatives. The financial markets for financial options and derivatives are so complex today that few in senior management can effectively manage the risks that lie therein.

As a result, greed can be served in many forms through complex trading strategies. No wonder, when Alan Greenspan was discussing the issues of corporate governance post-Enron and WorldCom with the Federal Reserve Board, he said: 'It is not that humans have become any more greedy than in generations past. It is that the avenues to express greed have grown so enormously.'

Kenneth Lay and Bernard Ebbers, the disgraced chief's of Enron and WorldCom respectively, were lauded and applauded as the world's greatest CEO's only a few years ago.

Take this quote from ChiefExecutive.net in December 2001: 'Bernard Ebbers of WorldCom placed first among value-creating CEOs for the past two years.' Or take this interview with Kenneth Lay, CEO of Enron, with Business Week in August 2001, 'We think the company is on solid footing, and we're looking forward to continued strong growth. We had a very, very strong first half, including second-quarter net income up 40%, earnings per share up 32%, and operational physical volume delivery up 60%. In the last five years, we have had 25% per year compounded annual growth in earnings per share.'

What could have brought these firms and individuals down to their knees so suddenly?

You guessed it, turbo-charged options and derivatives trading using highly complex trading strategies, arbitrage, credit derivatives and so on.

When WorldCom went belly-up, no-one could tell how much the firm had lost. Initially, losses were estimated at $4 billion, then $7, $9 and most recently $11 billion. The reason is that the complex trading strategies employed by the firm to buck revenues were only discovered gradually after their collapse. Meanwhile, Enron went bankrupt in December 2001, but by summer 2002 had $6 billion in cash sitting in the bank. . .thanks to a range of energy options forward contracts and futures coming good.

Until you can accurately measure the risk exposures created by complex, turbo-charged trading strategies, no firm is safe from corporate collapse.

As a result, we should see as much focus upon creating technology solutions that accurately report and analyse risk exposures, operational risk and value-at-risk, as we do for solutions that allow the creation of complex options, derivatives and futures instruments.

Even with that technology capability, management within institutions will still need to be highly vigilant towards operational risk from the human perspective. After all, the Duffy's and Rusnak's were only exploiting the same loopholes that Leeson wormed through ten years before.

That is where Sarbanes-Oxley kicks in. In the case of Lay and Ebbers, their excuse is 'aw shucks', as in 'aw shucks, I'm only the Chief Executive and it was the Chief Financial Officer who messed up – I don't understand the financial stuff'.

Suffice to say, that Sarbanes-Oxley rules out that defence and so there should be much more vigilance in the echelons of power to demonstrate accountability and integrity.

In the case of financial instruments, that should mean that if you do not understand it, do not buy it. Now, that could get interesting as it should mean that much more creativity to generate future instruments that deliver high returns whilst clearly outlining the risks inherent in such products.

As both Sarbanes-Oxley and Basel II make clear, the human aspects of risk are just as important as the technological, and the two must work hand-in-hand if we are to protect our corporate and financial futures.

SIBOS Blogs

Each year SWIFT, the bank owned and run as a co-operative which supplies secure, standardised messaging to nearly 8,100 financial institutions in over 200 countries, runs a major exhibition and conference called SIBOS. At SIBOS, all of the world's leading payments professionals gather and Chris ran a daily blog at the 2005 and 2006 shows on Finextra.com. These blogs proved quite popular, and are provided here in their entirety.

SIBOS Blog 2005: Copenhagen, Denmark

SUNDAY, 4 SEPTEMBER 18:22 (UK)
A YEAR OF ANTICIPATION

Well, here we are on our way to another conference and tradeshow, although this one is an exception. SIBOS. The very name of it conjures up images of something out of Star Trek. . .whoops, sorry, that was Siborg.

Anyway, as usual, I'm at an airport about to board a flight to meet a bunch of bankers and vendors and gossip, learn, see and think about the future of our industry, the latest state of affairs and the things that make us get up in the middle of the night and go 'gee' – or is that just me?

In order to prep for this particular journey, I have my usual range of things in the suitcase, but here are the four most important items:

1. insect repellent – to deter the most ardent vendors;
2. amphetamines – to ensure you hear the presentations you really have to remember;
3. nytol – to ensure you don't hear the presentations that you really don't want to remember; and, of course,
4. super-strength overnight hangover cure, as SIBOS does always remind me of an annual banker's cocktail party.

Mind you, that all changed last year when Heidi Miller woke us up with a call to action. In case you've forgotten about that, you can read her words at Heidi Miller's Speech at http://www.swift.com/index.cfm?item_id=43378 and my response on what has happened since SIBOS 2004 can be seen in Chapter 17.

So, I'm sitting in the airport lounge this year actually excited and expectant about this year's show, with some great sounding sessions that I will treasure repeating to my family over dinner on Friday night, when we all return home.

A good example is 'Treasury markets: the changing landscape from execution to settlement – could processing efficiencies eliminate the back office?' That is the sort of session that always gets the attention of the guys down at my local watering hole, when we get together to revel in engaging anecdotes and stories of the week we have had. Then there are a couple that really hit the attention like 'Tools for Anti-Money Laundering'. . .I have always wanted to know how to do that. Even better is the engagingly short title 'TARGET2' – simple and straight, but did they miss TARGET1? Will we ever know?

Seriously, this year's conference does have a great line-up and, in the light of Giovannini, MiFID and SEPA, along with SWIFTNet, PE-ACH and PE-DD, and increasing competitive impacts from PayPal and others, the show should be good this year. And the theme could not be better – Transformation.

So, between the bastions of our industry such as Jacob Wallenberg and George Mathewson, and the new ideas to be presented by Leonard Schrank on SWIFT's Vision for 2010, and a few SWIFT drinks or too with the vendors, bankers, consultants and practitioners at this year's show, I can't wait.

See you in Copenhagen tomorrow morning folks and here's to the first session. Ah yes, how to launder a few euros. . .

MONDAY, 5 SEPTEMBER 11:51 (DENMARK)
NOT SO SWIFT

Woke up to a foggy Copenhagen this morning after arriving late last night into a foggy Copenhagen. Of course, I immediately grabbed the SIBOS conference programme and began thumbing through the dog-eared pages re-marking the sessions to attend and then jumped onto the conference bus.

That's when the troubles began, as SIBOS began its 2005 agenda with a 2,000+ person queue in the main lobby as delegates stood in line to have their photos taken as part of increased security measures.

One-and-half hours later I eventually crossed the threshold.

Now, where's the queue for coffee begin. . . ?

MONDAY, 5 SEPTEMBER 15:38 (DEN)
FIRST SESSION HITS THE SPOT

Off to the first session, Return On Investment (ROI) in technology chaired by TowerGroup's very own Dushyant Shahrawat. Dushyant was joined on stage for 90 minutes by Tom Abraham of Citigroup, Wolfgang Gaertner of Deutsche Bank and Andre Vanden Camp of ING, all focused upon the discussion of ROI.

And it was pretty interesting, particularly as they all seemed to agree that the financial models we use for working out the justifications for IT investments are fundamentally flawed. Tom summed it up well when he said: 'We have these elaborate and sophisticated financial models with ROI, IRR and NPV but the margin of error that leads to decisions is substantial. At the end of the day, you are taking a bet.'

Bottom-line – and that's a good word when it comes to ROI – is that, after half a century of making IT investments, we still have no idea how well those investments perform. . .we just have more sophisticated ways of justifying making them.

On that note, onwards and upwards to the first plenary session where Jaap Kamp and Leonard Schrank outline SWIFT's vision for the future.

MONDAY, 5 SEPTEMBER 18:34 (DEN)
TELLING TALES

Back to the hotel and thinking about what a great opening session we just experienced which began with Jaap Kamp and Leonard Schrank praising Heidi Miller for waking us all up at SIBOS last year. And boy, has SWIFT woken up. But, before we go there, let's start at the beginning.

Mr Kamp introduced Jacob Wallenberg whose credits are longer than my blogs, but include vice-chairman of SEB, chairman of Investor AB and board member of SAS Airlines and ABB. He's also a sailor in his spare time.

Mr Wallenberg gave us all an insight into the state of our industry from the viewpoint of 20 years of deregulation and re-regulation.

In particular, today, Mr Wallenberg talked around the challenges of transformation in the context of SEPA. For more background on some of these areas, refer to the Chapter 5, 'The European Union unravels' and Chapter 18, 'The future of European payments'.

The message he gave was that he was 'personally embarrassed' by the way banks had failed to transform in response to these challenges, and cited the time it takes to make a retail payment between banks, as compared to an electronic payment on the internet to illustrate the point.

In conclusion, he thanked 'the apathy of our customers who are more likely to get divorced than challenge their bank relationships' but went on to say that a bank's position is not given but earned, and that bank's ignore that fact at their peril. . .a little like Hans Christian Anderson's story of the emperor's new clothes when the emperor is, in fact, naked!

On to Messrs Kamp and Schrank who were not telling stories or fairy tales but giving us a vision as to how they have rethought SWIFT in light of Ms Miller's comments last year.

Jaap Kamp first of all talked us through the process and then Lenny gave us the headline – SWIFT is going to move from being the 'global financial community's foremost messaging infrastructure' in 2006 to the 'global financial community's foremost transaction management infrastructure' by 2010.

This came around through a whole raft of soul-searching and I think Jaap's review of SWIFT's strategic options was particularly revealing. SWIFT had discussed the following seven options going forward:

1. continue to increase savings in financial institutions operational and transaction costs;
2. increase global straight through processing capabilities in conjunction with the Giovannini process (more on that tomorrow);
3. increase SWIFT's role in pan-industry initiatives such as SEPA;
4. standardise worker remittance practices especially for the BRIC (Brazil, Russia, India, China) markets;
5. standardise bank-to-corporate connectivity globally;
6. use SWIFT's standards to improve supply chain management and reconciliation processes;
7. involve SWIFT policy more to improve anti-money laundering and anti-terrorism capabilities for the financial community.

The vision offered covers all of these and more. You will be able to read this in depth on the SIBOS site, so enough of the discussion of their presentation in this blog. Suffice to say I thought it gave us all hope that SWIFT had listened last year, learned and at least was prepared to put a stake in the ground to say here's what we are going to do. Leonard Schrank did say that it would be at least a year before they could present the detailed picture so Sydney 2006 will build upon this theme and vision announced here.

So that's it for day one of SIBOS work.

Now onto night one of SIBOS fun.

I am told the DTCC are throwing a big shin-dig tonight, but DTCC sounds too much like the DT's for me and my liver can only take one or two thrashings a week...it's an age thing you know. So, I'm out for a quiet dinner with a few colleagues – and if you believe that, you will believe me when I say that I understudied for Hans Christian Anderson. So here's to an evening of tales, stories and merriment. Talk again tomorrow.

TUESDAY, 6 SEPTEMBER 10:24 (DEN)
FROM BRICKS TO CLICKS

Strangely – considering the excesses of the night before – I managed to get to the first session today on BRIC. BRIC is Brazil, Russia, India and China. I kind of think they also need Kazakhstan in there as well to make it a proper BRICK. Then maybe you need Canada, Lithuania, Iran, Cambodia and Korea to join in for a CLICK too.

BRIC actually turns out to be the key economies that the world looks toward for the future. And for those who want a piece of the action – like Richard Brown's Citigroup who were the only non-BRIC bank presenting in this session – it means investing for the long term as Citi has been in most of these economies for over a century.

For those in the BRIC community, it means challenge. The key challenge being finding the skills, education and leadership to compete on the global stage. And those skills are typically being imported from the developed economies' banks – like Citigroup.

We all say share and share alike.

Meantime, where's that coffee queue?

TUESDAY, 6 SEPTEMBER 13:16 (DEN)
TRANSFORM OR DIE

The big theme of this year's SIBOS is transformation. Finally, our industry is waking up to the fact that if we sit in our old, silo function structures with legacy systems we will not survive.

Opening the second plenary session today, Johan Kestens, head of marketing for SWIFT began with an interesting number – 34%. Then another one – 24%. And finally 9%. Thirty-four per cent is the average cost of payments to a bank's overall spend, 24% is the average payments revenues generated as a result, and 9% is the profitability. The 34% stat is the headline issue because the 9% figure is going down. You only need to look at yesterday's Finextra headlines for Cap Gemini's estimate that banks will lose EUR29 billion due to SEPA to realise that profits are going to be eroded. That is why we need to tackle the 34% of costs to maintain our margins or go out of business.

Johan was joined on stage by Mark Greene of IBM, Leo Apotheker of SAP, Yawar Shah of JPMorgan (and also deputy chairman of SWIFT) and Erik Dralans of ING. As one participant described it – 'the mother of all panels'.

The general consensus seemed to be that banks were too slow to transform, not bold enough or far reaching enough in their change programmes, and were continually being set their agenda by external parties such as the regulators. As Leo said, 'your corporate customers are fed up with you because they cannot understand why a fedex parcel can be processed straight through whilst a simple payment cannot'.

Erik Dralans then gave a good insight into transformation using the example of ING Direct. ING Direct is the largest global direct banking operation with distribution in eight countries, 14 million customers and €170 billion in deposits. Erik put all of this down to a simple product and process structure, focused execution, smart technology and great customer understanding. I tend to think a competitive interest rate also helped.

Erik's point was that you can grow, innovate and build business if you apply your mind to it, but you need vision, discipline, execution and persistence. And that was the theme of transformation – vision, discipline, execution and persistence. That is how you do it.

The conclusion being that it is time to stop talking about transformation now and start doing it.

TUESDAY, 6 SEPTEMBER 19:00 (DEN)
SEPA: CREATING A BORDERLESS EUROZONE

As usual with conferences, I'm in a great hotel in a beautiful city in a wonderful country and I just know I will not see any of it. However, I will see lots of conference rooms, exhibition halls, restaurants and bars. More of that later. First, to the action this afternoon.

After transforming some food and water, I wandered down to the conference room to hear the latest on SEPA – the Single Euro Payments Area. I wrote three reports on SEPA earlier this year, and reckon that it will mean banks in Europe will need to spend an additional $4.5 billion on infrastructures in 2007 to be SEPA compliant by 2008. That is when SEPA should be operational. And that $4.5 billion spend is over and above the $6 billion European banks are already spending today on keeping their ACHs and RTGS systems running. In other words, European banks will be spending $10.5 billion in 2007. Now, if you want to know more about SEPA, a good place to find out more is at the official website of the EPC, the European Payments Council (www.europeanpaymentscouncil.org).

And it was the EPC who were running the show this afternoon with Charles Bryant, secretary general of the EPC, chairing a panel of key members from among the leading banks of Europe. The first panel participant to take the podium was Gerard Hartsink, a leading exponent of SEPA, Chair of the EPC and a global ambassador for ABN Amro. Gerard made it totally clear that the EPC is committed to making SEPA a reality, with a roadmap drafted in December 2004 ready for ratification of the final rulebooks this month and a live SEPA infrastructure in place by January 2008. That is in line with European Central Bank's requirements of SEPA being operational by 2008 and mandatory for all euro cross-border payments by 2010.

Other panel members then detailed how this would happen, with Christian Westerhaus of Deutsche Bank detailing the plans for a Pan-European Direct Debit infrastructure and Mark Hale of Barclays Bank explaining the plans for Credit Transfers. Finally, Alfredo Rodriguez of BBVA joined the throng and explained the standards that would be implemented for SEPA to be a reality.

Of all of this, the most intriguing headlines were that there will be mandatory time cycles for instructions of payments to be completed, with a direct debit being processed in under two days and a credit transfer in less than three days. There will also be improvements to cash management, with Gerard Hartsink stating that banks lose over $21 billion a year due to poor cash management processes and structures. It almost makes you wonder how any bank makes a profit. Therefore, as part of SEPA there will be SECA. Now, SECA is even more interesting because it is a Single European Cash Area, rather than a Single Euro Cash Area. In other words, cash management and processing in SECA will apply to all of the EU's 25 countries, plus Iceland, Norway, Liechtenstein and Switzerland. Interesting. After all, SEPA – the Single EURO Payments Area – only applies to the Eurozone, which is just 12 countries.

It seems clear that SEPA is just stage one of a plan by the ECB and the EPC to make all of Europe a single, seamless financial trading area that can compete with the USA. And that's really what SEPA, MiFID, the Financial Services Action Plan and all that stuff is about – making Europe a highly competitive trading zone.

Anyway, as you can gather, I can talk about this stuff for hours – especially as I've written about 120 pages of research on the subject – so I better move on.

After SEPAing, I got a text message from an old friend at Clear2Pay, so I entered the exhibition halls yet again. I haven't said much yet about the exhibition, but it is the normal impressive array of vendors with a few – like IBM, Misys and SWIFT themselves of course – standing out purely for the sheer size of their exhibit areas. I also enjoy collecting gifts and entering competitions as we go around these booths, so here's fingers crossed to winning the Vespa or Sony Playstation or Hawaiian holiday or all of them. Will let you know if I'm successful.

A fast chat with my friends and then on to a nice quiet dinner with some other folks this evening. I hear rumours of parties with SunGard and Checkfree and, although tempting, after last night I think I will just retire to my room and watch Danish movies. No – stop it. I can hear you thinking rude thoughts – honestly, these ones are clean.

See you tomorrow.

WEDNESDAY, 7 SEPTEMBER 08:35 (DEN)
THE PARTY AFTER THE NIGHT BEFORE

Good morning. Nice and bright and early on a sunny morning in Copenhagen. I'm feeling fresh and revived having gone to bed at 3 a.m. after parties with all the firms in the SIBOS world – so much for retiring early and watching movies.

The last party was Nordea's which was a fabulous affair focused on karaoke. Now, I love karaoke at the worst of times – you should hear my 'Mack the Knife' – so this was perfect stomping ground for finishing the evening.

Anyway, today looks good with a range of sessions from Giovannini to future standards. A quick coffee and off to the first session.

WEDNESDAY, 7 SEPTEMBER 10:52 (DEN)
I DREAM OF GIOVANNINI

Great first session today as I haven't yet got fully to grips with Giovannini and the idea of single clearing and settlements infrastructure for Europe. Alberto Giovannini was joined by various luminaries from the industry and proceeded to explain why the 15 barriers to achieving change were in place, how they were going to be eliminated and what they meant.

The star of the show had to be Bob Wigley, managing director of Europe, Middle East and Africa for Merrill Lynch who engaged the audience from the first line with a classic joke worth recounting here.

Alberto Giovannini, Charlie McCreevy (the European commissioner for the internal markets) and Pierre Francotte (CEO of Euroclear) go to heaven to ask God a question. First, Alberto asks God: 'When will my 15 barriers to a single European clearing and settlement infrastructure be in place?' God thinks about this and replies 'sometime in the 22nd Century' and Alberto goes away crying.

Then Pierre asks God: 'When will my infrastructure be used as the preferred single clearing and settlement system for Europe?' Again, God considers this and says 'sometime in the 22nd Century' and Pierre goes away crying.

Finally, Charlie McCreevy asks God: 'When will we have a single European financial markets that does not require legislation to make it happen?' God thinks about this and says 'one day. . .but not in my lifetime' and starts crying.

Big laugh and then on to the real focus of what Giovannini can achieve. The aim is for one central counterparty system and central depository. There are 15 barriers and gradually they are being eroded. But slowly. Most of the issue lies with national agendas apparently. As Alberto Giovannini stated: 'In order for this to work, it is absolutely essential that the European Commission and national governments play their roles effectively.'

Equally, as with with SEPA and MiFID and the other changes in Europe, there has been much talking about transformation with relatively little implementation. As Sophie Gautie of Banque National de Paribas (BNP) stated: 'Until recently it was taboo to talk about the end game.'

But we are getting towards the end game and it is clear that as with all of these regulatory changes, if the industry does not engage in the process then it will be steam-rollered into making it happen.

A roller coaster ride is in store.

WEDNESDAY, 7 SEPTEMBER 15:39 (DEN)
LOWERING STANDARDS

In light of the ISO 20022 (www.iso20022.org) standard, also known as Unifi, which provides financial firms with a common platform for developing SWIFT and other messages in standardised XML formats, I sauntered into this morning's other session, '2025: a standards odyssey'.

The session started with Martine De Weirdt, SWIFT's head of standards, talking about the industry's past, present and future. I thought her opening line about SWIFT being created in the early 1970s to create a common language – a standard – was a good one, especially as that language is 'I just sent you an MT100 which will be followed by an MT202, but I'm leaving MT72 blank.' That's almost as memorable as 'vorsprung durch technik'.

The session's highlight was Hugh Palmer of Société Generale who opened his pitch with a slide that said something along the lines of the following: 'Standards are like space travel. They cost millions, are developed in a slow and painful process, are mostly fiction, and are created by the few to be imposed upon the many.'

That just about sums up standards! There were a few other TWISTs to the conversation that hit the TARGET, but mostly this was about XML, XML, XML.

After lunch, it was then back into the exhibit hall for what is called 'vendor briefings'. Now, why is it that they are called 'briefings' when no vendor is ever brief?! Anyway, my insomnia has been cured.

When I came out of my briefings, I then headed for a few of the bank stands. You've got all the key global players here such as JPMorgan, HSBC, ABN Amro to name just a few. ING are giving away some great cuddly toy lions which are hunted for like gold dust whilst Barclays Bank has, for me, the best exhibit of all of them.

The Barclays Premiership Trophy – you know, the one that Chelsea bought. . .sorry won, last year. So yes, I got my photo taken with the trophy and really do think I have that David Beckam profile.

You can stop laughing now. You can. Please.

WEDNESDAY, 7 SEPTEMBER 17:18 (DEN)
WORK IS FOR THE DRINKING CLASSES

It's day three of SIBOS and already I feel my liver screaming for some rest. No sooner does the clock strike three o'clock in the exhibition hall than all the exhibitors start plying alcohol on poor unsuspecting delegates. That would be OK if it was not for the fact that some of those delegates have spent half of the time in Copenhagen absorbing copious amounts of the wretched brew already. No matter, when in Denmark do as the Danes do – or is that when in SIBOS do as the Sibes do – and so we embark on another round of aperitifs before dinner.

First to my friend at EDS for a glass of white wine, then to S1 and Dovetail where everyone had gathered for drinks, onwards to Voca who are buzzing with SEPA news, and then finally to Wall Street Systems.

The last visit was made primarily to enter their contest to win an England football shirt. Not just any old shirt, but one signed by my twin David Beckham and also Wayne Rooney. Now that is a prize worth winning as, for those who do not know, England play Northern Ireland tonight in the World Cup Qualifiers and Beckham and Rooney are hopefully going to be our star players. In fact, I also hear that Omgeo are running a great party in one of the downtown bars to see the match so that one is quite tempting.

Alternatively, a whole bunch of folks just got on buses to go to Sweden. I have no idea why they are going to Sweden and I don't think they have either, except that JPMorgan reckon that when in Denmark do as the Danes do and go to Sweden. So there's the JPMorgan party in Sweden, Omgeo's in Copenhagen and about five or six other things I could go to. So. . .

Well, I am not going to lie again and talk about quiet nights in and early to bed or other baloney. For me, I'm just going to see how the evening pans out. Have a great time wherever you are and see you tomorrow for the final run-in to the real SIBOS party.

THURSDAY, 8 SEPTEMBER 07:56 (DEN)
BUNCH OF LOSERS

England lose their world cup qualifier 1–0 to Northern Ireland and everyone calls for the manager's head. Meantime, Denmark – who beat England 4–1 in a recent friendly – beat Georgia 6–1 and everyone in Copenhagen parties. I guess that is similar to banking – there's always winners and losers.

The winner today has to be me as I managed to quietly extricate myself from the bar before midnight and got a good night's rest. Sleep was so good in fact that I get to SIBOS at 7:30 and there's no-one here. It's weird being at such a large show on your own. Nevertheless, it made the demonstrations on the booths interesting.

So it's the final day of SIBOS and countdown to the main party which I'm ready for. Here's to the Leningrad Cowboys and a final day of work, rest and play.

THURSDAY, 8 SEPTEMBER 10:06 (DEN)
SWIFTIFICATION

First session I opted for today was entitled 'What's driving 21st century securities automa-tion – the Nordic & Baltic experience', where Kjell Arvidsson group CEO of the Nordic Central Securities Depository Group coined a new word for the 21st Century, 'SWIFTifica-tion'. Apparently, the Nordic securities market is 'SWIFTified' after the implementation of the corporate actions standard ISO15022 (www.iso15022.org) which, along with ISO 20022 provides for convergence between SWIFT and FIX.

Next up, Markku Pohjola, deputy group CEO and head of group processing and technology for Nordea Bank, opened with a thank you to the other panellists for being so complementary about the Nordic markets. Apparently, 'the rest of Europe is much lousier than the Nordic Region in this perspective'.

Back on the exhibition floor, where I hooked up with Karen Wendel of Identrus, who yesterday announced plans to work with TWIST to produce new standards for identity management.

TWIST chairman Tom Buschman said that this was needed because 'so far the banks have not been willing to come up with a common standard for corporates'.

After that it is back into the thick of things for a quick walk by the Wall Street Systems stand to see if I won the signed England football shirt. Nope. But now they are giving away the England football team with the shirt.

THURSDAY, 8 SEPTEMBER 13:49 (DEN)
THE PITTER-PATTER OF LARGE FEET

I get to the EBA's session on their new offerings for SEPA (the Single Euro Payments Area) and the room is a sell-out. This is the first session I've been to where it is standing room only. In fact, it was so full, I actually had to kick six or seven of the bodies out of the way at the entrance to get into the room. I think I got away with it as I explained I worked for one of the vendors.

You probably all know lots about the EBA, the Euro Bankers Association (www.abe.org), and their different offerings so I won't bother going into too much background detail. Nevertheless, I was a little amused at the opening when Giorgio Ferroro, chair of the EBA, said that this session would cover 'STEP1, STEP2 and many other Steps in the future'. Obviously, this pitter-patter of euro banker's feet is building into a crescendo, although I'm not sure I can keep up with their dancing movements.

The session covered three major areas of EBA focus.

First, enhancing EURO1 and STEP1 with improved liquidity management by allowing subsidiaries of bank group's to directly connect and so allowing a bank to aggregate their group-wide euro-based liquidity.

Second, creating a concentric credit transfer and direct debit capability into STEP2 to enable both cross-border and domestic payments processing.

Third, delivering a priority payment capability so that a customer can make a cross-border payment within four hours of placing the order including the full transfer of funds between accounts.

What followed then was a gallop through each area with a whole raft of presenters – I think I counted there were eight. The presentations were mixed between the EBA's own people and guest spots from bank friends ING, BBVA and SEB who endorsed the approach. Overall, building on Tuesday's 'SEPA: creating a borderless Eurozone' (see Blog 18:00 on 6th) it is clear that the EPC and EBA are trying hard to be ready for SEPA by January 2008.

The session also had a few areas of disagreement. For example, the BBVA spokesman said that everyone would logically move to a centralised system for the economies of scale, efficiencies and cost savings. I don't think Marion King of Voca UK or Jad Khallouf of STET France would agree with that.

Equally, in the first session this morning on the Nordic Securities industry, one of the other things Markku Pohjola of Nordea said is that it is 'better to have a commercial stock exchange rather than a utility owned by market participants because it makes the exchange more customer focused and competitive'. That does call into question the logic of going with a bank-owned Pan European ACH (PE-ACH) when there are now several commercial organisations operating more functionally-rich ACH's. That is why the EPC has recognised there will be multiple PE-ACHs.

The bottom-line is that SEPA will happen; STEP2, EURO1 and TARGET2 will play a strong role, as will Voca, STET, Interpay and others; and we will have a Eurozone that is capable of competing with any other geography's financial industry by some time around 2010 or soon after.

The gentleman from SEB put it best. If you are a German and you have a holiday home in Spain, you will soon be able to pay all your Spanish bills from your main bank account in Germany, rather than having two accounts. That is the point of SEPA. Bring it on.

After the session, we all dived into the luncheon hall and the many European bankers associated with SIBOS tucked into their non-euro lunches (we are in the Danish Krona country here).

Meantime, England's cricket team are fighting another battle called 'beat the Aussies and win the Ashes'. For me, I just hope they don't emulate our football team and snatch defeat from the jaws of victory. Speaking of which, I'm just going to snatch that chocolate cake into the jaws of Skinnery.

THURSDAY, 8 SEPTEMBER 18:49 (DEN)
FINAL FAREWELLS

So here is the final entry to this week's blog for those who have been kind enough to read it. For those who haven't, jeg har set sler der ser bedre ud end dig. My Danish is improving as I'm told that means 'I've seen better looking donkeys than you' but if it's really offensive then even better still.

We had a great finishing to this week's SIBOS with Sir George Mathewson, chairman of the Royal Bank of Scotland, and Finn Otto Hansen, head of clearing and settlement strategies for DnB NOR Bank ASA.

Sir George began with an insight into how a small Scottish bank has become the sixth largest bank in the world by market capitalisation. You have to respect the man as he is a legend, along with Fred Goodwin. What amazes is that it is all good, tried, trusted and simple lessons he has learned along the way that have made the bank so successful.

For example, Sir George stated that the hostile acquisition of NatWest would never work due to the challenges of IT. The merger of IT systems would be the largest project of its kind ever attempted by any bank and no-one believed it could succeed. . .except the Royal Bank of Scotland management team.

How did they do it? Through a 'clear business plan with low risk' that minimised any impacts to client relationships, staff, tight deadlines, clear objectives, accountabilities and incentives and no branch closures. It sounds so beautifully simple and yet so few bank management teams can implement these ideas effectively. But Royal Bank of Scotland has done so in spades.

He finished with some insights on the challenges SWIFT faces for the future, which includes SEPA, allowing corporate users' access to SWIFT, SWIFT's relationships with the debit and credit card operators and financial supply chain management. In particular, I thought his comments about corporate access to SWIFT were quite telling when he said, 'if we fail, our customers will find a way to do it without us'. And that has been one of the key lessons for me this week.

The industry, as always, is at a critical juncture but that juncture has been brought around through the internet. Without it, banks had proprietary ways to stop people questioning their role. Now, customers can find ready alternatives to banking systems.

Which leads quite neatly to Mr Hansen's summary of this week's SIBOS. Using video highlights of the week's presentations, Finn Otto led us through the key message we are to take away. These were articulated best by Yawar Shah, deputy chairman of SWIFT, in the plenary on Tuesday. 'The Trade Services Utility (TSU), Giovannini, SEPA and Corporate Access. These are the four things that will make the difference in the next five years.'

There were other great comments in the closing video series, including the following:

'SEPA is inevitable. Let's accelerate the inevitable'. (Leonard Schrank)

'The core of the problem is lack of standards'. (Alfredo Giovannini)

'No matter how controversial, corporates will eventually have direct access to SWIFT'. (Steven Groppi)

Although my personal favourite had to be Michael K. Clark's (like Mr Groppi, also of JPMorgan Chase) comment: 'We do one million and five hundred thousand faxes a day to process payments. . .get rid of the faxes.'

The net result is that banks are aware that if they do not deliver value to customers, someone else will. Transform or be transformed.

After the closing plenary, I finally strolled the exhibit hall, smelled the air for the last time – and boy did it smell – watched wealthy bankers and vendors fighting for the last gifts and freebies on the booths and enjoyed the oiling process building up to tonight's final SIBOS party for 2005.

I would report on this one but I think you have had enough (or maybe I have). So my own final thoughts in closing.

First, it was a great SIBOS this year covering all the key topics. Having said that, half of SWIFT's business in now on the securities side and it was surprising that no mention was made of MiFID, the Markets in Financial Instruments Directive. For the securities side this is as big as SEPA and I have been on the Working Parties investigating this Directive. Depending upon its final definitions it could be as impactful as Y2K with our estimates as high as $9 billion of change costs, averaging $22 million per sell-side player, over the next three years. MiFID is as big, if not bigger, than SEPA.

Second, Copenhagen is a wonderful city full of wonderful people who smile, enjoy our company and are very engaging.

That is it for SIBOS 2005 – see you all in Sydney from October 9th through 13th next year.

SIBOS Blog 2006: Sydney, Australia

FRIDAY 6 OCTOBER, 21:20 (UK)
ANOTHER YEAR, ANOTHER SIBOS

This year we're celebrating 28 years of SIBOS, and yet it doesn't seem like 28 years since this annual banker's jamboree began in Brussels. More like 48 if my liver has anything to say about it.

This year, we're all in sunny Sydney, Australia, land of blistering heat and strange creatures, such as Kangaroos, Koala Bears and Dame Edna Everage. Anyways, I've been practising for this year's SIBOS by spending the 12 months since Copenhagen partying around the world in order to be able to withstand the onslaught of cocktail parties, drinks do's and liquid lunches that always go on 24×7 during the SIBOS shindig. Or that's my excuse. After all, SIBOS does stand for Sober and Informed Bankers Often Staggering. A bit like the old adage about the difference between a supermarket trolley and a banker – you can't get that much drink into a supermarket trolley!

So, we're all gearing up for big days and nights out down by the billabong. Having said that it's not about raising glasses this year, it's about raising ambitions. That means doing more and growing, as discussed in this month's Finextra commentary. I don't intend to repeat that stuff here therefore, except to say that the big difference for me this year is that I'm going as a guest of SWIFT. That is in order to chair the SEPA session which I expect to see y'all attend, or I'll be coming after you later to find out why you missed it!

Anyways, I'm here at Heathrow, checked in and eager to rock and roll. I was looking at the Aussie immigration forms and got confused about the question to do with having a criminal record – didn't know that I still needed one.

Rather than making too many Aussie jokes, we'll just stick with the one about how after my BA flight lands the plane carries on whining for five minutes after the engines are turned off. That's the way the Aussies know the Pommies have arrived.

Have a great week in the land of didgereedoos and boomerangs, and I'll wake up on Monday with a few ideas about banking. For the moment I'm going to stick to a few ideas of sleep.

SUNDAY, 8 OCTOBER, 20:00 (AUSTRALIA)
LAND OF SUNSHINE AND RAIN

Arrived in Sydney at 05:55 local time, which is 20:55 in the UK, or five to nine at night. Made the usual calls home. 'Hi ma, I made it to the other side of the world'; 'Hi darling, nope I haven't seen any kangaroos yet'; 'Honey, gotta go, there's an aborigine in the road.' The last one may sound made up, but there was an aborigine in the road. Around Circular Quay there were quite a few on Sunday actually, selling and playing didgeridoo's and original artworks. The rock aborigine didgeridoo band may not sound like a great seller on myspace.com, but he was certainly doing well yesterday around the harbour with the tourists.

Checked into the hotel and with a slight stretch of the neck...argh...there we go...yes...you can just about see the Opera House from here.

Funnily enough, it is actually an Opera House, as in they do sing a lot and wear Viking helmets, rather than just being a famous landmark. It kind of reminds me of that old Brit-Aussie thing around:

Q: What's the difference between Australia and Yoghurt?

A: Yoghurt has a culture.

Not very fair I admit and so, on the other hand, three Australian surgeons are in a bar arguing which patients are the easiest to operate on. One says 'technologists, because all of their organs are like connections to USB ports – you just connect and disconnect them'. The second reckons, 'It's bankers, because all of their organs are numbered for ease of access and valuation.' The third says, 'No, it's Brits, as they are spineless, heartless, gutless...'

Anyways, back to bizzo. SIBOS. SIBOS cannot be avoided here. You walk through the airports, there's signs everywhere. You get to Darling Harbour and the bridges are covered in SIBOS flags. You enter the Convention Centre and it's all there. Book in, have your piccie taken and register.

All of that done, the rest of yesterday was spent watching people trying to look cool in t-shirts and shorts. You could spot the SIBOS attendees as they were the ones wearing the socks and sandals.

Looking forward to Monday, my agenda includes a few official duties over an IBM lunch and a SWIFT dinner – although I'll take my time over it – and the highlight of the day is going to be the opening plenary session with Yawar Shah, SWIFT Chairman; Lenny Schrank, SWIFT CEO; and David Morgan, Westpac CEO. My feeling is that much of the focus around this session will be the BRIC economies and, obviously SWIFT2010.

That'll do for now. Will report back when there's some real news and views...

MONDAY, 9 OCTOBER, 09:15 (AUS)
EUROCLEAR OFF

The trouble with any conference is you start the day in a hotel where loads of other SIBOS people reside. Therefore, what is meant to be a nice, leisurely breakfast morning, becomes a bean-fest of 'Saw your article on MiFID the other day – do you have any idea what you're talking about' and 'oh hi, you know that crap you wrote about us – we'll get you back'. SIBOS week begins. . .

That was followed by the normal bout of senile moments where you go, 'I know your face, what's your name again?' and 'oh jeez, I was supposed to be on booth F-something or other half an hour ago, where the **** is it?'

Apart from that, a very easy 'no worries' morning, followed by a pleasant lunch with the masters of the universe, namely IBM's great and the good of SIBOS who they've hand-picked for a free lunch. Again, one of the more interesting guests was a didgeridoo and an aborigine. . .maybe there's a theme emerging here?

Back to the main halls for the Securities session, with the optimistic title 'Securities Market Reform – heaven, hell or purgatory?' There was also a surprise guest at this one, a certain Jean-Michel Godeffroy of the ECB who was discussing the post-SIBOS arranged announcements of a TARGET2 for Securities. This is meant to be some sort of centralised Euro-clearing operation and is the reason I attended, as next to Jean-Michel was Pierre Francotte, CEO of Euroclear. A good punch-up should have ensued.

Instead, it was all very polite and nice. Jean-Michel said all the banks were behind it. Pierre asked what 'it' was, and Jean-Michel said 'we don't know yet. After a due period of consultation and feasibility analysis, we will tell you early next year'. A gentleman from ABN AMRO then asked from the audience, 'is "it" going to be mandatory?' and Jean-Michel said 'yes but no but yes but no but yes. . .'

Someone suggested it might be good to debate this further next year. A collective sigh of relief.

Back to the exhibition hall to find a vendor or bank booth with free coffee or water (too early for anything else yet – three parties lined up tonight already) and on to the plenary. . .

MONDAY, 9 OCTOBER, 17:45 (AUS)
THE LEMMING CULTURE

The first plenary was introduced with a 'joyful welcome to Sydney' from the Australian Girls Choir, who were very melodic and uplifting. They sang about how much they loved Australia. This was followed by a leading Australian politician, who talked about how much he loved Australia, who was followed by the CEO of Westpac, who told us how much he liked banking in Australia. Yes, I am converted and have now emigrated. . .

Actually, the main session was pretty good with David Morgan, CEO of Westpac, making a heartfelt plea to leave banks alone and let them self-regulate. There's too much regulation out there and when, in 1817, the Bank of New South Wales was formed – later to become Westpac – the bank brought 'order to anarchy'.

This was a theme Mr Morgan repeated several times because he was making it clear that it is only 'when the private sector fails to regulate itself properly that the banks, and their customers, take a beating. That is when the government has to step in to regulate the system.' In other words, banks must avoid screwing up in order to keep the regulators off their back.

He also pointed out a few other challenges, namely the issues of online security and authentication, and the threats of new non-bank entrants in the payments space. In this regard, he said something that I hear often.

He said that another major obstacle, and I quote, 'is the consequence of our own creation'. This is our own caution. Non-traditional providers invest ahead of the curve and drive change but, frankly, they are on our turf. We are not by nature pioneers in technology, and technology has been the growth curve of payments in recent times. Customers like their banks to be stable, predictable and reliable, which is why we are followers rather than leaders.'

Customers like their banks to be followers rather than leaders?

I don't think so. Two reasons.

First, all of the innovation in technology today is being driven by customers – iPods, PSPs, DVD and Slingshot TV Broadband, Mobile Telephony, MySpace, YouTube, RSS, Blogs...you name it. Banks are not keeping up with the pace of customers change usage of technology, and so customers are demanding that banks change faster.

Second, the European CEO of PayPal recently made this comment to me: 'the banks laughed at our three year business plan and said we'd be lucky to achieve it in ten years. We achieved it in nine months. If PayPal was run with a banker's mentality, we wouldn't exist.' That is why non-traditional providers are on your turf Mr Morgan.

And customers lke their banks to be followers rather than leaders? No way. It is bankers who like their banks to be followers rather than leaders.

This can be corroborated by another convention I attended last week, where the CFO of one of the world's largest banks had a presentation that started with a picture of a lemming and finished with a picture of a tortoise.

He started by talking about bankers all following each other like lemmings, sometimes over cliffs, and that even if banks invest in innovations they are still tortoises...only faster tortoises. Banks are slow because they are risk averse, and it is not the customer who drives this. It is the banker's mentality.

The challenge is to raise the game; be more energetic, enthused and focused; raise ambitions...whoops. Raising ambitions – that's the theme of the show.

So, Yawah Shah, Chairman of SWIFT and Leonard Schrank, CEO, then did a double act around raising ambitions. However, I'm not going to repeat the content here because it's covered in my overview of the SWIFT Strategy (see Chapter 17: SWIFT changes in wholesale payment).

Off to the evening events and a few parties plus maybe a few bankers throwing themsleves into the harbour...like lemmings?

TUESDAY, 10 OCTOBER, 12:36 (AUS)
EUROPE AND ASIA

This morning covered several extremes around the world of banking.

The first was SEPA. No, not the Standardising Electronic Payments in Asia forum, but the Single Euro Payments Area.

Having said that, it does seem strange in many ways to be discussing Europe in Australia, but the audience seemed to be interested as about 400 turned up at 9:00 a.m. to be entertained by Gerard Hartsink, Chair of the EPC and SEVP at ABN AMRO; Jean-Yves Garnier of Natexis; Marco Bolgiani who runs Unicredit's Global Financial Services; Vincent Herlicq of AGF; and, of course, yours truly.

It was all very gentlemanly. The main focus being around 1 January 2008 – are we ready? Seventy-five per cent of the banks in the audience said yes but, according to research outside this meeting 75% of banks are not ready. Equally, no-one in the audience thought corporates were ready although I suspect that corporates will not do anything about SEPA before the banks get their act together.

The best comment of the session came from Monsieur Herlicq, who is representing the corporate community as a Board Member of AFTE, the French Treasury Association. As a Frenchman he said, 'SEPA? Je ne sais pas!' which translates for those who need it, as SEPA means 'I don't know' in French. I don't know.

On then to the plenary which was all about lands of rising ambitions, Asia. Good session and a fantastic opening video which, if you really want to know the importance of Asia, you have to see.

The session members included:

- Dominic Barton (moderator), Chairman – Asia, McKinsey & Company;
- Vincent H. C. Cheng, Chairman, Hong Kong and Shanghai Banking Corporation;
- John McFarlane, CEO, Australia and New Zealand Banking Group Limited;
- Rajnikant Patel, CEO, Bombay Stock Exchange Limited;
- Masamoto Yashiro, Senior Adviser, Shinsei Bank, Ltd and Director, China Construction Bank.

discussing the opportunities and risks in the BRIC economies.

The opportunity is that of the 6.5 billion people on this planet, half of them live in Asia and are rapidly rising as affluent new consumers. In fact, around a billion mass affluent consumers will appear in the BRICs over the next decade.

There is also no established capital market in China, an early market in India, and fledglings elsewhere. With a capital market of little substance about to explode in economies growing at almost 10% CAGR there is definitely going to be a juggernaut of financial wealth to be found in the BRIC economies over the next decade, especially as these markets are liberalised to foreign investors.

The other conclusion was that the fact these guys went through a financial meltdown in 1997, the Asian Financial Crisis, means they have now learned their lessons and are robust for the future, as far as they can be.

I recently got to write a load of stuff about China and India which will appear in Finextra commentaries in November and December. Meantime, if you want to know what's really going on, then visit McKinsey's website – loads of free research analysis on China and India.

So, off to lunch. Can't make me mind up whether to go for a Chinese or Indian take away – hot and spicy – or something French or Italian – traditional and requiring a long sleep afterwards. . .

TUESDAY, 10 OCTOBER, 17:52 (AUS)
CHINA AND A DOSE OF SOA

After a lunch that comprised a Wongyu Beef thing – you may think I mean Wagyu Beef, but I do mean Wongyu which I think is the Aboriginal word for 'mess' but don't quote me on that – it was off to the conference session to hear more about what's happening in Asia and, specifically, China.

China's financial markets open fully to foreign investment and competition as from 11 December 2006 'on paper', and should result in full market capabilities. Bearing in mind that China's markets may be a fraction of the size of Europe's and America's today, that is not the point. It is what these markets will mean in 10 to 20 years.

In the spirit of this year's SIBOS, this was also a panel debate comprising:

- Thomas Achhorner, Vice President and Director, IT and Financial Services Operations Practice, Asia, The Boston Consulting Group;
- Qian Ouyang, Executive Vice President, China Citic Bank;
- K. K. Tse, Executive Vice President, State Street Bank and Trust Company;
- Richard Yorke, Chief Executive Officer, China, The Hongkong and Shanghai Banking Corporation Limited.

who had a healthy discussion about the state of China – or the State of China if you prefer – and the bottom-line is that we always over-estimate the speed of change and under-estimate the impact. China is like that. We all expect big change tomorrow, but it will be more like 10 years or more before we really realise the impact.

This point was made by K. K. Tse who discussed mutual funds in China which were nothing in 1998 but are now worth $70 billion, which is more than Singapore's and Hong Kong's mutual fund markets. This is still tiny compared to America's over $8 trillion industry, but the question is how long before China's mutual funds industry outweighs America's. 10 years? 20? Make your own conclusions.

Other interesting facts included:

- China's growth rates have averaged 9.6% CAGR over the last 25 years, a record in world history for economic expansion;
- in the last five years, foreign direct investment in China's banks has been worth $21bn, with $18bn invested in 2005 alone;
- a third of all new worldwide banking revenues came from China, 2001–05 ($130bn);
- Shangdong has bank loans that are worth in total more than Russia's loans as a country and more than double all of Brazil's; and
- there are more people learning English in China than people who speak English as their native language worldwide.

Having said all that, it still does not explain what the Chinese call their best cups, saucers, dishes and plates.

Then it was off to see IBM for a discussion about 'SOA: is it a cure-all?' My Dutch friend told me that SOA is actually a Dutch word for a Sexually Transmitted Disease, which was a bit of a bum note to begin with, but the panel had a good discussion and convinced me that SOA is actually a reality. The technology works, is reliable and proven. It's the bank mentalities and legacies that hold it back. Or so they seemed to say.

Anyways, I'm now off to spend the evening on a large Catamaran courtesy of Voca. There's something about lolling around inside a Big Cat all night that seems rather alluring. . .

WEDNESDAY, 12 OCTOBER, 09:54 (AUS)
MAKE SEPA COMPULSORY

A late start today after an enjoyable evening floating around Sydney harbour. . .on a boat that is. The party went on till eleven and I bumped into various bankers and technologists having a ball with the main excitement being gambling with fake chips for a prize of a Satellite Navigation system. Amazing how ruthless the bankers became as they fought for those chips and played Black Jack, Caribbean Poker and Roulette. Not so much James Bond as Ned Kelly, as the action heated up to a crescendo where one player put all their chips on the number 45 on the roulette table and, hey presto, won big time. Apparently, this caused everyone else to try and find the bar steward...

Ah well, up late this morning to see the SIBOS Issues headline came from yesterday's SEPA session I chaired. Gerard Hartsink, Chair of the EPC and SEVP at ABN AMRO, responded to a question re self-regulation versus more regulation with the line 'if the tax authorities don't use the new standards, SEPA will never become a reality. If they don't move forwad, consumers will never buy into the concept'.

Anyways, off to SEPA out of the hotel and sneaker into the conference...

WEDNESDAY, 12 OCTOBER, 17:43 (AUS)
CORPSE

Just been to the most interesting session of SIBOS so far which was on Corporate Access to SWIFT, apart from the SEPA session of course.

The first reason it was of interest is because I'm really keen on supply chain automation and getting banks and corporates to work better together.

The second reason is that the session was held in the Parkside Ballroom here at the Convention Center. I hadn't been in that room before but it's a massive great cocktail lounge, with hi-tech tables with voting systems and PC screens. But the real kicker is that each table is illuminated and can change colours. In the darkened room, it reminded me of some great disco club lounge...I was just waiting for our esteemed panel to arrive and start singing and dancing.

Alas, no singing or dancing but plenty of good information.

Johan Kestens, Head of Marketing for SWIFT, did a deft job of steering the panel through a 90 minute Q&A, with the panel comprising:

- Michèle Fitzpatrick, Managing Director for Sales and Account Management, Wall Street Systems;
- Mark Hodgkinson, General Manager, Shell Treasury Centre East, Shell;
- John Murphy, Managing Director, Trade & Transaction Services, ANZ Banking Group Limited; and
- Gianfranco Tabasso, Chairman, Payments Commission, European Association of Corporate Treasurers.

Johan began by telling us about the three ways that corporates can now gain access to SWIFTNet, namely through treasury counterparty operations, MA-CUGs and the lastest Standardised CORPorate Environment for SWIFTNet, or SCORE.

Lucky it wasn't called CORPorate Standardised Environment...

Having said that, Johan also said 'we're good with acronymns' and then gave us NMGs, the BPC, CAG, BVG, MG, along with SCORE...all in about the space of a minute. I kept up but TLA's have always been my strength.

Whoops, didn't say that a TLA is a Three Letter Acronymn.

Anyways, Johan had us digi-voting with 57% of the audience saying that corporates would benefit most from corporate access...duh, that was a hard one wasn't it?

What should be the priority for banks? Forty-three per cent of the audience voted for enabling legacy applications for SWIFTNet, which was more than double the next choice.

What is the most important things for SWIFT to do? Forty per cent voted for making joining and connecting for corporates easier, again more than double the voting over the next choice.

The most vocal panellist throughout was Mr Murphy from ANZ who, as a banker, may have felt he had the most at stake. A few comments can be summarised as:

- 'corporate access has been discussed at the last two SIBOS's and I think we have to move on from there to getting it done';
- 'banks that focus on the 0.0001 cents charges for transactions will not be at SIBOS in five years because they will be out of business';
- 'we are great at building new systems, but awful at closing down the old ones which is why we have so much legacy out there'; and
- 'banks have moved too far into systems development and too far away from what they are good at, namely banking'.

but the best interaction was the laugh of the day when Michèle Fitzpatrick of Wall Street Systems said that payments should be more like airline ticketing – 'I flew here through four cities with four airlines with one ticket and one price.'

Johan responded: 'SWIFT is the other way around – we give you complex tickets but we never lose your luggage.'

Nuff said. . .

THURSDAY, 12 OCTOBER, 00:49 (AUS)
LATE NIGHT LAUNDRY

Instead of lunch, I decided to wander around the exhibit hall and soon discovered that the exhibitors knew their audience. It began with a wine tasting at the Reuters stand with an expert sommelier who asked me to taste and name seven different Aussie wines. Apparently 'nectar' didn't suffice, although it works for beer, so after copious slurps, gargles and spittoons that covered the gulps, I got through about two litres and staggered away. . .

. . .only to fall into the CitiGroup booth where an expert sommelier persuaded me to taste another few Aussie wines. Don't ask me how many but they were pretty good. And just as I fell off the CitiGroup stand I landed in the ABN AMRO bar where they offered G&T, R&C, M&S – you name it.

Finally extricated myself back to the conference for the LMA session. Sorry, ALM session. Nope. . .Ant-e mon-ey lawn-der-ring sesh or AML. That's better. . .

So I staggered into the AML session, which was by invitation only, and was surprised that no-one asked me whether I was invited. Especially as I had 200,000 brand new, crisp $100 Aussie notes in my bag. Ah well, there you go.

Not a bad session, although it was only meant to be 45 minutes and I suspected that having six panellists would be a challenge. And it was. After 45 minutes, only four speakers had achieved their aim of standing on stage. . .and I had to go!

Best speaker in this session was Felicity Yoal of CitiGroup who clearly explained the issues. I was going to go into depth here but it was by invitation only and as I was about to tell you who did what, how, etc, I was asked to keep it quiet.

As a man of principle, this was hard to accept but then they offered to take my notes and pass them through the Cayman Islands, no questions asked, so. . .an offer is an offer.

Back to the exhibit hall and the IBM booth where I chaired a final debate on SEPA. The theme was 'Will SEPA be a success?' and a prestigious panel comprised:

- Gerard Hartsink, Chair of the EPC and SEVP of ABN AMRO;
- Mark Hale, Head of Payments at Barclays Bank;
- Paul Burstein, Corporate Treasury at GE; and
- Alec Nacamuli of IBM – the only person we know who has attended every single SIBOS since the Show started in 1978.

The result was an overwhelming vote for SEPA being in place by 2008 and the banks delivering, but no-one using it by 2010 due to inaction by member states, governments, regulators and corporates. Pretty much the same message as yesterday's panel in the main session (see earlier blog).

Meantime, a final conference note from today's proceedings is that I heard the session chaired by David Bannister for the Standards Forum was entitled 'The Truth About Standards'. This was in the digi-voting stadium and, amazingly, the vote at the start had 4% **more** people voting that standards were important than at the end. In other words, the audience thought that standards were less important at the end than at the start – shocking news and maybe that is the truth about standards: they aren't important? Or maybe that's the truth about the SWIFT community in Sydney: standards aren't important to them. That can only be because SWIFT is the standard I guess.

Anyways, you may be wondering what I am doing entering a blog at 1:00 in the morning rather than being out on the town, as most folks would be in a typical SIBOS week. Well, Mr Skinner is taking a brief respite in order to be fresh for tomorrow night's big party. The final evening is always meant to be a biggie so, always best to be controlled on the Wednesday.

Kind of reminds me of the story of two bankers in a bar where one says, 'do you know much about the euro?' and the other says 'the euronals over there'.

THURSDAY, 12 OCTOBER, 10:26 (AUS)
MILES AND MILES

Late to bed and early to rise. You have to rise early around here as it's a fair old walk to get around. Sure, you can take a taxi but in a beautiful city with blue skies, sunshine. . .oh yea, weather's cleared up nicely and again, being British, it's pretty important to us to know our weather forecast so here it is:

Thursday

Fine. Sunny.

Current Temperature: 24°c

3 Day Forecasts:

Friday

Fine. Sunny.

Min: 19°c **Max:** 33°c

Saturday

Fine. Late change.

Min: 21°c **Max:** 33°c

Sunday

Chance early shower.

Min: 17°c **Max:** 24°c

Monday

Chance showers.

As I was saying, late to bed and early to rise to get a good walk to the Convention Centre which, btw, is in Darling Harbour whilst hotel is in Circular Quay. That's about a 3k walk each way. Someone then told me that from the entrance of the convention centre to the back of the exhibition hall is 1k. Add on about 0.5k to the conference rooms and we must be walking about 10k a day minimum. Strewth – no wonder everyone looks whacked out. . .or maybe it was the JPMorgan, Misys and other parties last night that went on into the wee small hours.

Ah well, off to hear all about 'Risk: disasters, terrorism, epidemics, fraud'. . .sounds like fun!?

THURSDAY, 12 OCTOBER, 14:29 (AUS)
CATASTROPHIC RISK

The extremely exciting sounding 'Risk: disasters, terrorism, epidemics, fraud' wasn't bad actually.

Subtitled 'Catastrophic Risk' it featured:

- Harry Newman, Director FIN, SWIFT (Moderator);
- Mike Fish, CIO, SWIFT;
- Lester Owens, Managing Director, Global Cash & Trade, Deutsche Bank;
- Neil Gallagher, Homeland Security Executive, Bank of America.

There was meant to be a fifth panelist, but he had been wiped out with serious illness last week and couldn't make it. Sounds like a catastrophic risk got him to me.

In the spirit of this year's SIBOS we also had another bout of digital voting. Here's the main results, fyi:

What organisation do you work for?

Bank	58%
Industry utility/market infrastructure	15%
Securities firm	5%
Software provider	5%
Other	17%

Which of the following catastrophic risks is the biggest threat to your business?

Fraud	46%
Natural Disasters	22%
Terrorism	17%
Epidemics	15%

How often do you carry out crisis simulations?

We don't	23%
Every 5 years	2%
Every 2–3 years	11%
Every year	41%
Every quarter	13%
Don't know	10%

Who should take the lead in devising our industry's collective response to risk?

Governments	17%		
Industry owned utilities	11%	}	
Industry bodies/associations	43%	}	54%
Risk is best left to each individual firm to manage	28%		
Don't know	1%		

Of the many 'best practices' initiatives that you've heard today, which do you believe is the most important in mitigating risk?

Design for security and resilience from the start	11%		
Communicate	12%		
Be realistic, flexible and up-to-date with BCP	19%	}	
Exercise BCP regularly and realistically	44%	}	63%
Get the cutler right	11%		
Run a resilience and risk security program	3%		

Lots of great commentary around these themes, including some fantastic comments from Neil Gallagher, Homeland Security Executive, Bank of America, whose role was created after 9/11. Neil was previously in counter-terrorism in the FBI and led investigations into the Lockerbie PanAm 103 crash, the first attack on the World Trade Centre in the 1990s, and the Oklahoma City bombing. An example of just a few of his comments:

> At one point, we heard of a prospective cyberattack. We asked the victim what is the difference between being intruded through a cyber attack versus being threatened or impacted by a terrorist attack? The response was there is no difference.

> In the 1980's there were a wide range of terrorist organisations. They were always then looking for something and had demands. The outbreak of Al Qaeda has no demands though. Their act is their statement.

> We had a tabletop exercise with the senior management of BoA, and gave them the exercise we ran in the FBI for senior government officials. The management were busy, walking in and out and didn't want to do it. I said look, just give me one hour. What we learned is that we had solutions to any issues that came up, but the thing they hadn't thought about is the impact of outside influences from government and law enforcers. So the management believed that they had all of the issues, contingencies and scenarios that could possibly happen covered . . . in theory. Then, I threw in an example in this scenario the idea that during this crisis we were trying to deal with as a fictional example, the mayor of the town enforced an emergency curfew. The whole town was locked down. The bank management looked at me, and asked what would happen if they carried on with the plan as it was written if this new factor – a town lockdown – was enforced. The answer was that we'd all be arrested. They had no answer to that one.

Great stuff and lots of other good insights like that one too.

Ah well, off to lunch with the Standards Forum and the European Commission then the final plenary before SIBOS 2006 officially closes.

That'll be a shame as Sydney's been wonderful.

Meantime, the big buzz in the news this morning is the Sydney Morning Herald's delight over the fact that ANZ has withdrawn their $5m budget from the Daily Telegraph and given it to them, This was all due to an inaccurate story the Telegraph ran about outsourcing Aussie jobs to India in the bank's call centre's. ANZ said it wasn't call centre jobs, it was just IT jobs. Apparently, that's ok then as the papers are now apologising big time and the banks scored a point.

Result: I'm outsourcing this column to Chennai next year.

THURSDAY, 12 OCTOBER, 18:56 (AUS)
THE END IS NEAR. . .

So that's it. Another year, another SIBOS. Next year it's Boston and then Vienna in 2009, by which time SEPA **will** be a reality.

The show this year has been good, with a wide ranging agenda from derivatives to low value payments, from SEPA to the BRICs and from clearing banks through to corporate access. I even got a little moment of stardom in the final video vignette on SEPA – thank you Mr VT guys.

The highlights for me were #1 – the major, big time news that the European Commission have responded to Gerard Hartsink's call to enforce SEPA across Europe's member states by asking all Eurozone government bodies to migrate to SEPA-based infrastructures. 'This is a major response and demonstrates the power of SIBOS', said Eva King who made this announcement during the closing plenary. Big news, big response and major movement forwards. . .

Other major news in the closing plenary?

On the BRIC economies:

'Shell has $6–$7 billion in China. We find ourselves squeezed between an economy that is rapidly expanding and an infrastructure that does not support it. It's getting there but it's not joined up yet.' (Mark Hodgkinson, General Manager, Shell Treasury Asia)

'If SWIFT is going to succeed in the region it will have to change its business model. Today, SWIFT is perceived a s a largely Euro-centric operation, specializing in the cross-border business and is some sort of IT vendor. Hiring an exec in the region and based in the region will change some of that.' (Lynn Mathews, SWIFT Board Member and Westpac Executive Director)

'An executive told me that they had a survey of their Indian graduates, and asked how many of their students wanted to start their own business. 95% said yes. If we had the same survey in Europe, 95% would probably want to work for the European Commission.' (Lenny Schrank, CEO, SWIFT)

On Derivatives:

'The next catastrophe in the financial world is credit derivatives. The amounts being offloaded to pension and other funds are too great. What is less understood is the explosion of the hedge fund business in OTC derivatives. They focus on how to structure the products and the result is that the middle and back office is a mess.' (Jacques Philippe Marson, President and CEO, BNP Paribas, and SWIFT Board Member)

On Corporate Access:

'The issue for the banks is that corporates are going to rapidly understand what is possible here and what can be done, and if the bank does not respond fast enough then they are going to find another bank that is.' (Lynn Mathews, SWIFT Board Member and Westpac Executive Director)

'One challenge you have here is the role of corporates at this sort of event. For example, would you, as banks, bring your corporate clients here to join this event?' (Mark Hodgkinson, General Manager, Shell Treasury Asia)

In conclusion, SIBOS has been a good show this year. Sydney is a great location and the Aussie's aren't so bad after all.

A little like the discussion between an Aussie Banker and a British Banker overheard in the bar last night.

The Aussie banker said, 'I'm clearly viewing the world differently to you as I'm much more cosmopolitan. For example, I've got a lineage that has a little bit of Irish, a little bit of Scottish, a bit of British, a lot of Asian influence and a huge amount of Australian. What do you think of that?'

The Brit banker retorted, 'I'm glad your mother was so liberal.'

There will always be good competition between us Brits and the Aussies but, at the end of the day, it's only because we Brits are jealous of the beautiful state of NSW, Australia and the brilliant lifestyle these guys enjoy. . .

. . .and the fact that most of their kids are living in London having a great time.

Take care Sydney and hello Boston 2007. See you there,

G'day.

Chris

Appendix
Original Articles

Below is the full list of the original articles and publication dates that comprise the chapters of the Future of Banking. These may all be found at www.finextra.com.

30th November 2006
Hidden dragons
http://www.finextra.com/fullfeature.asp?id=845
In the second of a two-part report, Chinese banking reforms and the emergence of a new superpower.

6th November 2006
Crouching tigers
http://www.finextra.com/fullfeature.asp?id=828
In the first of a two-part report, an in-depth look at the emerging Indian and Chinese banking markets.

6th October 2006
Blogging from SIBOS
http://www.finextra.com/sibosonline/finsibosblogs.asp

4th October 2006
SWIFT2010
http://www.finextra.com/fullfeature.asp?id=819
At SIBOS 2006 in Sydney, financial messaging co-op SWIFT will unveil its strategy document for 2010, which focuses upon growing the corporate userbase, getting into derivatives and grabbing a slice. . .

4th September 2006
The banks that like to say no
http://www.finextra.com/fullfeature.asp?id=807
The poor quality of customer service in the typical British bank.

2nd August 2006
When two tribes go to war
http://www.finextra.com/fullfeature.asp?id=793
The many regulatory battles taking place in the financial markets around the world and wonders who will win.

4th July 2006
Video nasty
http://www.finextra.com/fullfeature.asp?id=782
Broadband video-servicing is set to shake the foundations of retail banking.

31st May 2006
Who are you?
http://www.finextra.com/fullfeature.asp?id=768
The issues of identity and proposes that two-level authentication is not enough.

2nd May 2006
The death of cash
http://www.finextra.com/fullfeature.asp?id=751
The birth of contactless payments and forecasts the ultimate demise of hard cash.

3rd April 2006
Tools of the trade
http://www.finextra.com/fullfeature.asp?id=743
In these times of increasing automation and regulation, how can an honest broker-dealer make a dollar or euro? Some would consider chucking it in and keeping it simple, whilst others are moving. . .

28th February 2006
Banks in a TWIST
http://www.finextra.com/fullfeature.asp?id=734
The work of the Transaction Workflow Innovation Standards Team (TWIST), the standards-setting body for large corporate treasurers.

3rd February 2006
The MiFID monster
http://www.finextra.com/fullfeature.asp?id=729
During February, the European Commission will release the final text for the Markets in Financial Instruments Directive before it is ratified by the European Commission to become law in 2007. What. . .

5th January 2006
Eurovision 2006: Part one
http://www.finextra.com/fullfeature.asp?id=719
The first installment of a two part commentary on the Payment Services Directive released in December 2005.

1st December 2005
Strained relationships
http://www.finextra.com/fullfeature.asp?id=709
Based upon extensive research by the Bank Administration Institute (BAI) in the USA of bankers and consumers, there is a major disconnect between bankers, who say their number one driver is to create. . .

2nd November 2005
The cashless, cardless society
http://www.finextra.com/fullfeature.asp?id=687
During the last decades we have seen several technology revolutions. The 1980s introduced the personal computer, the 1990s the internet and the 2000s the iPod.

6th October 2005
Never mind the quality, feel the width
http://www.finextra.com/fullfeature.asp?id=676
Measuring the value of technology investments is never easy, but it is becoming increasingly essential.

4th September 2005
Blogging at SIBOS
http://www.finextra.com/fullblog.asp?id=651
Chris Skinner reports live and direct from the SWIFT international banking and operations seminar in Copenhagen.

30th August 2005
Miller's challenge
http://www.finextra.com/fullfeature.asp?id=654
At last year's SWIFT conference, Heidi Miller, head of the treasury and securities services businesses at JPMorgan Chase, challenged the industry for making it too difficult for customers to achieve. . .

2nd August 2005
Faith in banking
http://www.finextra.com/fullfeature.asp?id=645
The opportunities created for Western banks by growth in Islamic Banking.

5th July 2005
European Union unravels
http://www.finextra.com/fullfeature.asp?id=638
The euro is facing its most serious challenge since its inception in 1999 and, as a result, so is SEPA and the Financial Services Action Plan.

6th June 2005

What goes around comes around

http://www.finextra.com/fullfeature.asp?id=571

Fifteen years ago, the hot topic on everyone's agenda was Business Process Re-engineering. A decade and a half later it's back on the agenda big time. Is this because no-one got it right the first. . .

4th May 2005

Best execution with best intentions

http://www.finextra.com/fullfeature.asp?id=609

Europe and America are introducing a wave of regulatory changes that are creating as much emotion as Basel II, with MiFID and RegNMS leading the way.

5th April 2005

Risky options

http://www.finextra.com/fullfeature.asp?id=600

Options and derivatives trading has led to a number of major corporate disasters, from Barings Bank to Long-Term Capital Management and from Enron to WorldCom. Is technology a help or a hindrance in. . .

1st March 2005

Business objects

http://www.finextra.com/fullfeature.asp?id=578

The case for more open source development in financial services.

31st January 2005

The future of European payments

http://www.finextra.com/fullfeature.asp?id=570

EU objectives for a single European payments area are forcing banks to address a complex spaghetti of conflicting and competing systems and standards. For many, outsourcing may be the only solution. . .

6th January 2005

2005: The year of the enterprise

http://www.finextra.com/fullfeature.asp?id=573

The key retail and investment market technology challenges for the coming year.

29th November 2004

The road from Baghdad to Zurich

http://www.finextra.com/fullfeature.asp?id=571

The discovery of $650 million in newly minted bills at a compound in Iraq triggered an investigation that led to the imposition of a $100 million Fed fine for UBS.

1ˢᵗ November 2004
Give fraud the finger
http://www.finextra.com/fullfeature.asp?id=558
Rising fraud levels means that banks can no longer afford to ignore the potential of biometrics.

4ᵗʰ October 2004
When animals collide: Tigers rip up the Longhorns!
http://www.finextra.com/fullfeature.asp?id=551
The next generation of PCs will transform consumer banking.

21ˢᵗ September 2004
Chips with everything
http://www.finextra.com/fullfeature.asp?id=507
The next five years will see chip-based technologies being delivered that will revolutionise the business of banking.

Index

Index compiled by Annette Musker